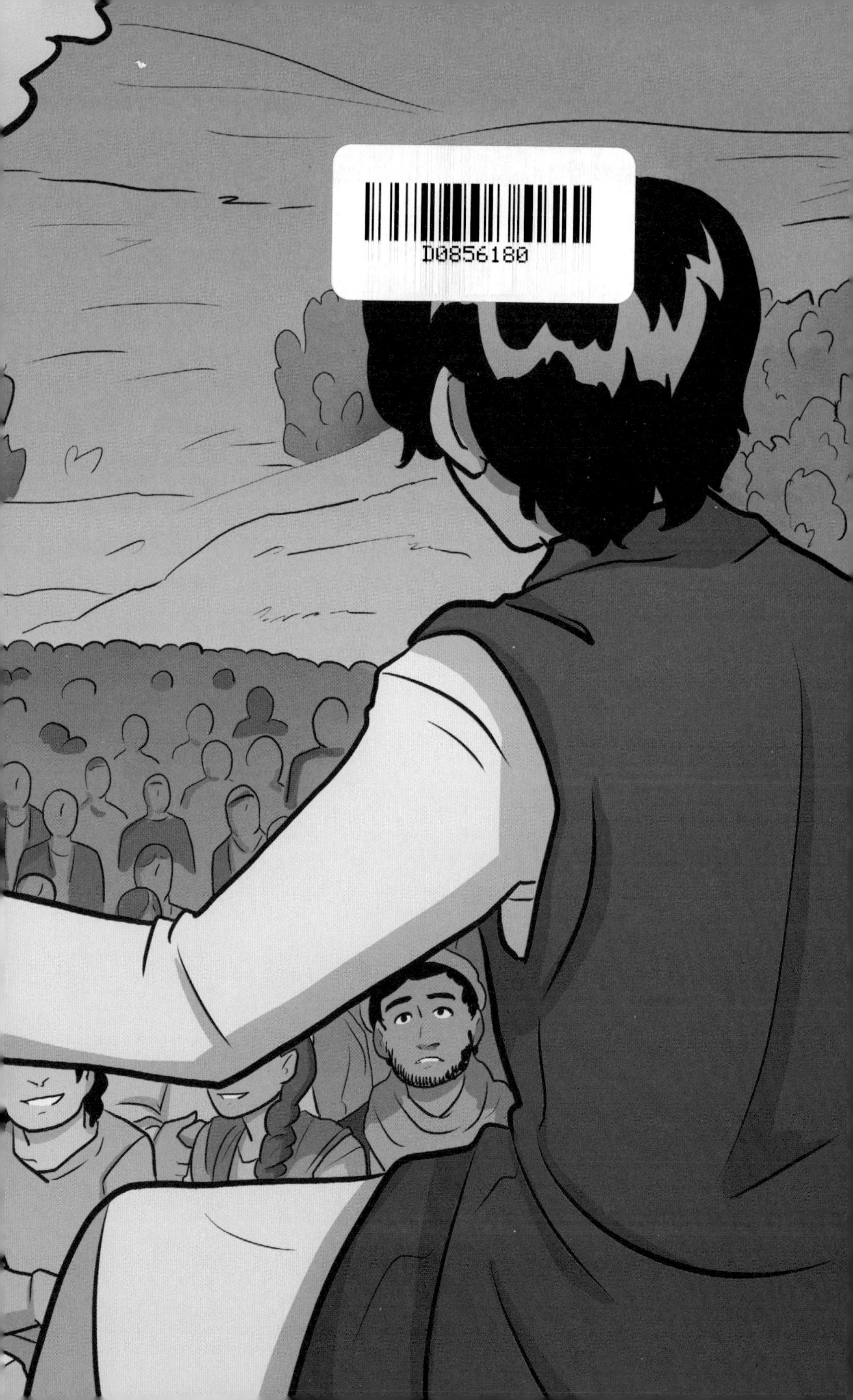

SHOW ME *HISTORY!*

JESUS

MESSENGER *of* PEACE!

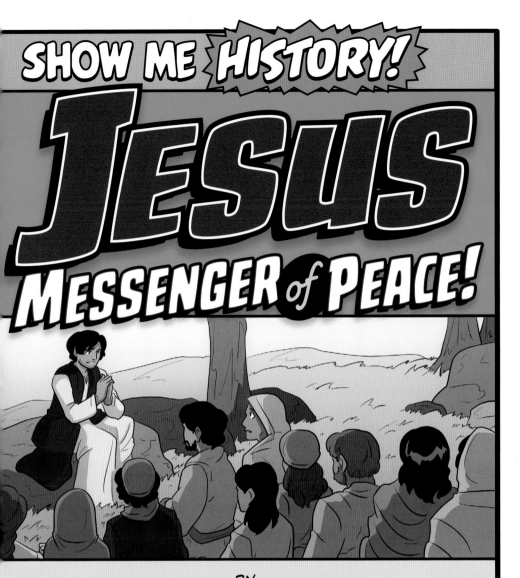

BY
JAMES BUCKLEY JR.

ILLUSTRATED BY
CAITLIN LIKE

LETTERING & DESIGN BY
SWELL TYPE

COVER ART BY
DERRICK DEVOE

PORTABLE
PRESS

SAN DIEGO, CALIFORNIA

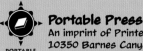 **Portable Press**
An imprint of Printers Row Publishing Group
10350 Barnes Canyon Road, Suite 100, San Diego, CA 92121
www.portablepress.com • mail@portablepress.com

Printers Row Publishing Group is a division of Readerlink Distribution Services, LLC. Portable Press is a registered trademark of Readerlink Distribution Services, LLC.

Correspondence regarding the content of this book should be sent to Portable Press, Editorial Department, at the above address. Author and illustrator inquiries should be sent to Oomf, Inc., www.oomf.com.

Portable Press
Publisher: Peter Norton • Associate Publisher: Ana Parker
Developmental Editor: Vicki Jaeger
Editor: April Graham Farr
Production Team: Jonathan Lopes, Rusty von Dyl, Julie Greene

 Produced by Oomf, Inc., www.Oomf.com
Director: Mark Shulman
Producer: James Buckley Jr.

Author: James Buckley Jr.
Illustrator: Caitlin Like
Lettering & Design by Swell Type: John Roshell and Forest Dempsey
Cover illustrator: Derrick DeVoe

ISBN: 978-1-64517-412-7

Library of Congress Control Number: 2020935513

Printed in China

24 23 22 21 20   1 2 3 4 5

A NOTE FROM THE AUTHOR

Hi, and thanks for picking up this volume of SHOW ME HISTORY! We'll meet our official narrators on the next page, but first I want to say a couple of things about the story you're about to read.

The story of Jesus is one of the most famous ever told. In the more than 2,000 years since it happened, it has been spoken, read, filmed, or drawn countless numbers of times. The story of Jesus is told in the Bible, mainly in the four parts called the Gospels. That's the story we have in this book.

Now, unlike in the other books in the SHOW ME HISTORY! series, we don't have as much historical proof for what is in this story as we do, for example, for the speeches of Martin Luther King Jr. or the writings of Alexander Hamilton. But we do have the four Gospels, and they tell a remarkable story.

Whether you believe it's all true or you're not sure, the fact remains that the story of this man's life has literally changed the world. That alone makes it a story to know.

Thanks for reading!

-- James Buckley Jr.

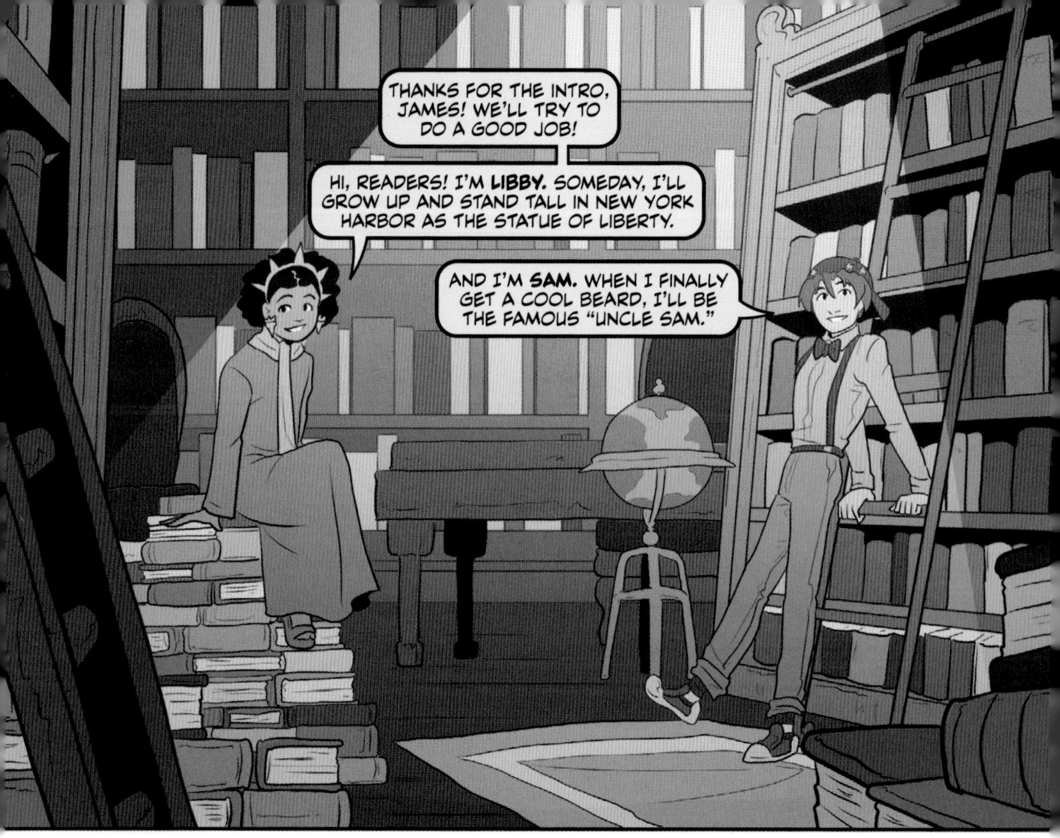
THANKS FOR THE INTRO, JAMES! WE'LL TRY TO DO A GOOD JOB!
HI, READERS! I'M **LIBBY.** SOMEDAY, I'LL GROW UP AND STAND TALL IN NEW YORK HARBOR AS THE STATUE OF LIBERTY.
AND I'M **SAM.** WHEN I FINALLY GET A COOL BEARD, I'LL BE THE FAMOUS "UNCLE SAM."

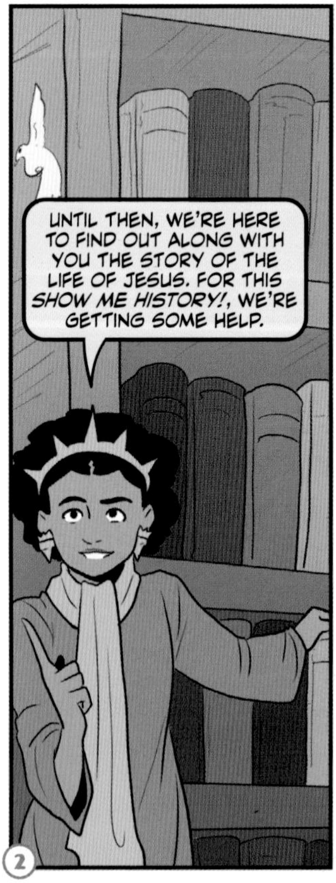
UNTIL THEN, WE'RE HERE TO FIND OUT ALONG WITH YOU THE STORY OF THE LIFE OF JESUS. FOR THIS *SHOW ME HISTORY!*, WE'RE GETTING SOME HELP.

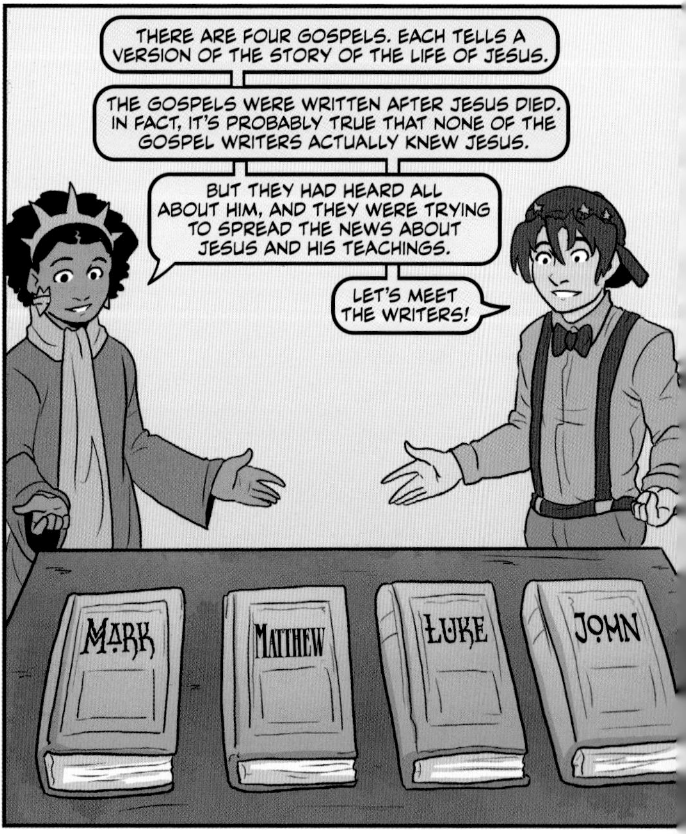
THERE ARE FOUR GOSPELS. EACH TELLS A VERSION OF THE STORY OF THE LIFE OF JESUS.
THE GOSPELS WERE WRITTEN AFTER JESUS DIED. IN FACT, IT'S PROBABLY TRUE THAT NONE OF THE GOSPEL WRITERS ACTUALLY KNEW JESUS.
BUT THEY HAD HEARD ALL ABOUT HIM, AND THEY WERE TRYING TO SPREAD THE NEWS ABOUT JESUS AND HIS TEACHINGS.
LET'S MEET THE WRITERS!
MARK
MATTHEW
LUKE
JOHN

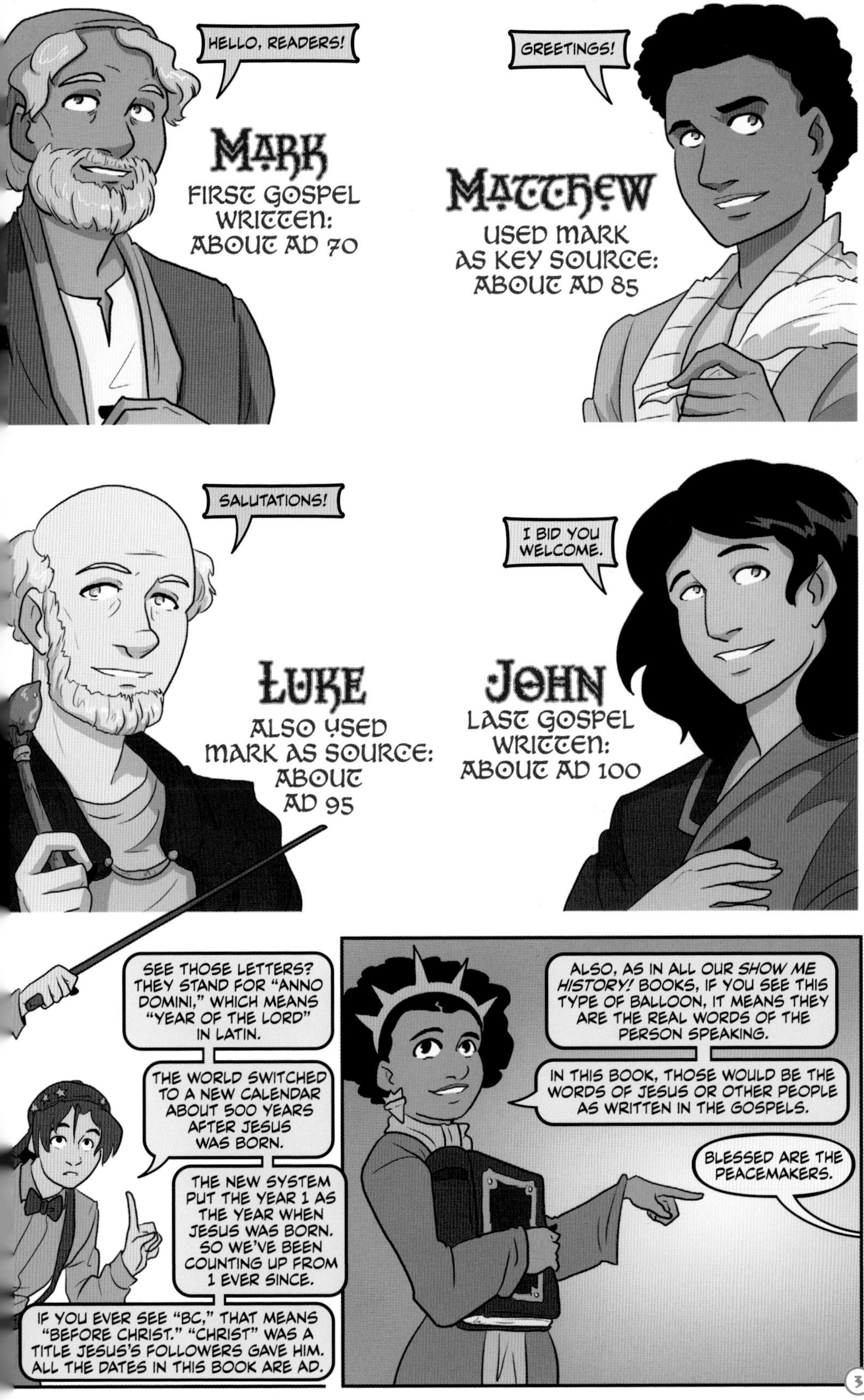

HELLO, READERS!
MARK
FIRST GOSPEL WRITTEN: ABOUT AD 70
GREETINGS!
MATTHEW
USED MARK AS KEY SOURCE: ABOUT AD 85
SALUTATIONS!
LUKE
ALSO USED MARK AS SOURCE: ABOUT AD 95
I BID YOU WELCOME.
JOHN
LAST GOSPEL WRITTEN: ABOUT AD 100
SEE THOSE LETTERS? THEY STAND FOR "ANNO DOMINI," WHICH MEANS "YEAR OF THE LORD" IN LATIN.
THE WORLD SWITCHED TO A NEW CALENDAR ABOUT 500 YEARS AFTER JESUS WAS BORN.
THE NEW SYSTEM PUT THE YEAR 1 AS THE YEAR WHEN JESUS WAS BORN. SO WE'VE BEEN COUNTING UP FROM 1 EVER SINCE.
IF YOU EVER SEE "BC," THAT MEANS "BEFORE CHRIST." "CHRIST" WAS A TITLE JESUS'S FOLLOWERS GAVE HIM. ALL THE DATES IN THIS BOOK ARE AD.
ALSO, AS IN ALL OUR *SHOW ME HISTORY!* BOOKS, IF YOU SEE THIS TYPE OF BALLOON, IT MEANS THEY ARE THE REAL WORDS OF THE PERSON SPEAKING.
IN THIS BOOK, THOSE WOULD BE THE WORDS OF JESUS OR OTHER PEOPLE AS WRITTEN IN THE GOSPELS.
BLESSED ARE THE PEACEMAKERS.

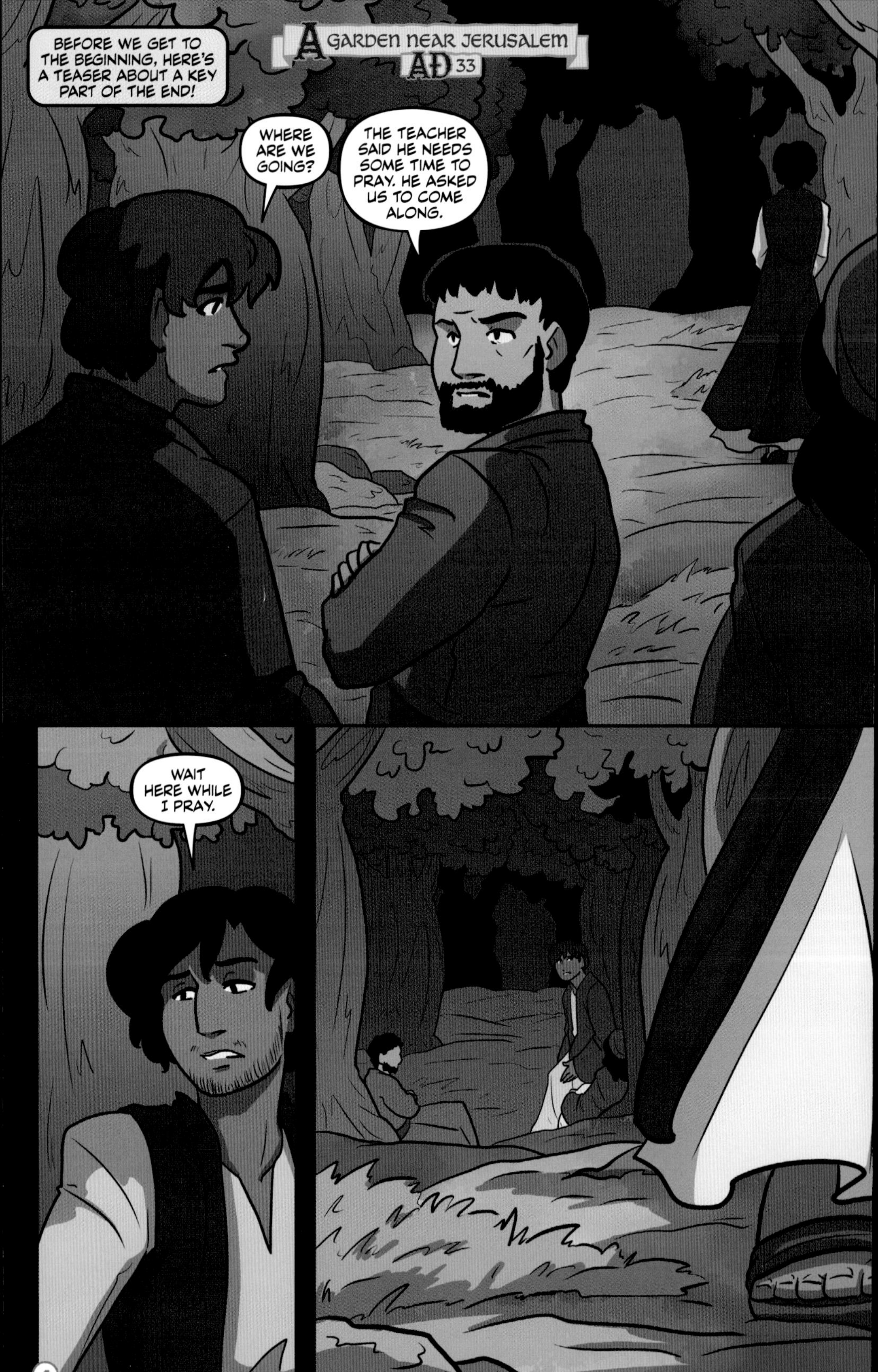
BEFORE WE GET TO THE BEGINNING, HERE'S A TEASER ABOUT A KEY PART OF THE END!
A GARDEN NEAR JERUSALEM AD 33
WHERE ARE WE GOING?
THE TEACHER SAID HE NEEDS SOME TIME TO PRAY. HE ASKED US TO COME ALONG.
WAIT HERE WHILE I PRAY.

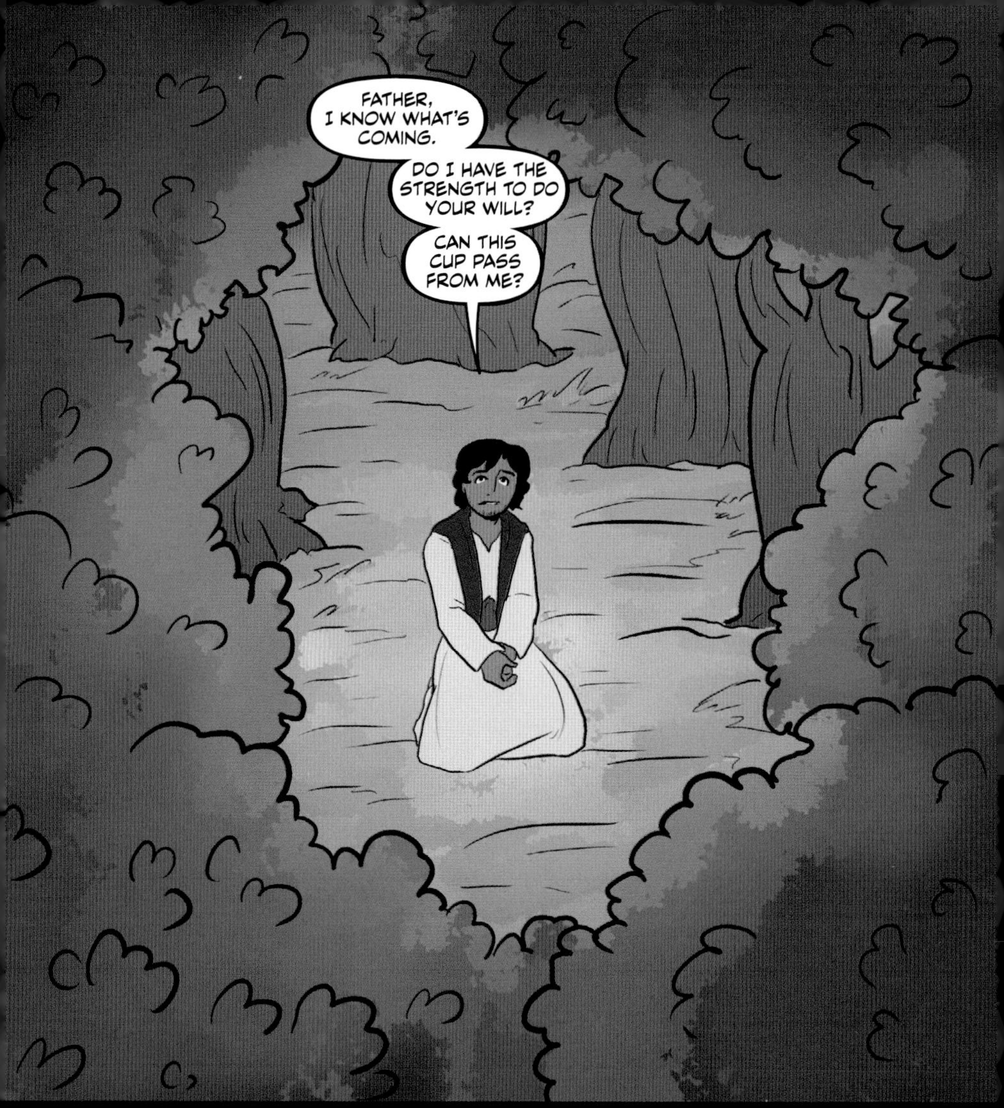
FATHER, I KNOW WHAT'S COMING.
DO I HAVE THE STRENGTH TO DO YOUR WILL?
CAN THIS CUP PASS FROM ME?

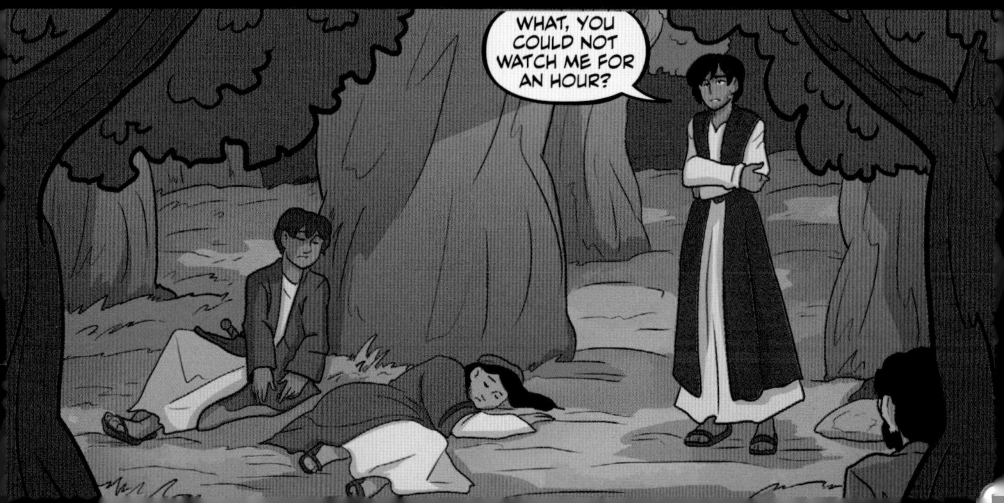
WHAT, YOU COULD NOT WATCH ME FOR AN HOUR?

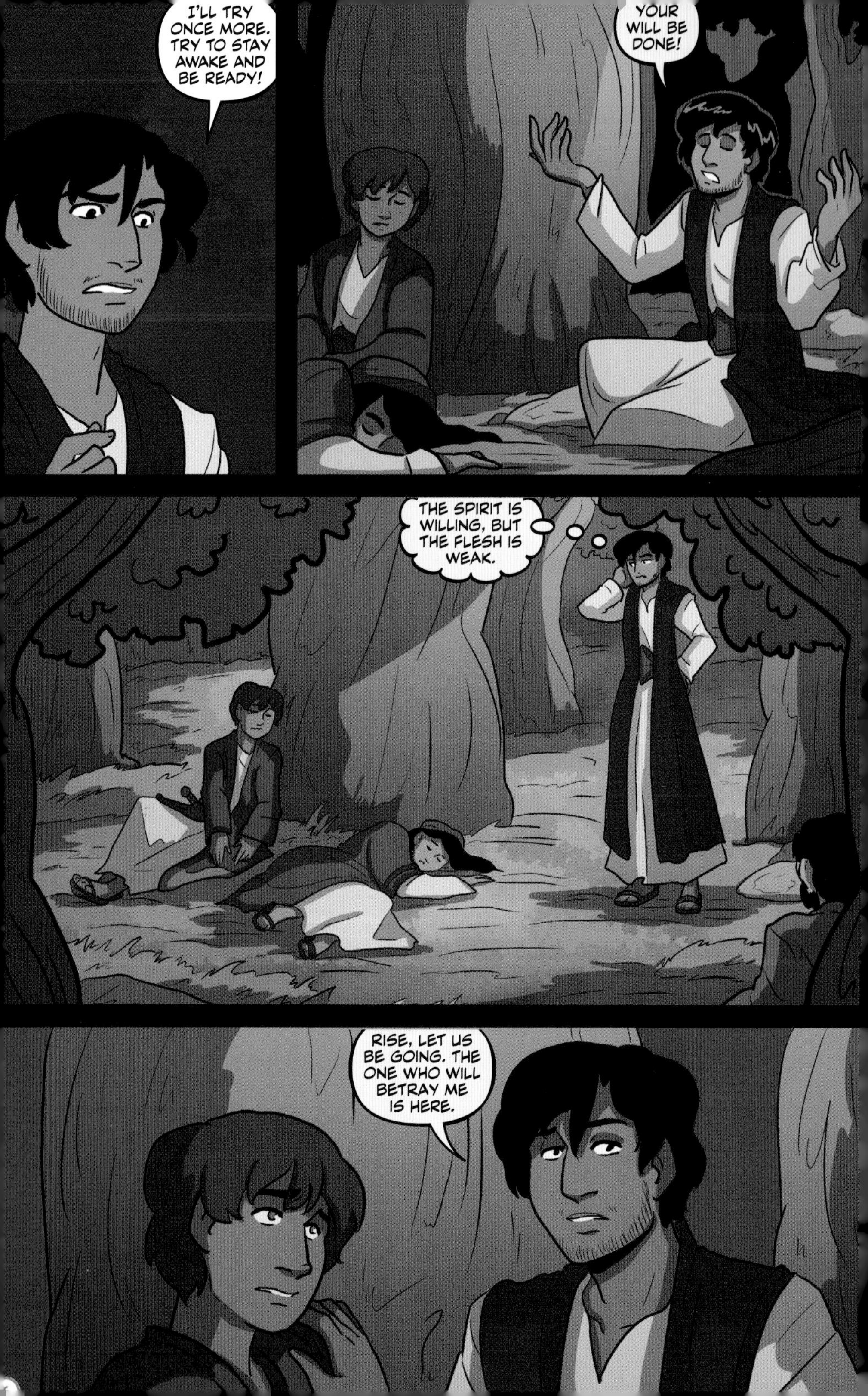
I'LL TRY ONCE MORE. TRY TO STAY AWAKE AND BE READY!
YOUR WILL BE DONE!
THE SPIRIT IS WILLING, BUT THE FLESH IS WEAK.
RISE, LET US BE GOING. THE ONE WHO WILL BETRAY ME IS HERE.

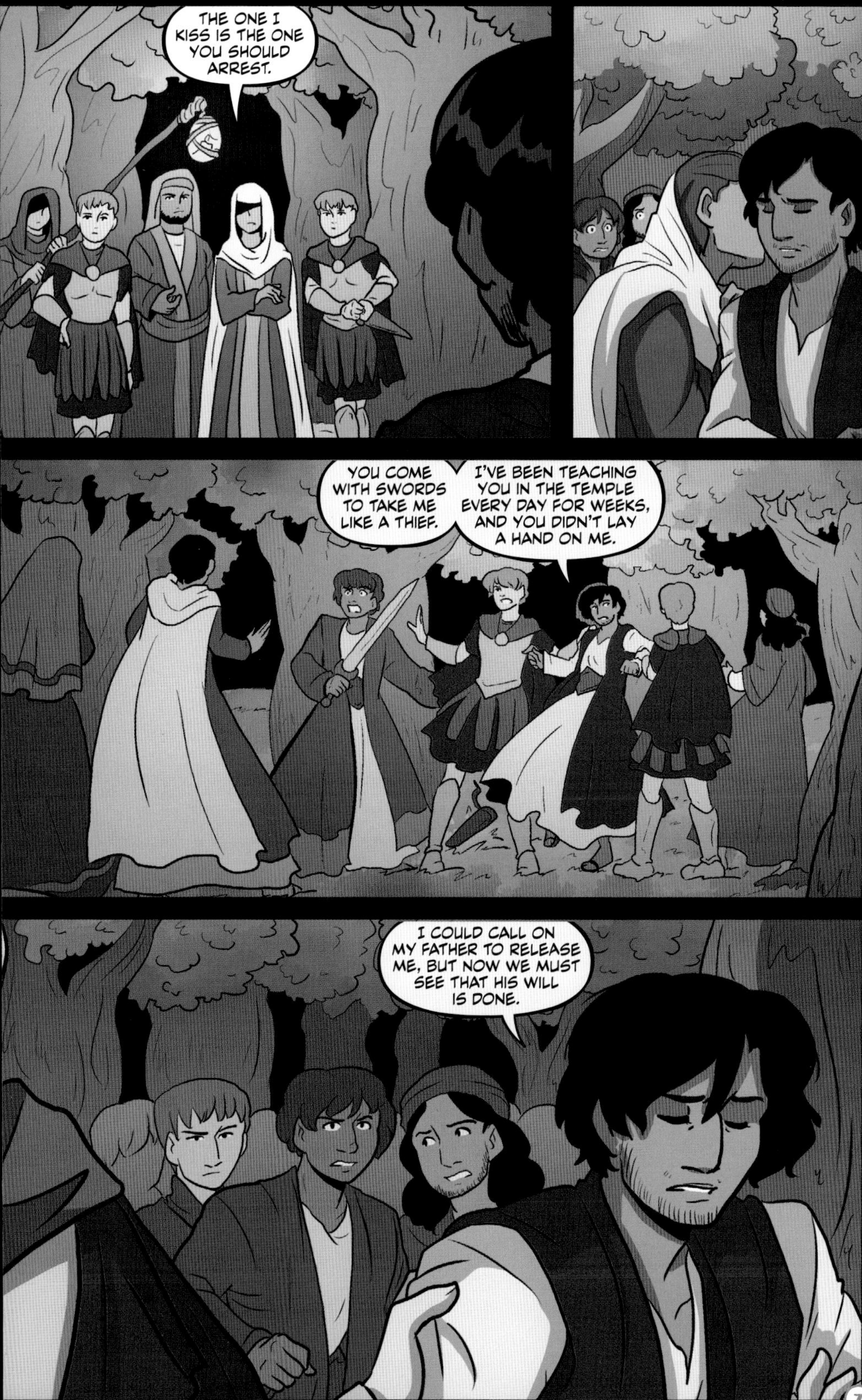

THE ONE I KISS IS THE ONE YOU SHOULD ARREST.
YOU COME WITH SWORDS TO TAKE ME LIKE A THIEF.
I'VE BEEN TEACHING YOU IN THE TEMPLE EVERY DAY FOR WEEKS, AND YOU DIDN'T LAY A HAND ON ME.
I COULD CALL ON MY FATHER TO RELEASE ME, BUT NOW WE MUST SEE THAT HIS WILL IS DONE.

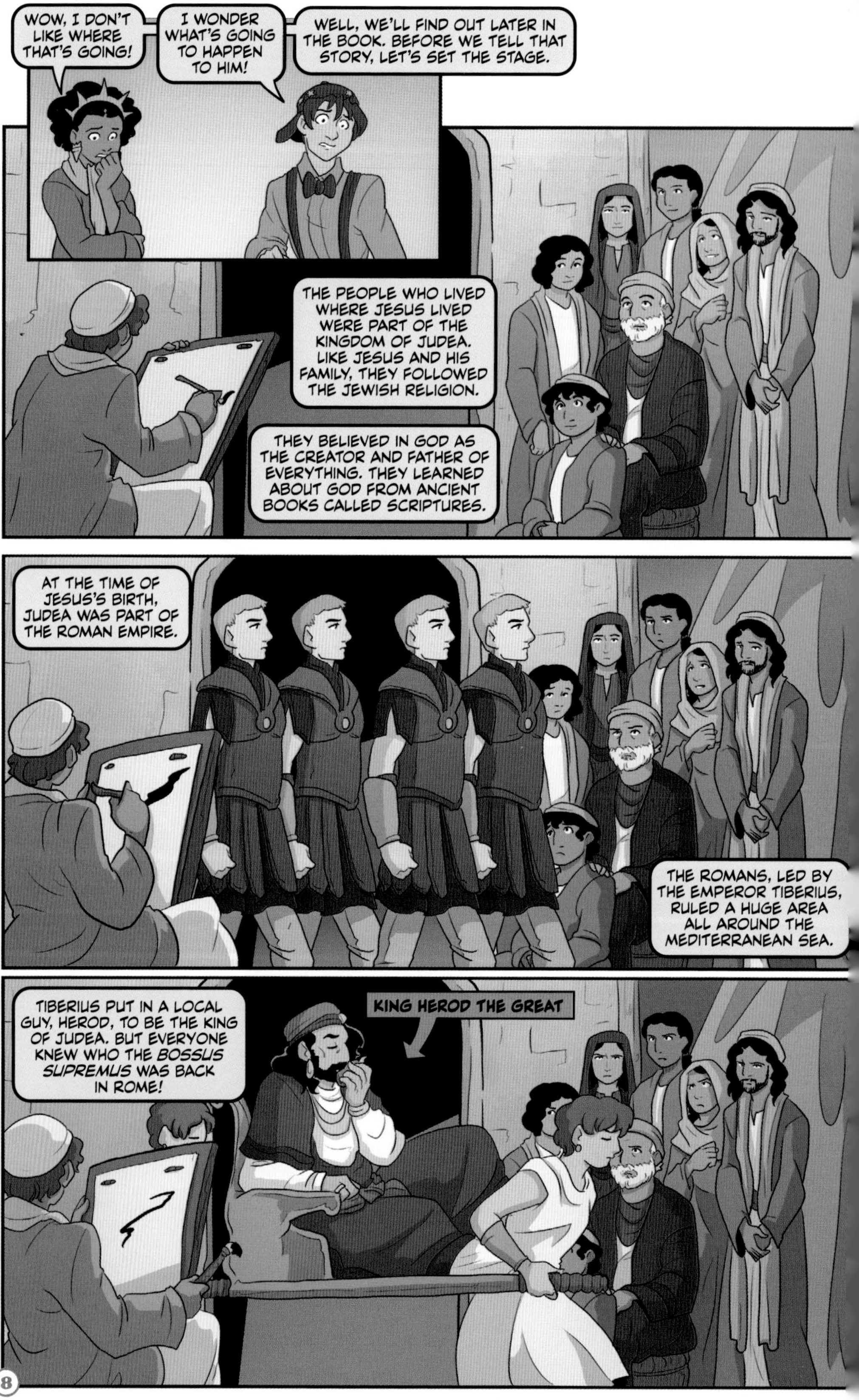

WOW, I DON'T LIKE WHERE THAT'S GOING!
I WONDER WHAT'S GOING TO HAPPEN TO HIM!
WELL, WE'LL FIND OUT LATER IN THE BOOK. BEFORE WE TELL THAT STORY, LET'S SET THE STAGE.
THE PEOPLE WHO LIVED WHERE JESUS LIVED WERE PART OF THE KINGDOM OF JUDEA. LIKE JESUS AND HIS FAMILY, THEY FOLLOWED THE JEWISH RELIGION.
THEY BELIEVED IN GOD AS THE CREATOR AND FATHER OF EVERYTHING. THEY LEARNED ABOUT GOD FROM ANCIENT BOOKS CALLED SCRIPTURES.
AT THE TIME OF JESUS'S BIRTH, JUDEA WAS PART OF THE ROMAN EMPIRE.
THE ROMANS, LED BY THE EMPEROR TIBERIUS, RULED A HUGE AREA ALL AROUND THE MEDITERRANEAN SEA.
TIBERIUS PUT IN A LOCAL GUY, HEROD, TO BE THE KING OF JUDEA. BUT EVERYONE KNEW WHO THE *BOSSUS SUPREMUS* WAS BACK IN ROME!
KING HEROD THE GREAT

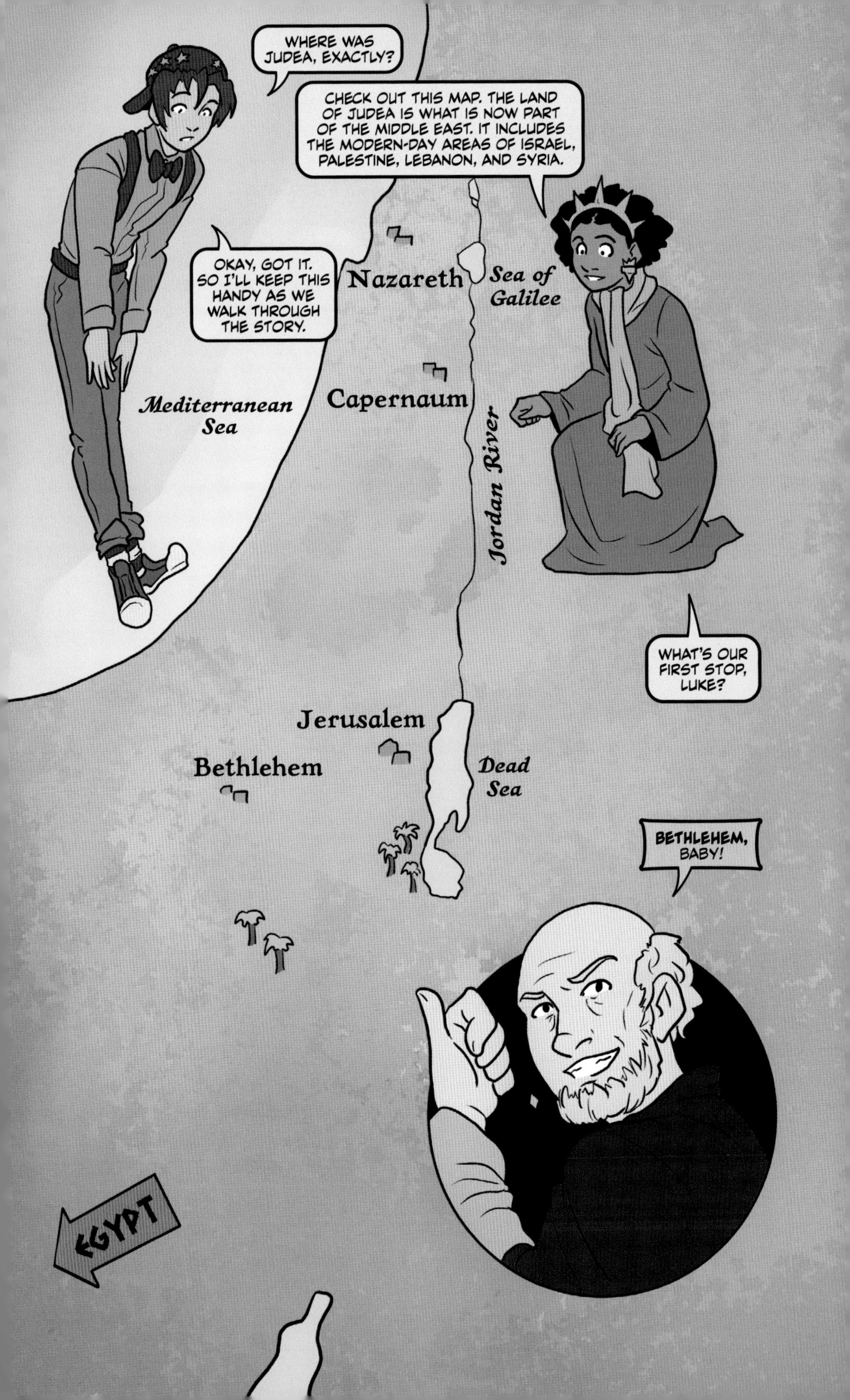
WHERE WAS JUDEA, EXACTLY?
CHECK OUT THIS MAP. THE LAND OF JUDEA IS WHAT IS NOW PART OF THE MIDDLE EAST. IT INCLUDES THE MODERN-DAY AREAS OF ISRAEL, PALESTINE, LEBANON, AND SYRIA.
OKAY, GOT IT. SO I'LL KEEP THIS HANDY AS WE WALK THROUGH THE STORY.
Nazareth
Sea of Galilee
Mediterranean Sea
Capernaum
Jordan River
WHAT'S OUR FIRST STOP, LUKE?
Jerusalem
Bethlehem
Dead Sea
BETHLEHEM, BABY!
EGYPT

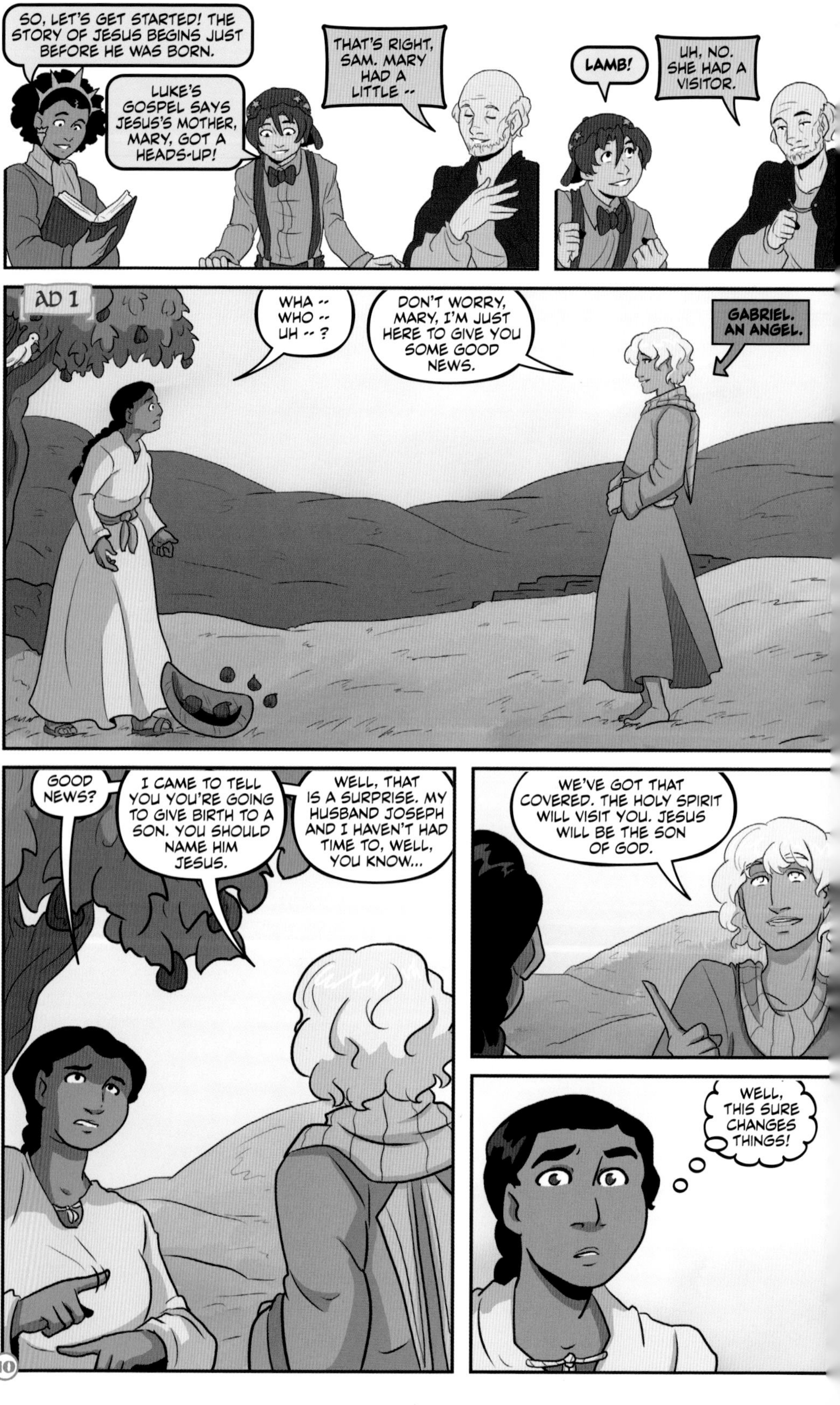
SO, LET'S GET STARTED! THE STORY OF JESUS BEGINS JUST BEFORE HE WAS BORN.
LUKE'S GOSPEL SAYS JESUS'S MOTHER, MARY, GOT A HEADS-UP!
THAT'S RIGHT, SAM. MARY HAD A LITTLE --
LAMB!
UH, NO. SHE HAD A VISITOR.
AD 1
WHA -- WHO -- UH -- ?
DON'T WORRY, MARY, I'M JUST HERE TO GIVE YOU SOME GOOD NEWS.
GABRIEL. AN ANGEL.
GOOD NEWS?
I CAME TO TELL YOU YOU'RE GOING TO GIVE BIRTH TO A SON. YOU SHOULD NAME HIM JESUS.
WELL, THAT IS A SURPRISE. MY HUSBAND JOSEPH AND I HAVEN'T HAD TIME TO, WELL, YOU KNOW...
WE'VE GOT THAT COVERED. THE HOLY SPIRIT WILL VISIT YOU. JESUS WILL BE THE SON OF GOD.
WELL, THIS SURE CHANGES THINGS!

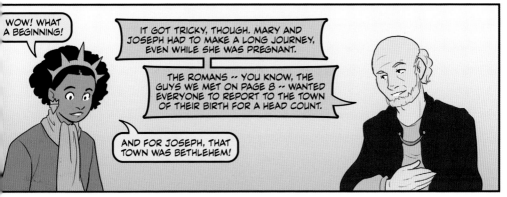

WOW! WHAT A BEGINNING!

IT GOT TRICKY, THOUGH. MARY AND JOSEPH HAD TO MAKE A LONG JOURNEY, EVEN WHILE SHE WAS PREGNANT.

THE ROMANS -- YOU KNOW, THE GUYS WE MET ON PAGE 8 -- WANTED EVERYONE TO REPORT TO THE TOWN OF THEIR BIRTH FOR A HEAD COUNT.

AND FOR JOSEPH, THAT TOWN WAS BETHLEHEM!

Welcome to BETHLEHEM "We're not famous yet!"

SORRY, FOLKS, I'M FULL UP. LOTTA PEOPLE BORN HERE OVER THE YEARS. THE TOWN IS PACKED!

I CAN LET YOU SLEEP IN THE STABLE IF YOU WANT.

NO VACANCY

THE STABLE? ISN'T THAT WHERE ANIMALS SLEEP? ICK!

WELL, IT'S NOT IDEAL, BUT WE'LL TAKE IT.

YES, TAKE IT! I'M GOING TO NEED A PLACE TO LIE DOWN **VERY** SOON!

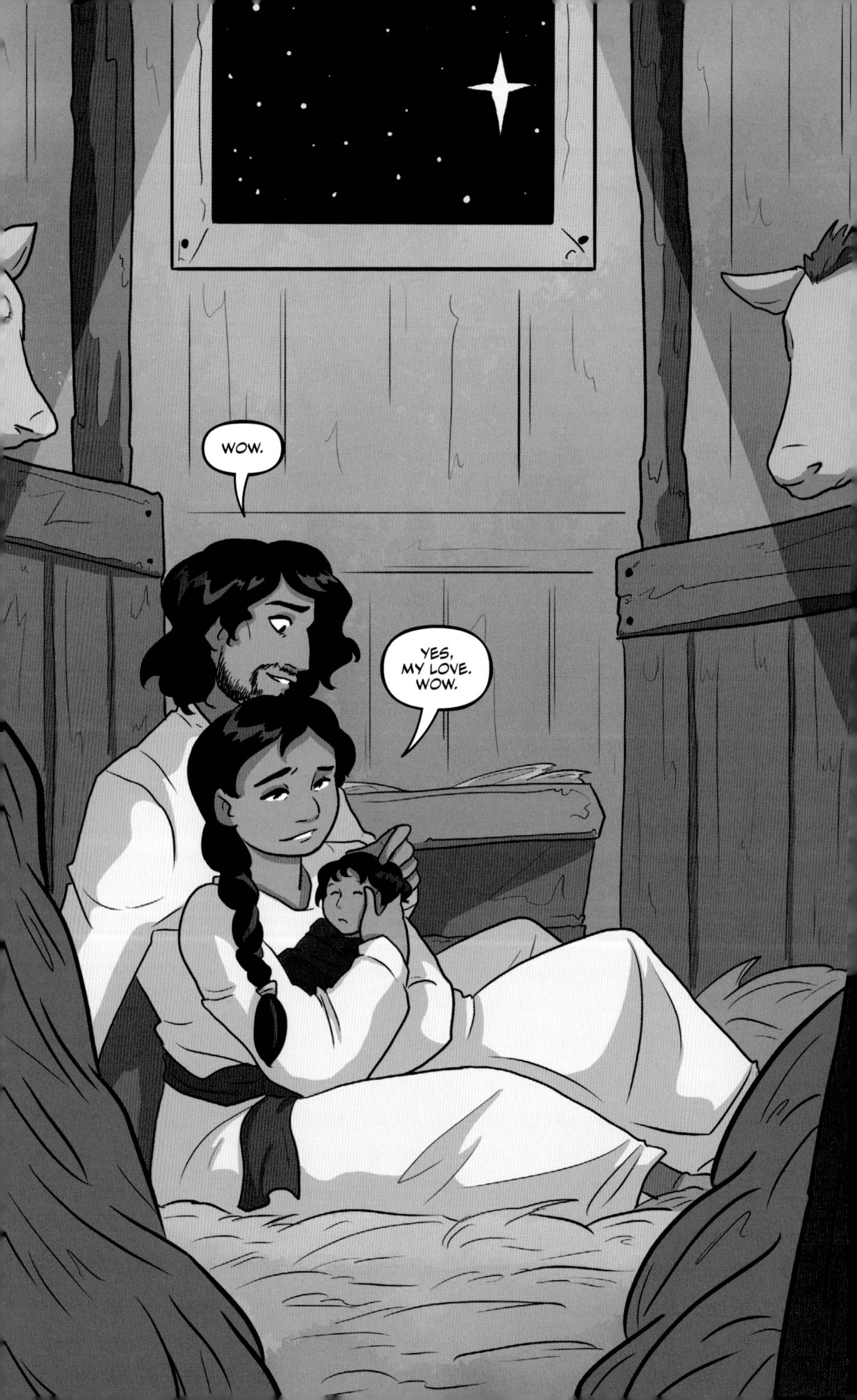
WOW.
YES, MY LOVE. WOW.

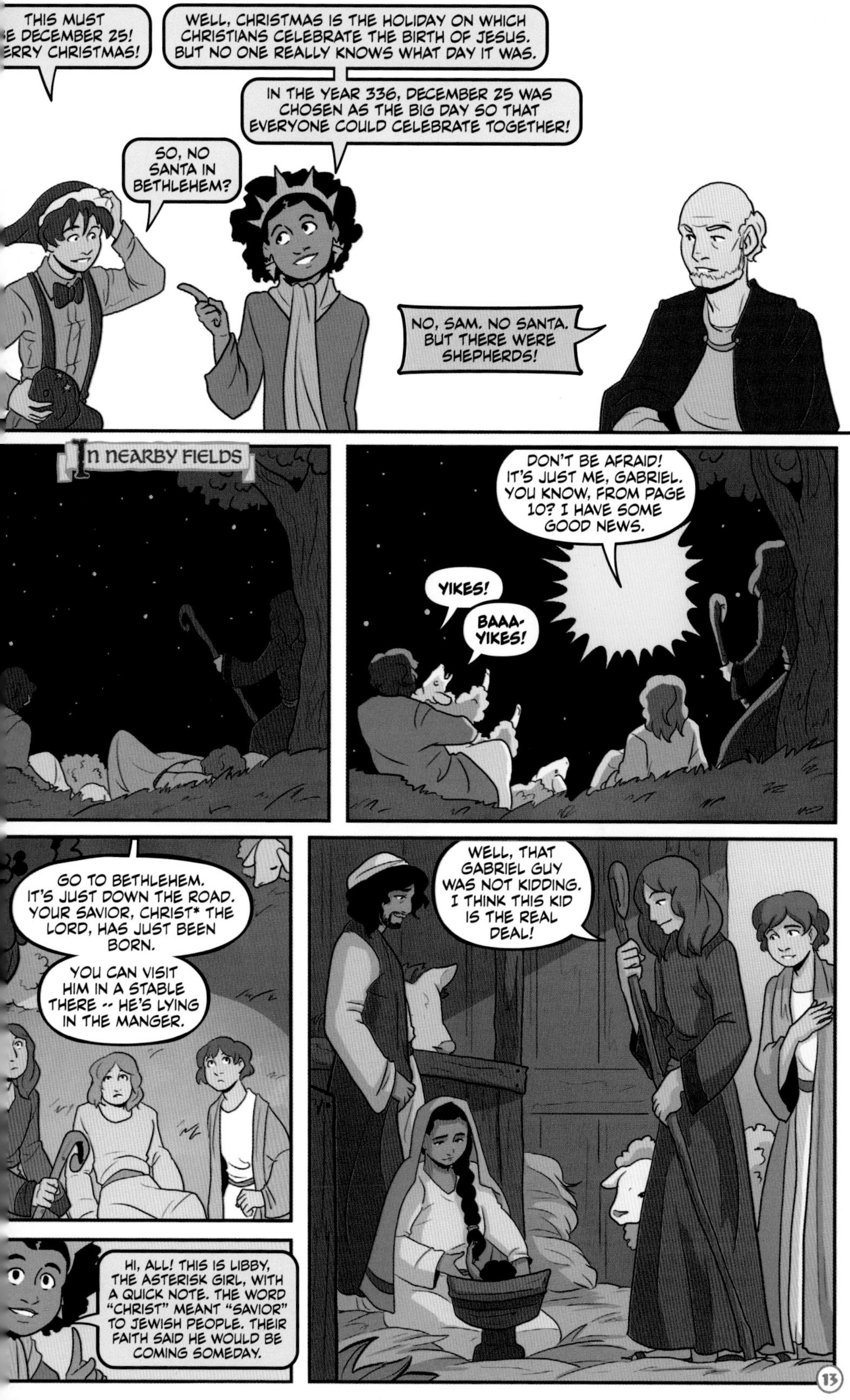
THIS MUST
E DECEMBER 25!
ERRY CHRISTMAS!
WELL, CHRISTMAS IS THE HOLIDAY ON WHICH CHRISTIANS CELEBRATE THE BIRTH OF JESUS. BUT NO ONE REALLY KNOWS WHAT DAY IT WAS.
IN THE YEAR 336, DECEMBER 25 WAS CHOSEN AS THE BIG DAY SO THAT EVERYONE COULD CELEBRATE TOGETHER!
SO, NO SANTA IN BETHLEHEM?
NO, SAM. NO SANTA. BUT THERE WERE SHEPHERDS!
In NEARBY FIELDS
DON'T BE AFRAID! IT'S JUST ME, GABRIEL. YOU KNOW, FROM PAGE 10? I HAVE SOME GOOD NEWS.
YIKES!
BAAA-YIKES!
GO TO BETHLEHEM. IT'S JUST DOWN THE ROAD. YOUR SAVIOR, CHRIST* THE LORD, HAS JUST BEEN BORN.
YOU CAN VISIT HIM IN A STABLE THERE -- HE'S LYING IN THE MANGER.
WELL, THAT GABRIEL GUY WAS NOT KIDDING. I THINK THIS KID IS THE REAL DEAL!
HI, ALL! THIS IS LIBBY, THE ASTERISK GIRL, WITH A QUICK NOTE. THE WORD "CHRIST" MEANT "SAVIOR" TO JEWISH PEOPLE. THEIR FAITH SAID HE WOULD BE COMING SOMEDAY.

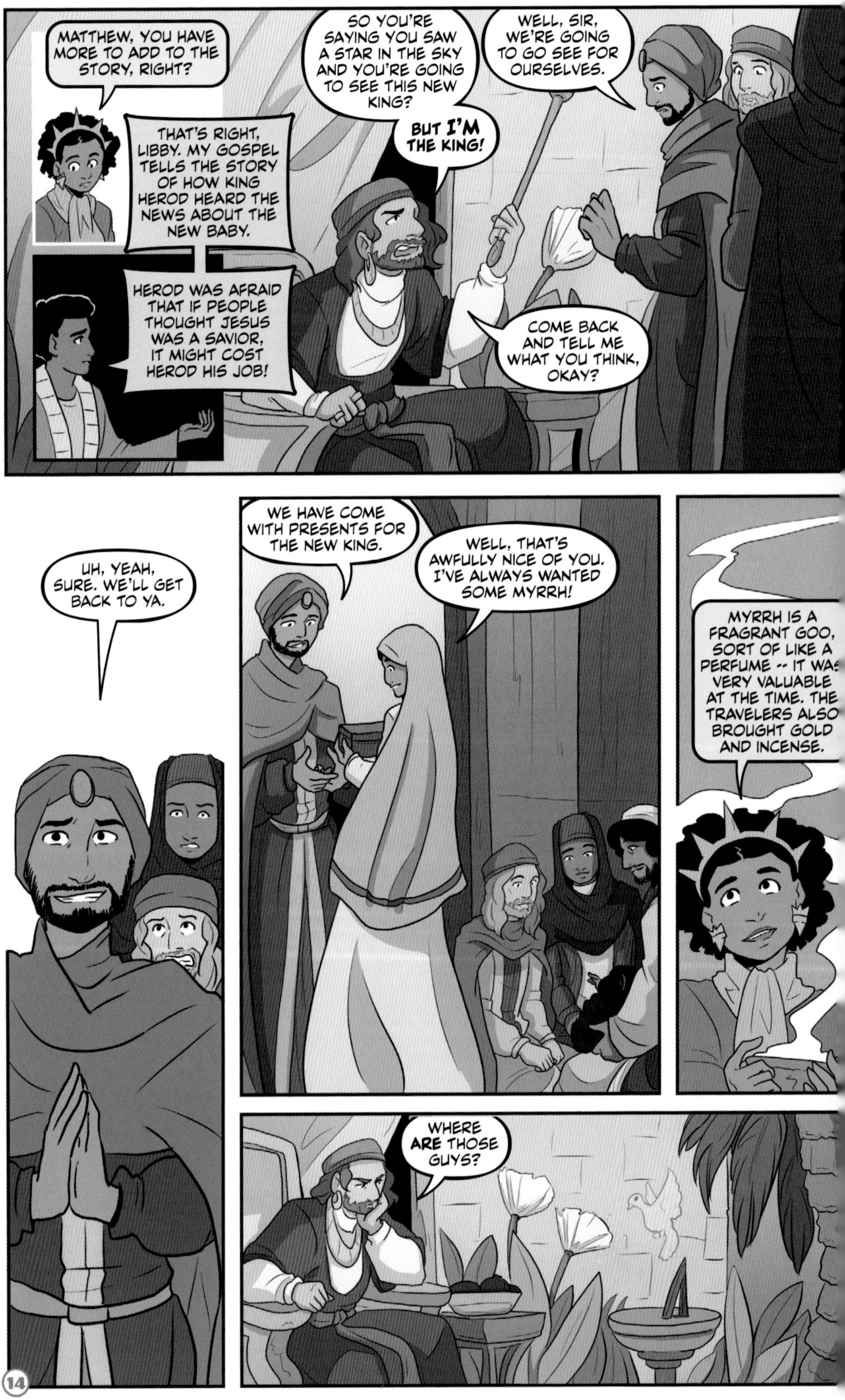
MATTHEW, YOU HAVE MORE TO ADD TO THE STORY, RIGHT?
SO YOU'RE SAYING YOU SAW A STAR IN THE SKY AND YOU'RE GOING TO SEE THIS NEW KING?
BUT I'M THE KING!
WELL, SIR, WE'RE GOING TO GO SEE FOR OURSELVES.
THAT'S RIGHT, LIBBY. MY GOSPEL TELLS THE STORY OF HOW KING HEROD HEARD THE NEWS ABOUT THE NEW BABY.
HEROD WAS AFRAID THAT IF PEOPLE THOUGHT JESUS WAS A SAVIOR, IT MIGHT COST HEROD HIS JOB!
COME BACK AND TELL ME WHAT YOU THINK, OKAY?
UH, YEAH, SURE. WE'LL GET BACK TO YA.
WE HAVE COME WITH PRESENTS FOR THE NEW KING.
WELL, THAT'S AWFULLY NICE OF YOU. I'VE ALWAYS WANTED SOME MYRRH!
MYRRH IS A FRAGRANT GOO, SORT OF LIKE A PERFUME -- IT WAS VERY VALUABLE AT THE TIME. THE TRAVELERS ALSO BROUGHT GOLD AND INCENSE.
WHERE ARE THOSE GUYS?

OKAY, ~~NE~~, I'LL DO ~~T~~ MYSELF.

THIS ORDER IS FOR YOU TO WIPE OUT ALL THE NEWBORN BABIES IN THE AREA. THAT'LL SHOW THAT SO-CALLED "KING"!

NO BABY IS GOING TO TAKE MY CROWN.

THIS SOUNDS PRETTY SCARY, MATTHEW. WHAT DID JOSEPH AND MARY DO?

THAT'S EASY -- THEY BAILED!

WELCOME TO EGYPT! TUT, TUT, TUT— YOU'LL HAVE A GREAT TIME!

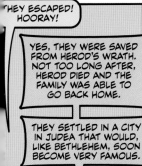

THEY ESCAPED! HOORAY!

YES, THEY WERE SAVED FROM HEROD'S WRATH. NOT TOO LONG AFTER, HEROD DIED AND THE FAMILY WAS ABLE TO GO BACK HOME.

THEY SETTLED IN A CITY IN JUDEA THAT WOULD, LIKE BETHLEHEM, SOON BECOME VERY FAMOUS.

I HOPE WE GET TO STAY HERE A WHILE. I'M GETTING TIRED OF RIDING THIS DONKEY!

Welcome to NAZARETH A Nice Place to Raise Kids

15

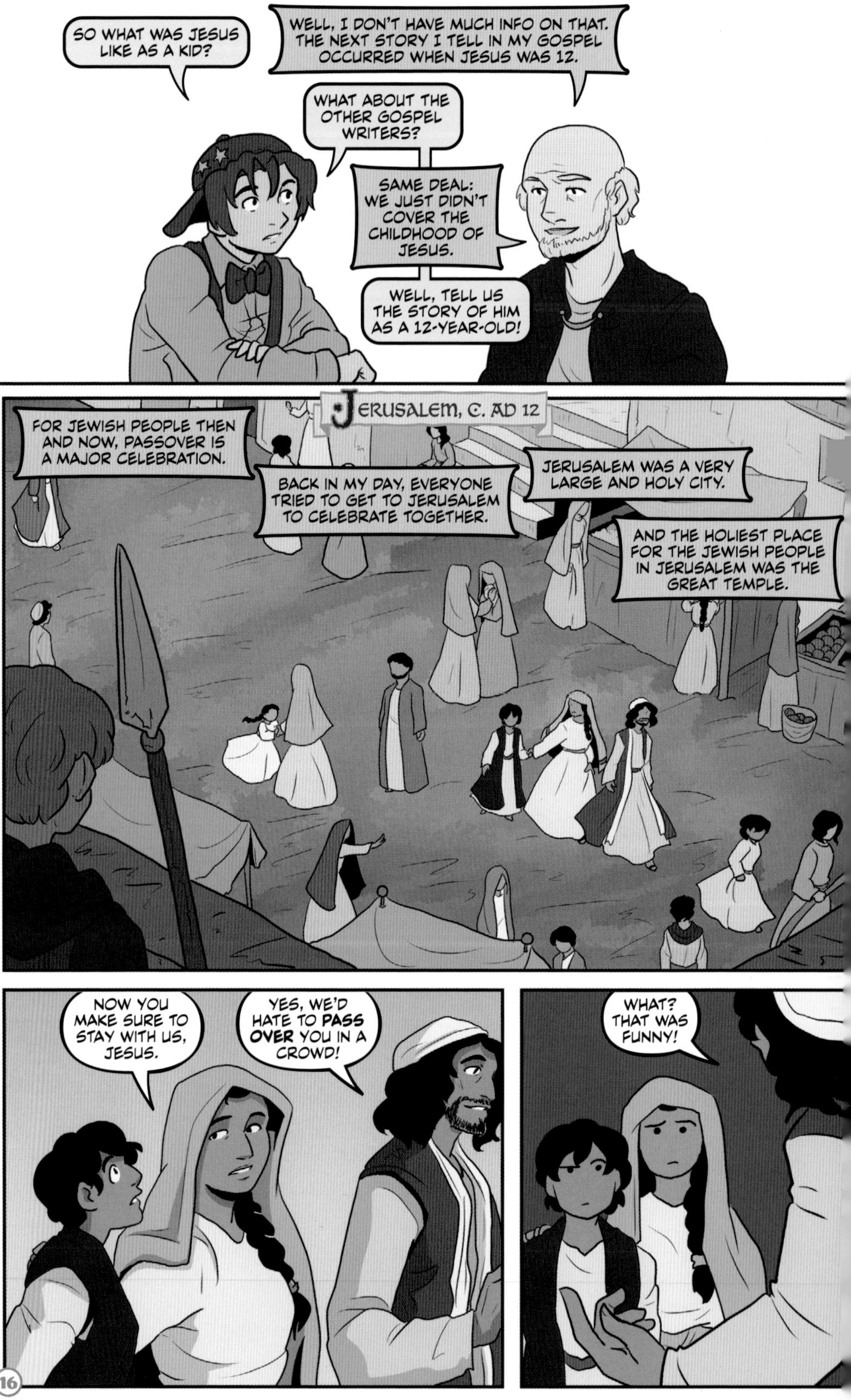
SO WHAT WAS JESUS LIKE AS A KID?
WELL, I DON'T HAVE MUCH INFO ON THAT. THE NEXT STORY I TELL IN MY GOSPEL OCCURRED WHEN JESUS WAS 12.
WHAT ABOUT THE OTHER GOSPEL WRITERS?
SAME DEAL: WE JUST DIDN'T COVER THE CHILDHOOD OF JESUS.
WELL, TELL US THE STORY OF HIM AS A 12-YEAR-OLD!
JERUSALEM, C. AD 12
FOR JEWISH PEOPLE THEN AND NOW, PASSOVER IS A MAJOR CELEBRATION.
BACK IN MY DAY, EVERYONE TRIED TO GET TO JERUSALEM TO CELEBRATE TOGETHER.
JERUSALEM WAS A VERY LARGE AND HOLY CITY.
AND THE HOLIEST PLACE FOR THE JEWISH PEOPLE IN JERUSALEM WAS THE GREAT TEMPLE.
NOW YOU MAKE SURE TO STAY WITH US, JESUS.
YES, WE'D HATE TO **PASS OVER** YOU IN A CROWD!
WHAT? THAT WAS FUNNY!

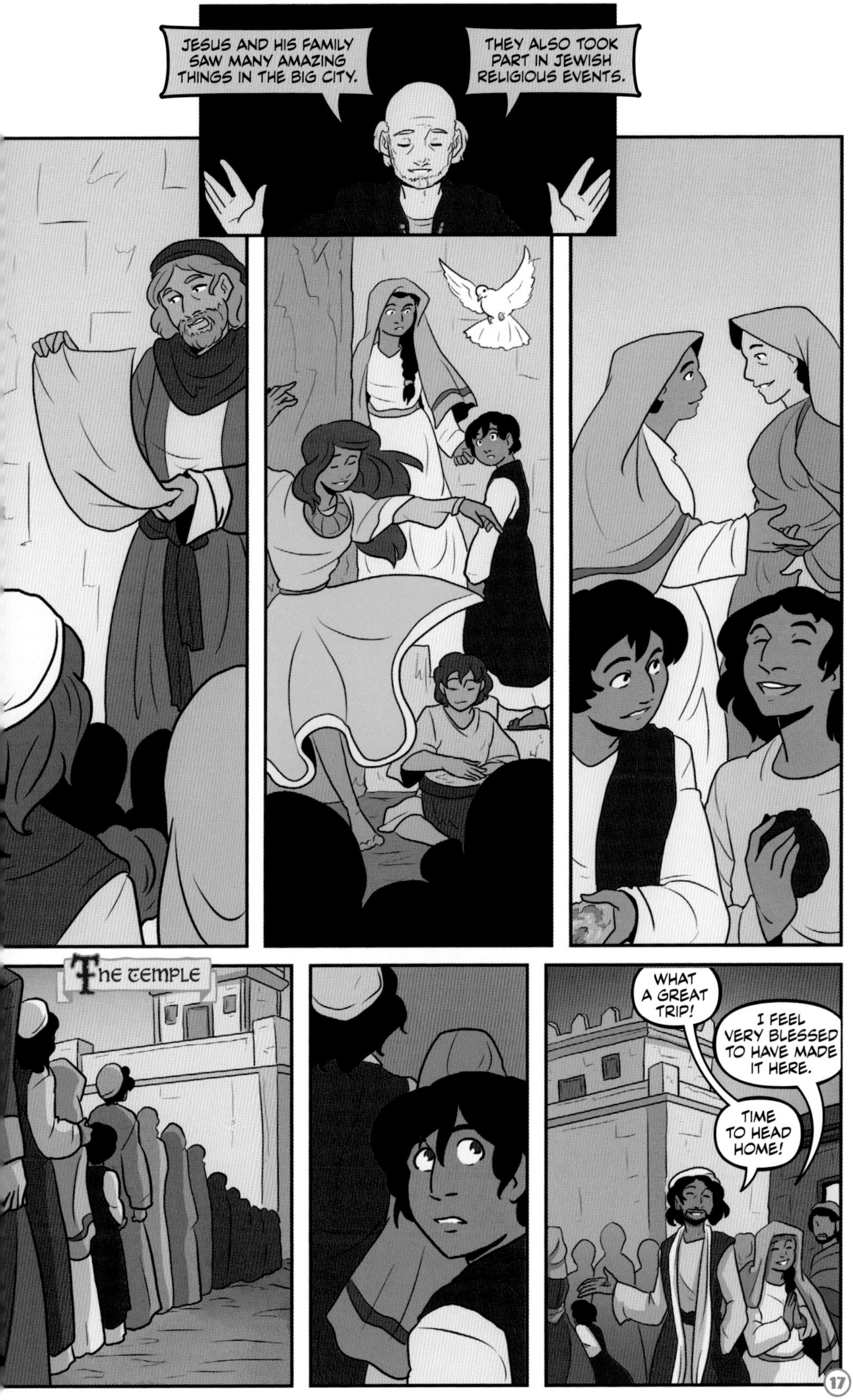

JESUS AND HIS FAMILY SAW MANY AMAZING THINGS IN THE BIG CITY.
THEY ALSO TOOK PART IN JEWISH RELIGIOUS EVENTS.
THE TEMPLE
WHAT A GREAT TRIP!
I FEEL VERY BLESSED TO HAVE MADE IT HERE.
TIME TO HEAD HOME!

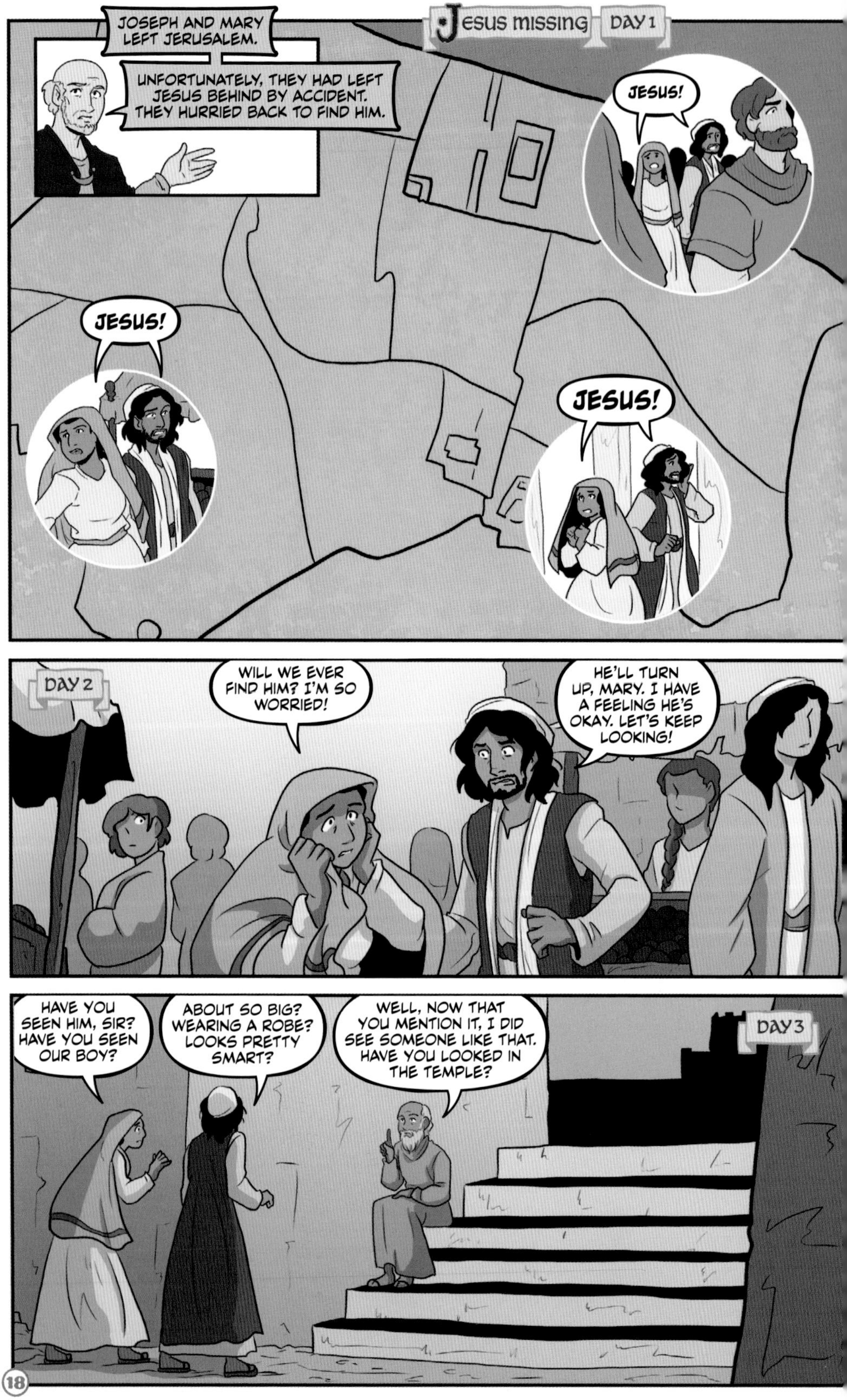
JESUS MISSING
DAY 1
JOSEPH AND MARY LEFT JERUSALEM.
UNFORTUNATELY, THEY HAD LEFT JESUS BEHIND BY ACCIDENT. THEY HURRIED BACK TO FIND HIM.
JESUS!
JESUS!
JESUS!
DAY 2
WILL WE EVER FIND HIM? I'M SO WORRIED!
HE'LL TURN UP, MARY. I HAVE A FEELING HE'S OKAY. LET'S KEEP LOOKING!
DAY 3
HAVE YOU SEEN HIM, SIR? HAVE YOU SEEN OUR BOY?
ABOUT SO BIG? WEARING A ROBE? LOOKS PRETTY SMART?
WELL, NOW THAT YOU MENTION IT, I DID SEE SOMEONE LIKE THAT. HAVE YOU LOOKED IN THE TEMPLE?

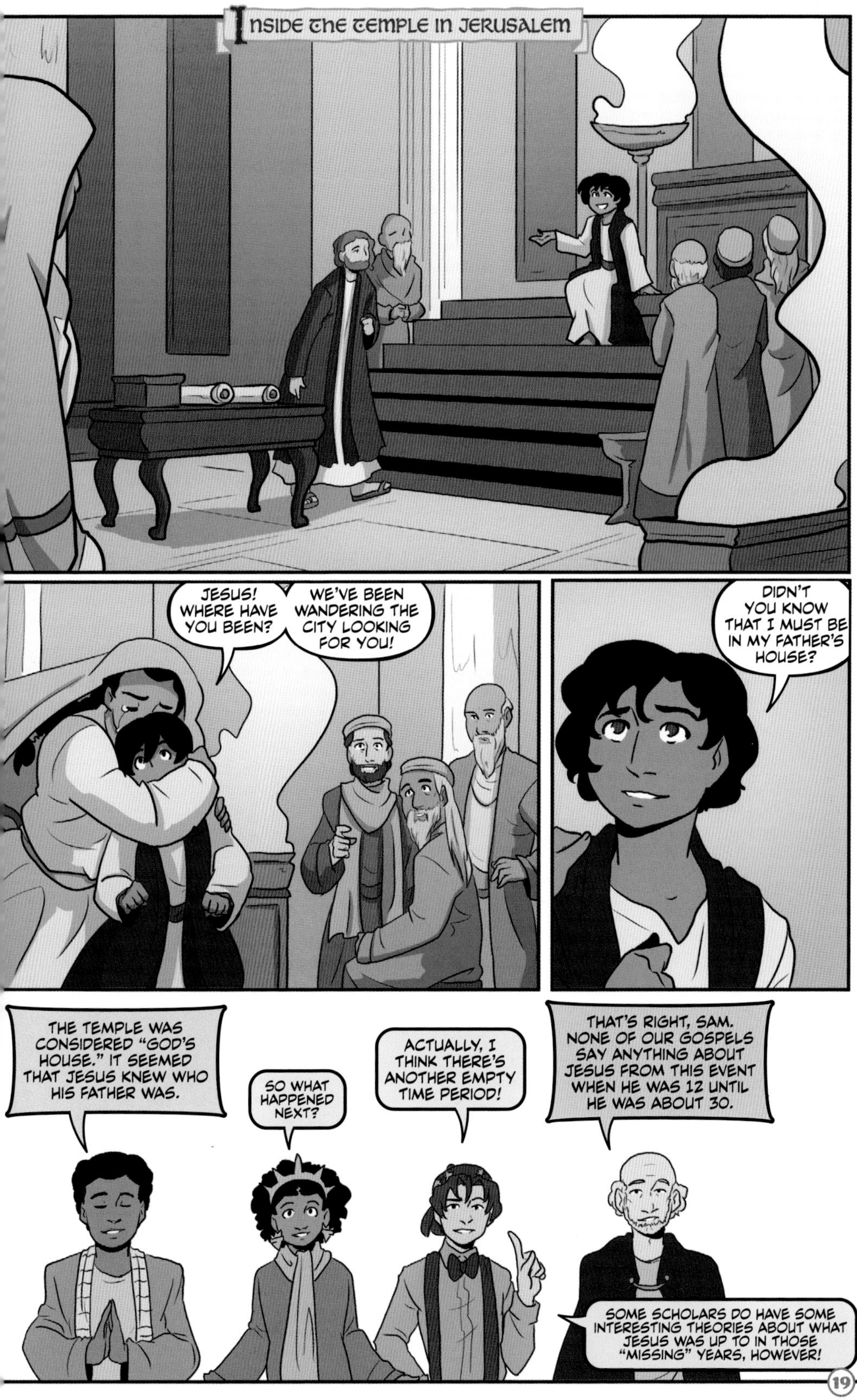
INSIDE THE TEMPLE IN JERUSALEM
JESUS! WHERE HAVE YOU BEEN?
WE'VE BEEN WANDERING THE CITY LOOKING FOR YOU!
DIDN'T YOU KNOW THAT I MUST BE IN MY FATHER'S HOUSE?
THE TEMPLE WAS CONSIDERED "GOD'S HOUSE." IT SEEMED THAT JESUS KNEW WHO HIS FATHER WAS.
SO WHAT HAPPENED NEXT?
ACTUALLY, I THINK THERE'S ANOTHER EMPTY TIME PERIOD!
THAT'S RIGHT, SAM. NONE OF OUR GOSPELS SAY ANYTHING ABOUT JESUS FROM THIS EVENT WHEN HE WAS 12 UNTIL HE WAS ABOUT 30.
SOME SCHOLARS DO HAVE SOME INTERESTING THEORIES ABOUT WHAT JESUS WAS UP TO IN THOSE "MISSING" YEARS, HOWEVER!

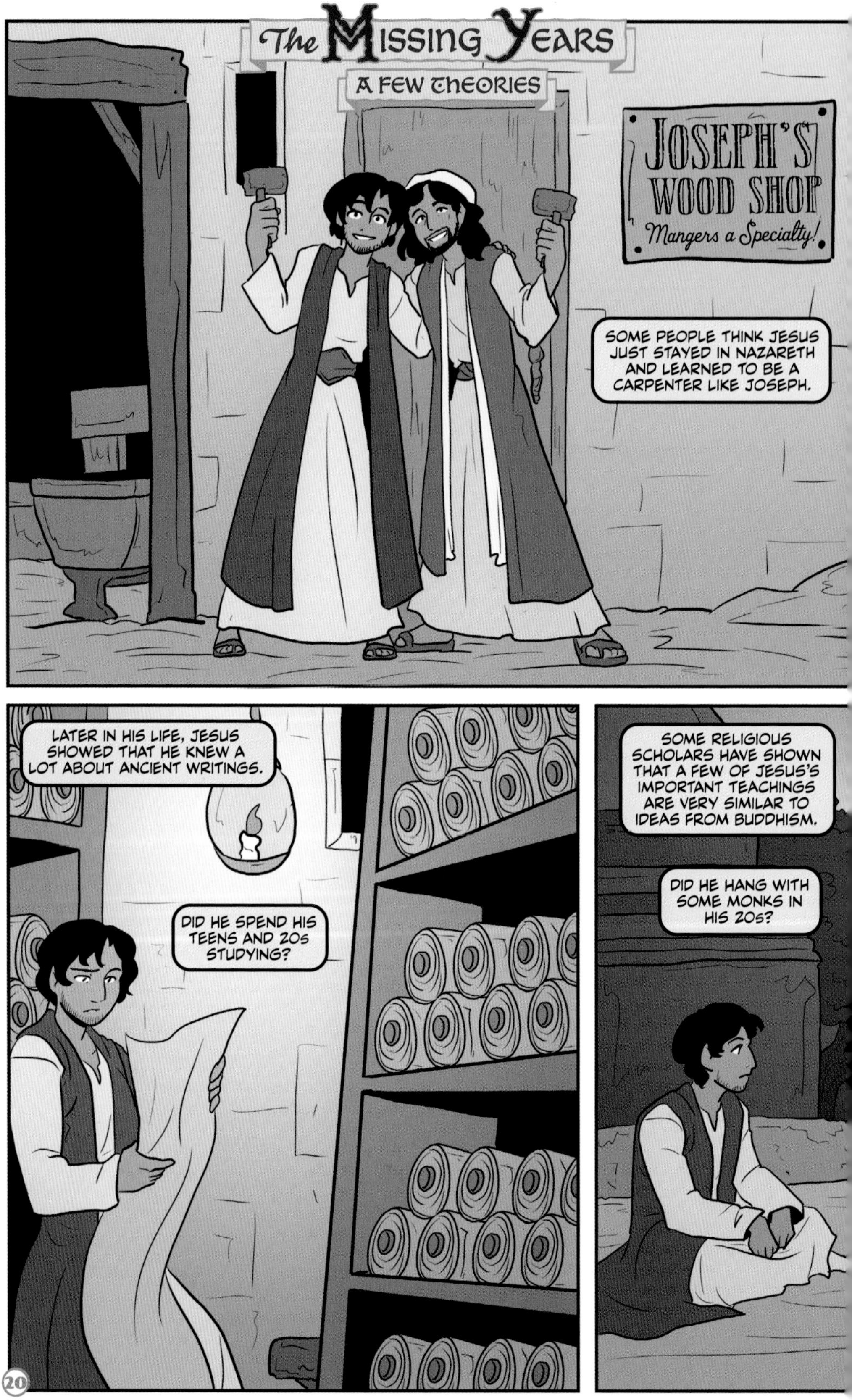
The Missing Years
A FEW THEORIES
JOSEPH'S WOOD SHOP Mangers a Specialty!
SOME PEOPLE THINK JESUS JUST STAYED IN NAZARETH AND LEARNED TO BE A CARPENTER LIKE JOSEPH.
LATER IN HIS LIFE, JESUS SHOWED THAT HE KNEW A LOT ABOUT ANCIENT WRITINGS.
DID HE SPEND HIS TEENS AND 20s STUDYING?
SOME RELIGIOUS SCHOLARS HAVE SHOWN THAT A FEW OF JESUS'S IMPORTANT TEACHINGS ARE VERY SIMILAR TO IDEAS FROM BUDDHISM.
DID HE HANG WITH SOME MONKS IN HIS 20s?

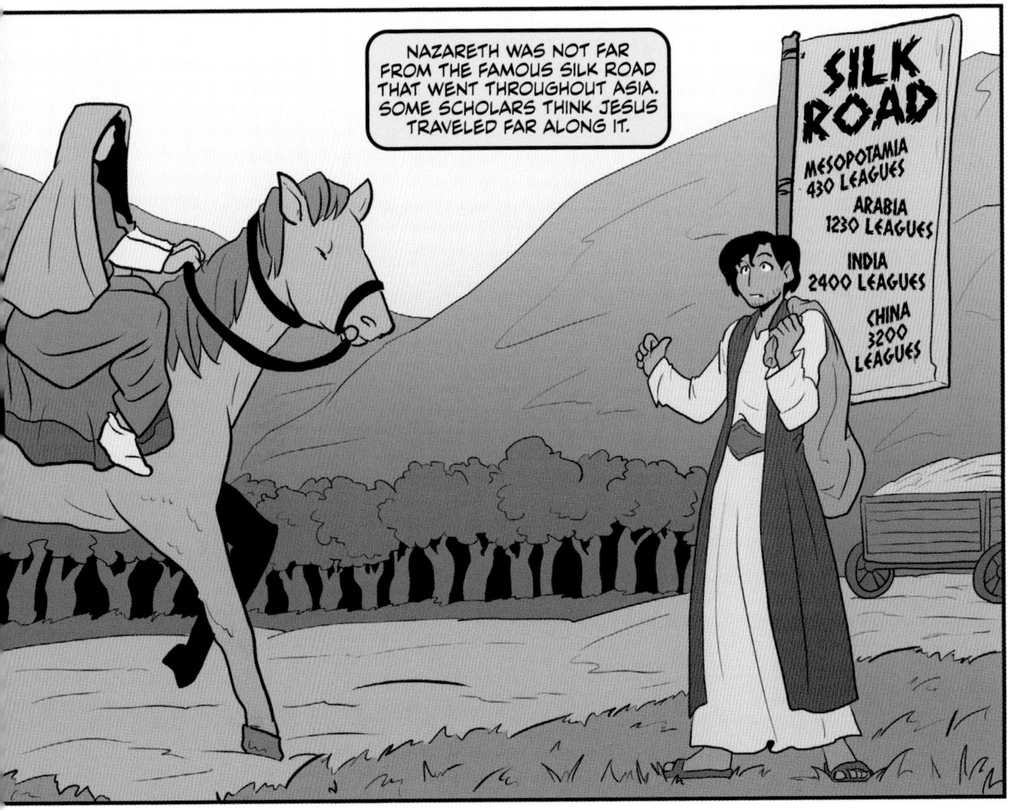
NAZARETH WAS NOT FAR FROM THE FAMOUS SILK ROAD THAT WENT THROUGHOUT ASIA. SOME SCHOLARS THINK JESUS TRAVELED FAR ALONG IT.
SILK ROAD
MESOPOTAMIA 430 LEAGUES
ARABIA 1230 LEAGUES
INDIA 2400 LEAGUES
CHINA 3200 LEAGUES

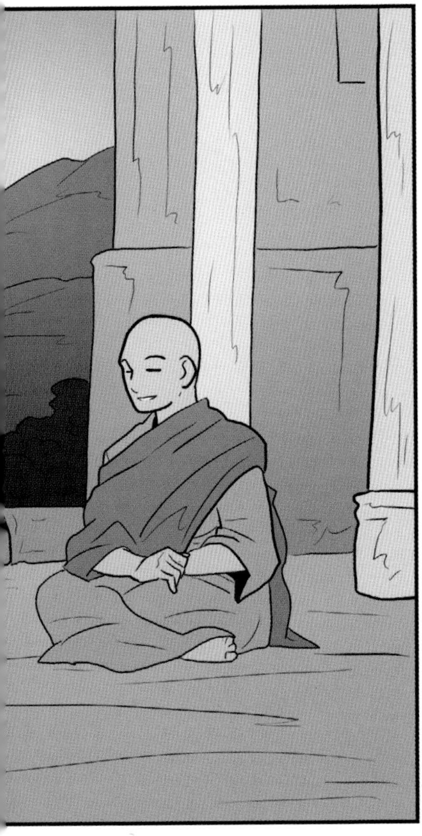

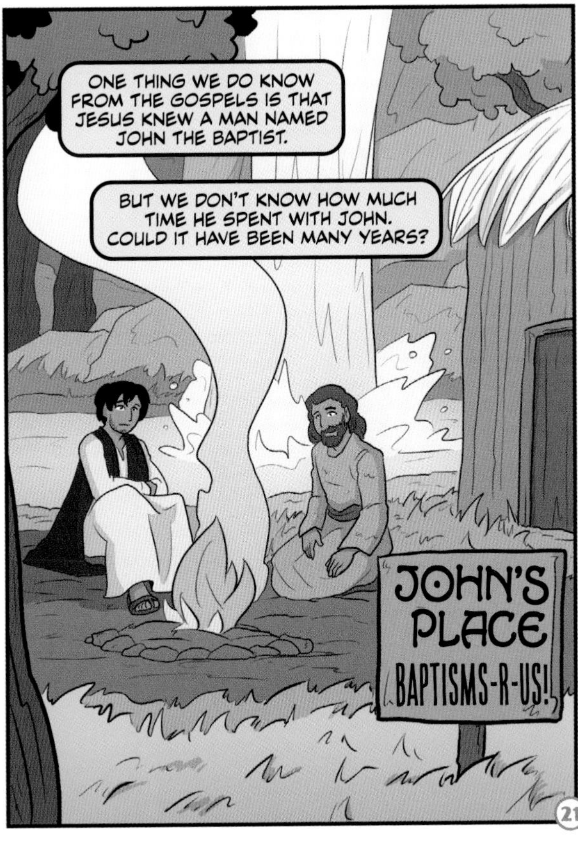
ONE THING WE DO KNOW FROM THE GOSPELS IS THAT JESUS KNEW A MAN NAMED JOHN THE BAPTIST.
BUT WE DON'T KNOW HOW MUCH TIME HE SPENT WITH JOHN. COULD IT HAVE BEEN MANY YEARS?
JOHN'S PLACE
BAPTISMS-R-US!

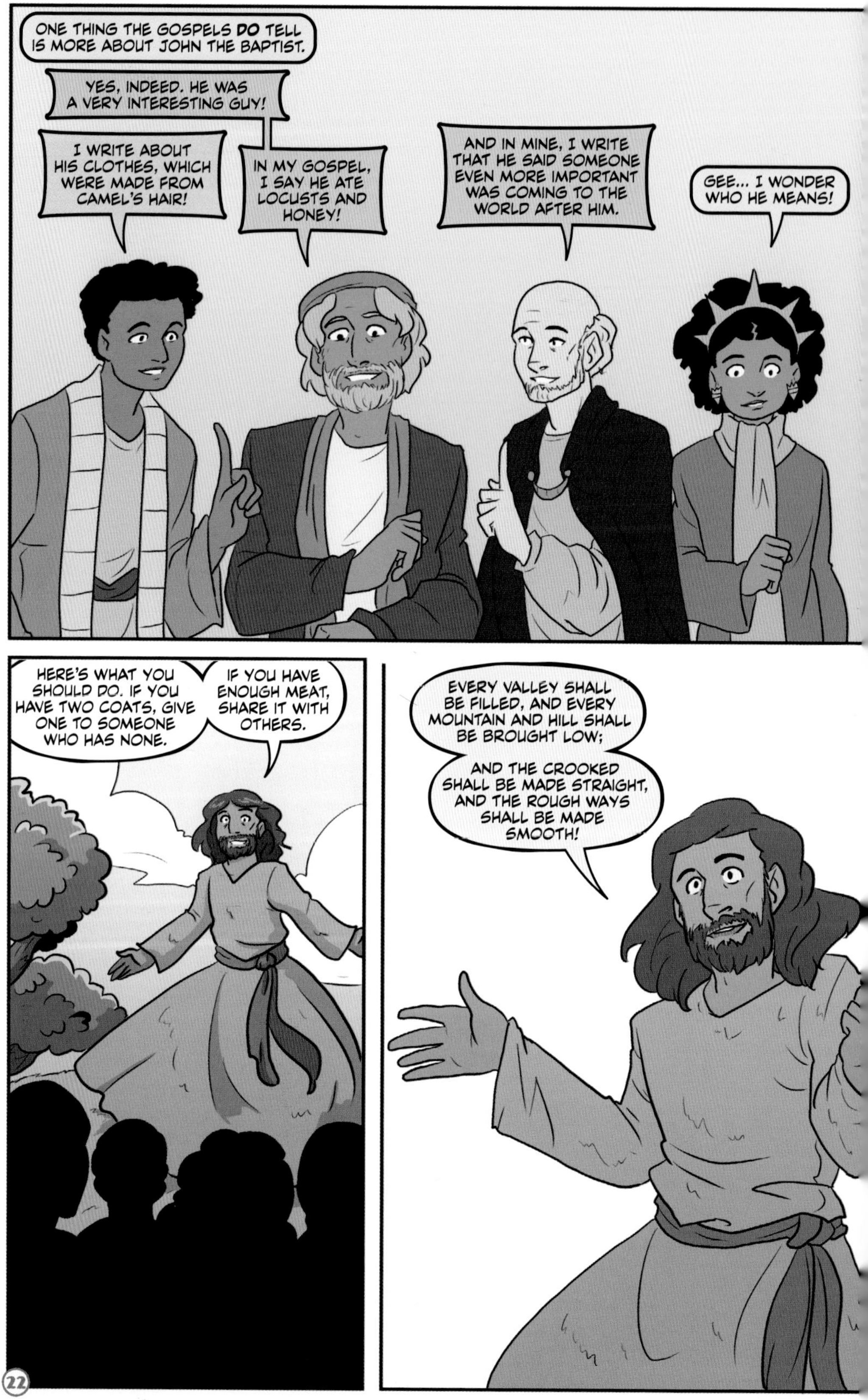
ONE THING THE GOSPELS DO TELL IS MORE ABOUT JOHN THE BAPTIST.
YES, INDEED. HE WAS A VERY INTERESTING GUY!
I WRITE ABOUT HIS CLOTHES, WHICH WERE MADE FROM CAMEL'S HAIR!
IN MY GOSPEL, I SAY HE ATE LOCUSTS AND HONEY!
AND IN MINE, I WRITE THAT HE SAID SOMEONE EVEN MORE IMPORTANT WAS COMING TO THE WORLD AFTER HIM.
GEE... I WONDER WHO HE MEANS!
HERE'S WHAT YOU SHOULD DO. IF YOU HAVE TWO COATS, GIVE ONE TO SOMEONE WHO HAS NONE.
IF YOU HAVE ENOUGH MEAT, SHARE IT WITH OTHERS.
EVERY VALLEY SHALL BE FILLED, AND EVERY MOUNTAIN AND HILL SHALL BE BROUGHT LOW;
AND THE CROOKED SHALL BE MADE STRAIGHT, AND THE ROUGH WAYS SHALL BE MADE SMOOTH!

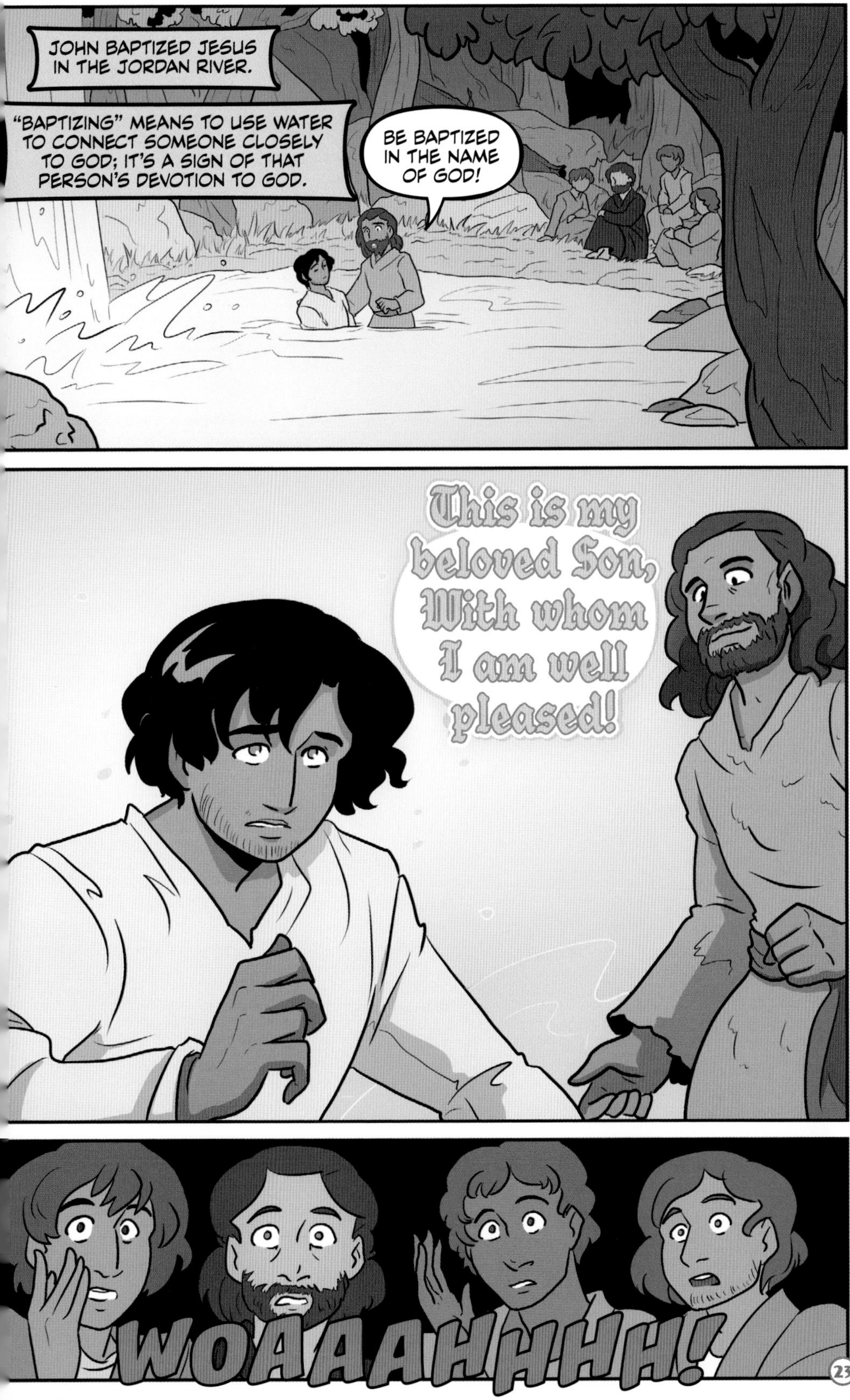
JOHN BAPTIZED JESUS IN THE JORDAN RIVER.
"BAPTIZING" MEANS TO USE WATER TO CONNECT SOMEONE CLOSELY TO GOD; IT'S A SIGN OF THAT PERSON'S DEVOTION TO GOD.
BE BAPTIZED IN THE NAME OF GOD!
This is my beloved Son, With whom I am well pleased!
WOAAAAHHHHH!

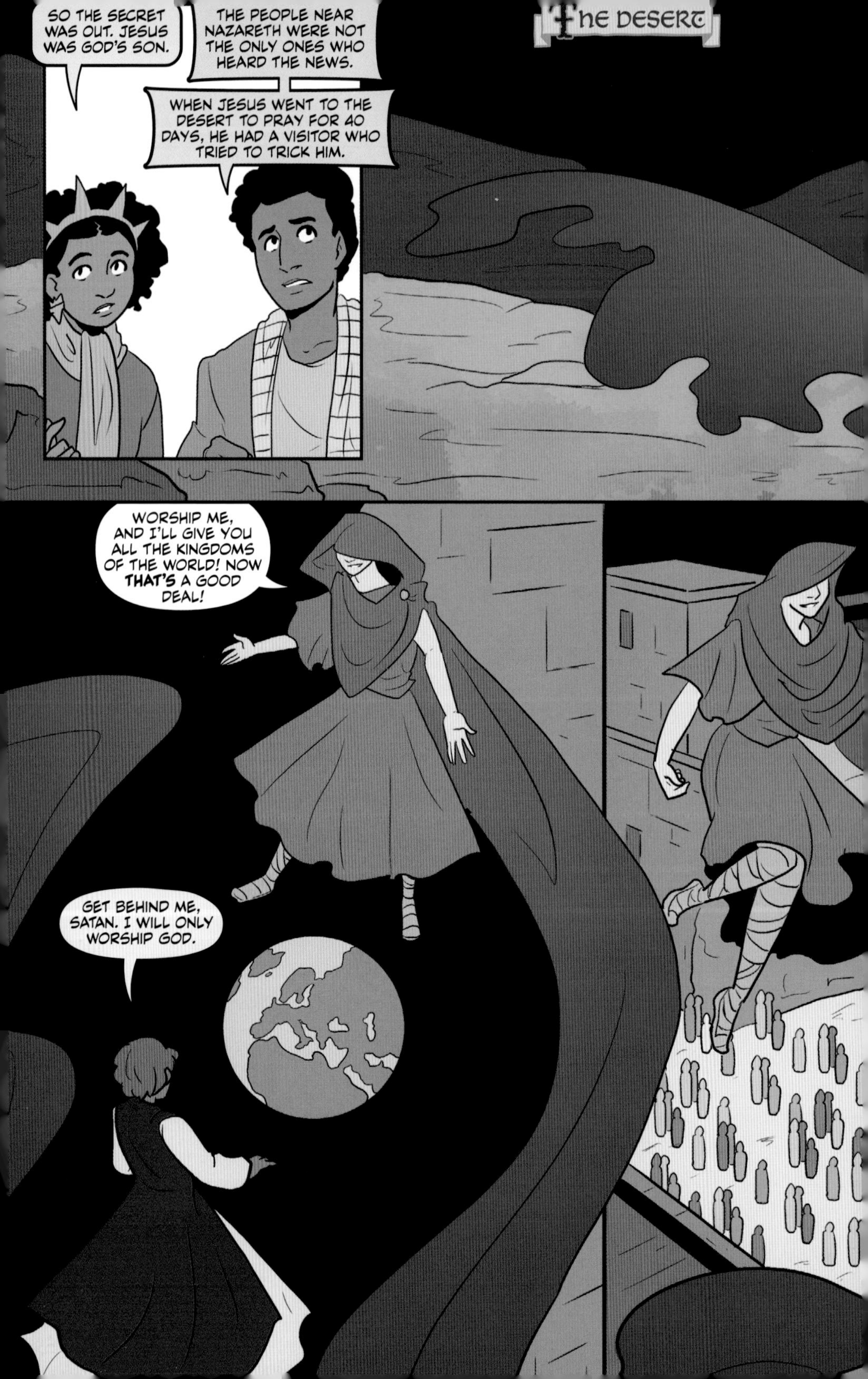
THE DESERT
SO THE SECRET WAS OUT. JESUS WAS GOD'S SON.
THE PEOPLE NEAR NAZARETH WERE NOT THE ONLY ONES WHO HEARD THE NEWS.
WHEN JESUS WENT TO THE DESERT TO PRAY FOR 40 DAYS, HE HAD A VISITOR WHO TRIED TO TRICK HIM.
WORSHIP ME, AND I'LL GIVE YOU ALL THE KINGDOMS OF THE WORLD! NOW **THAT'S** A GOOD DEAL!
GET BEHIND ME, SATAN. I WILL ONLY WORSHIP GOD.

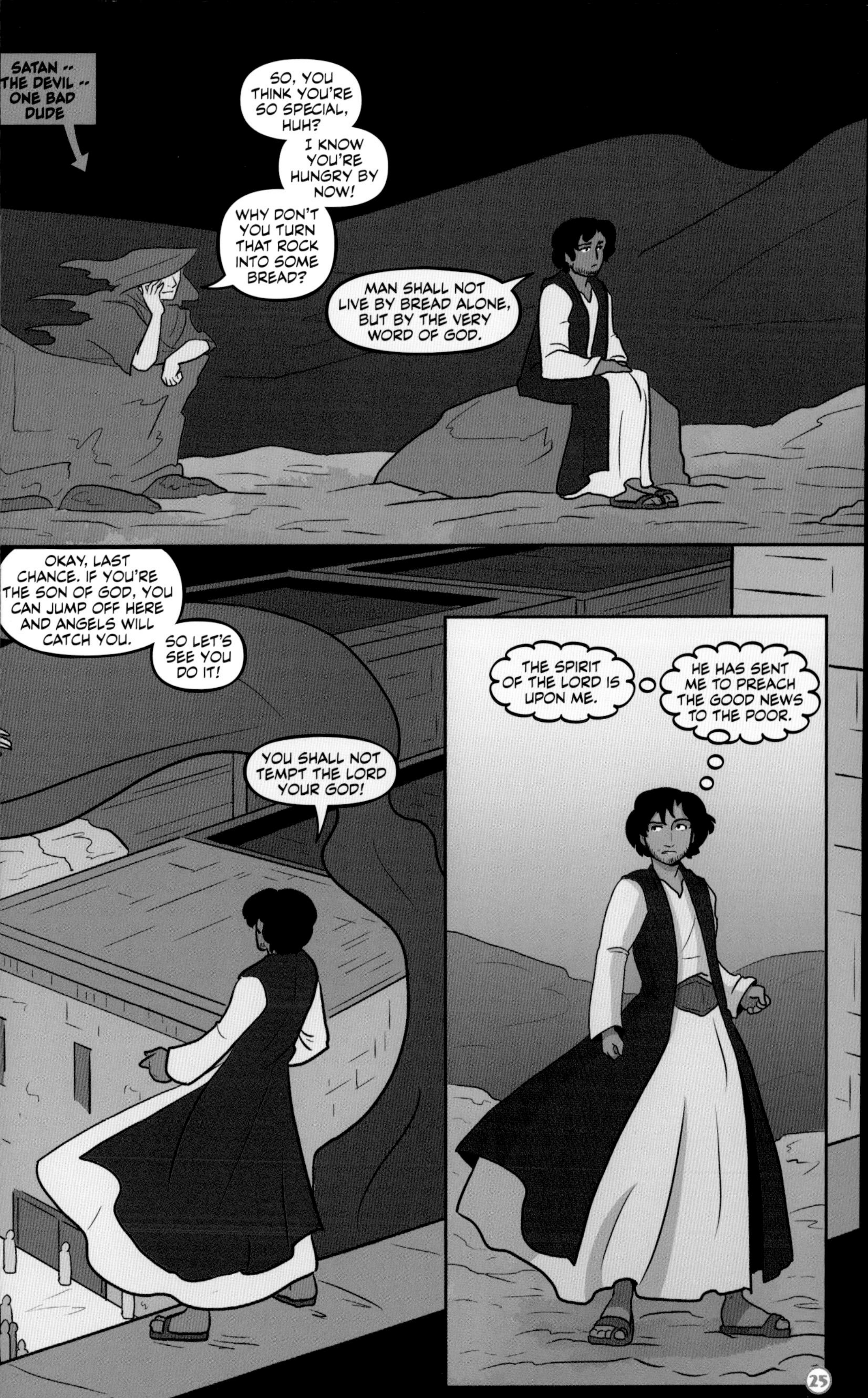

SATAN -- THE DEVIL -- ONE BAD DUDE
SO, YOU THINK YOU'RE SO SPECIAL, HUH?
I KNOW YOU'RE HUNGRY BY NOW!
WHY DON'T YOU TURN THAT ROCK INTO SOME BREAD?
MAN SHALL NOT LIVE BY BREAD ALONE, BUT BY THE VERY WORD OF GOD.
OKAY, LAST CHANCE. IF YOU'RE THE SON OF GOD, YOU CAN JUMP OFF HERE AND ANGELS WILL CATCH YOU.
SO LET'S SEE YOU DO IT!
YOU SHALL NOT TEMPT THE LORD YOUR GOD!
THE SPIRIT OF THE LORD IS UPON ME.
HE HAS SENT ME TO PREACH THE GOOD NEWS TO THE POOR.

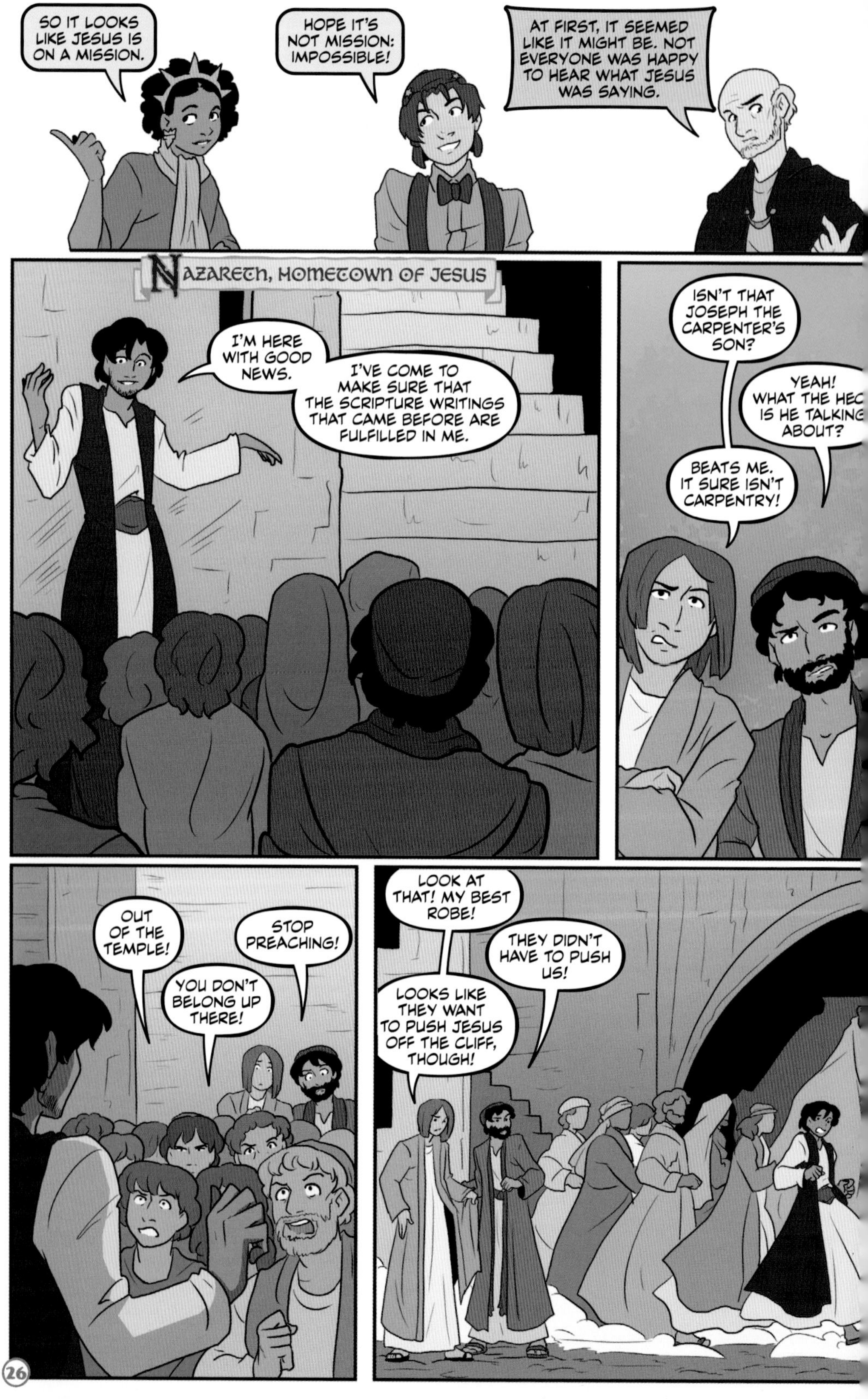

SO IT LOOKS LIKE JESUS IS ON A MISSION.
HOPE IT'S NOT MISSION: IMPOSSIBLE!
AT FIRST, IT SEEMED LIKE IT MIGHT BE. NOT EVERYONE WAS HAPPY TO HEAR WHAT JESUS WAS SAYING.
NAZARETH, HOMETOWN OF JESUS
I'M HERE WITH GOOD NEWS.
I'VE COME TO MAKE SURE THAT THE SCRIPTURE WRITINGS THAT CAME BEFORE ARE FULFILLED IN ME.
ISN'T THAT JOSEPH THE CARPENTER'S SON?
YEAH! WHAT THE HEC IS HE TALKING ABOUT?
BEATS ME. IT SURE ISN'T CARPENTRY!
OUT OF THE TEMPLE!
STOP PREACHING!
YOU DON'T BELONG UP THERE!
LOOK AT THAT! MY BEST ROBE!
THEY DIDN'T HAVE TO PUSH US!
LOOKS LIKE THEY WANT TO PUSH JESUS OFF THE CLIFF, THOUGH!

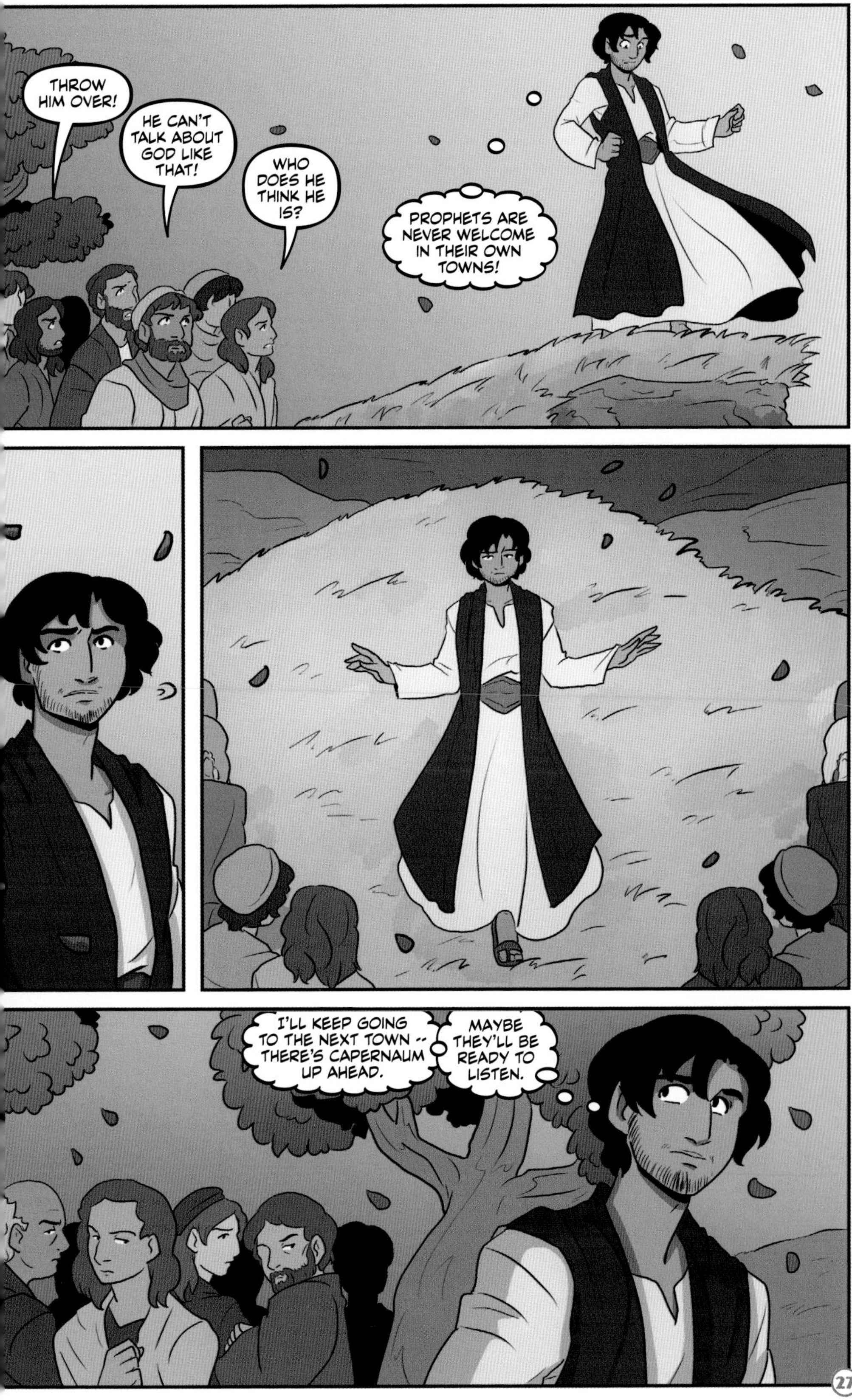
THROW HIM OVER!
HE CAN'T TALK ABOUT GOD LIKE THAT!
WHO DOES HE THINK HE IS?
PROPHETS ARE NEVER WELCOME IN THEIR OWN TOWNS!
I'LL KEEP GOING TO THE NEXT TOWN -- THERE'S CAPERNAUM UP AHEAD.
MAYBE THEY'LL BE READY TO LISTEN.

WOW, RUN OUT OF HIS OWN TOWN! THAT'S TOUGH.

WELL, HE WAS INDEED A MAN ON A MISSION. AND HE NEEDED HELP TO SPREAD HIS GOOD NEWS.

HEY, GOSPEL GUYS! HOW DID JESUS MEET HIS FIRST FOLLOWERS?

IT WAS LIKE THIS: JESUS WAS WALKING BY THE SEA OF GALILEE. ANDREW AND HIS BROTHER SIMON PETER WERE FISHING.

ANDREW SIMON PETER

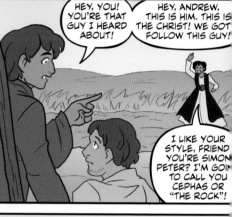

HEY, YOU! YOU'RE THAT GUY I HEARD ABOUT!

HEY, ANDREW, THIS IS HIM. THIS IS THE CHRIST! WE GOT FOLLOW THIS GUY!

I LIKE YOUR STYLE, FRIEND YOU'RE SIMON PETER? I'M GOIN TO CALL YOU CEPHAS OR "THE ROCK"!

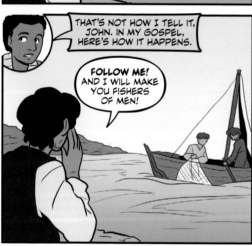

THAT'S NOT HOW I TELL IT, JOHN. IN MY GOSPEL, HERE'S HOW IT HAPPENS.

FOLLOW ME! AND I WILL MAKE YOU FISHERS OF MEN!

WELL, THAT'S CLOSE, BUT YOU LEFT OUT ONE COOL PART OF THE STORY.

HEY, FISHERMEN! HOW'S IT GOING?

LOUSY! WE'VE BEEN OUT HERE ALL DAY AND HAVEN'T CAUGHT A THING.

TELL YOU WHAT -- WHY DON'T YOU TRY ONE MORE CAST?

WHOA! A TON OF FISH! THAT WAS AWESOME! I'M GOING TO FOLLOW YOU ANYWHERE!

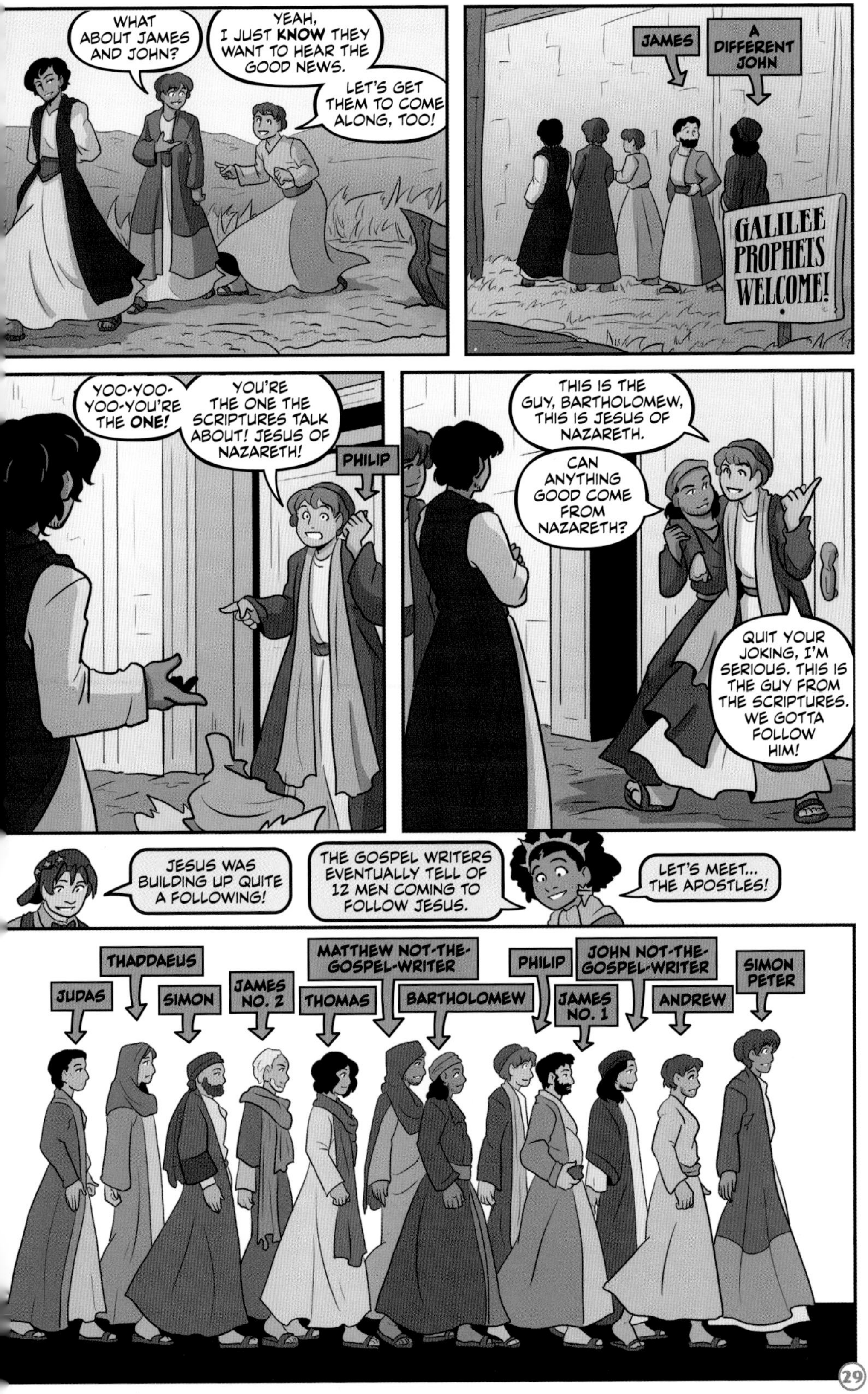
WHAT ABOUT JAMES AND JOHN?
YEAH, I JUST KNOW THEY WANT TO HEAR THE GOOD NEWS.
LET'S GET THEM TO COME ALONG, TOO!
JAMES
A DIFFERENT JOHN
GALILEE PROPHETS WELCOME!
YOO-YOO-YOO-YOU'RE THE ONE!
YOU'RE THE ONE THE SCRIPTURES TALK ABOUT! JESUS OF NAZARETH!
PHILIP
THIS IS THE GUY, BARTHOLOMEW, THIS IS JESUS OF NAZARETH.
CAN ANYTHING GOOD COME FROM NAZARETH?
QUIT YOUR JOKING, I'M SERIOUS. THIS IS THE GUY FROM THE SCRIPTURES. WE GOTTA FOLLOW HIM!
JESUS WAS BUILDING UP QUITE A FOLLOWING!
THE GOSPEL WRITERS EVENTUALLY TELL OF 12 MEN COMING TO FOLLOW JESUS.
LET'S MEET... THE APOSTLES!
JUDAS
THADDAEUS
SIMON
JAMES NO. 2
THOMAS
MATTHEW NOT-THE-GOSPEL-WRITER
BARTHOLOMEW
PHILIP
JAMES NO. 1
JOHN NOT-THE-GOSPEL-WRITER
ANDREW
SIMON PETER

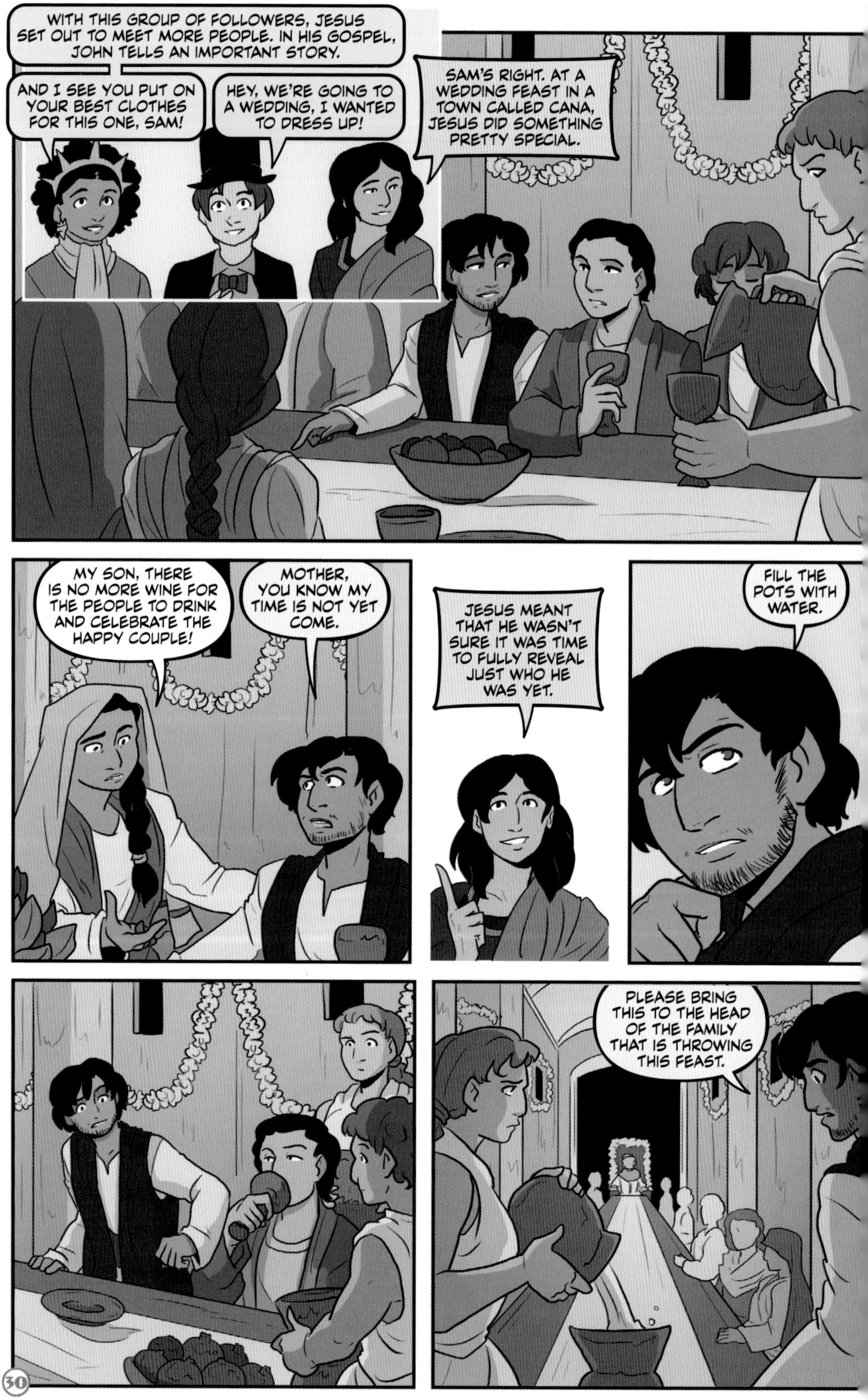
WITH THIS GROUP OF FOLLOWERS, JESUS SET OUT TO MEET MORE PEOPLE. IN HIS GOSPEL, JOHN TELLS AN IMPORTANT STORY.
AND I SEE YOU PUT ON YOUR BEST CLOTHES FOR THIS ONE, SAM!
HEY, WE'RE GOING TO A WEDDING, I WANTED TO DRESS UP!
SAM'S RIGHT. AT A WEDDING FEAST IN A TOWN CALLED CANA, JESUS DID SOMETHING PRETTY SPECIAL.
MY SON, THERE IS NO MORE WINE FOR THE PEOPLE TO DRINK AND CELEBRATE THE HAPPY COUPLE!
MOTHER, YOU KNOW MY TIME IS NOT YET COME.
JESUS MEANT THAT HE WASN'T SURE IT WAS TIME TO FULLY REVEAL JUST WHO HE WAS YET.
FILL THE POTS WITH WATER.
PLEASE BRING THIS TO THE HEAD OF THE FAMILY THAT IS THROWING THIS FEAST.

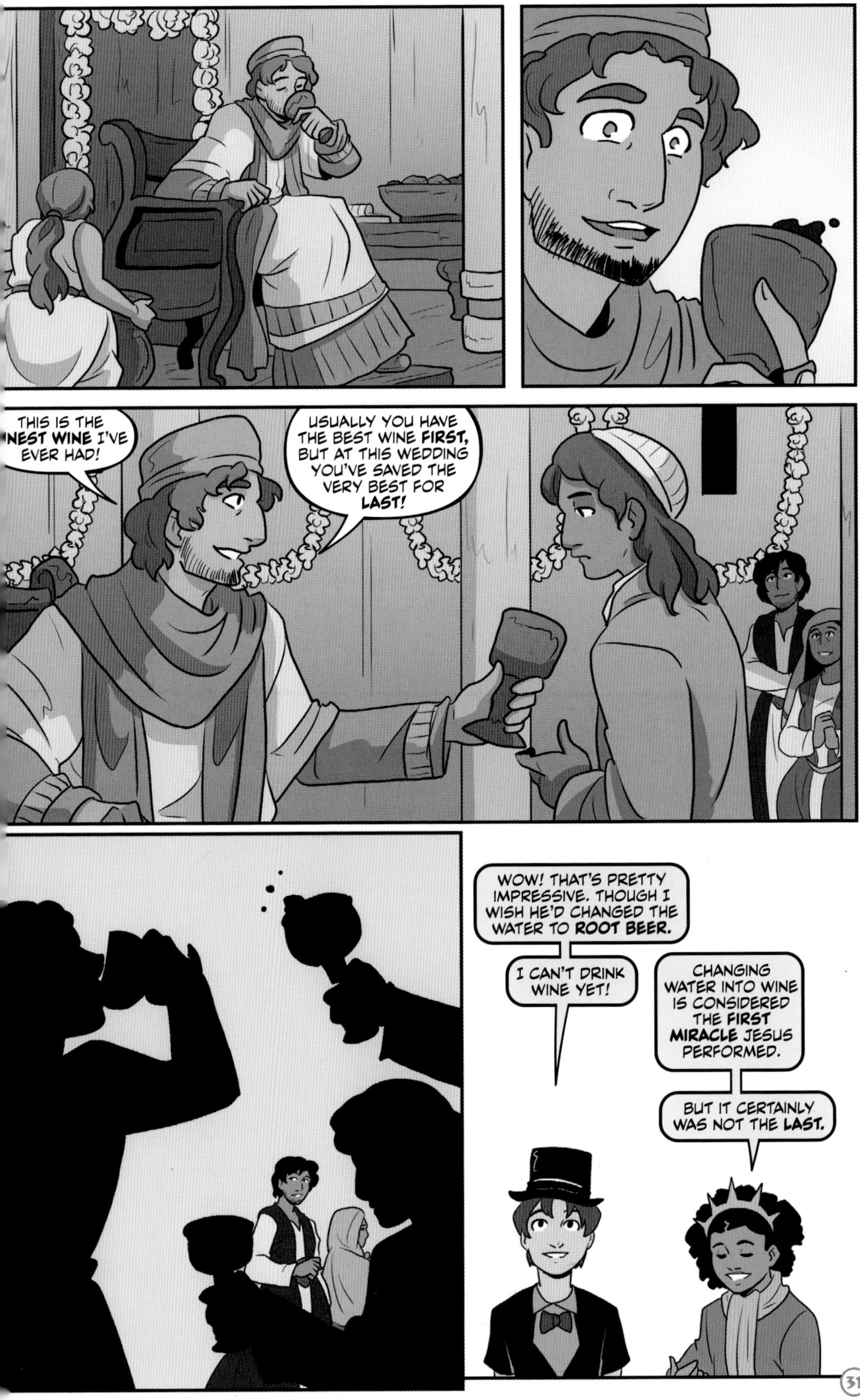
THIS IS THE NEST WINE I'VE EVER HAD!
USUALLY YOU HAVE THE BEST WINE FIRST, BUT AT THIS WEDDING YOU'VE SAVED THE VERY BEST FOR LAST!
WOW! THAT'S PRETTY IMPRESSIVE. THOUGH I WISH HE'D CHANGED THE WATER TO ROOT BEER.
I CAN'T DRINK WINE YET!
CHANGING WATER INTO WINE IS CONSIDERED THE FIRST MIRACLE JESUS PERFORMED.
BUT IT CERTAINLY WAS NOT THE LAST.

Some miracle moments!

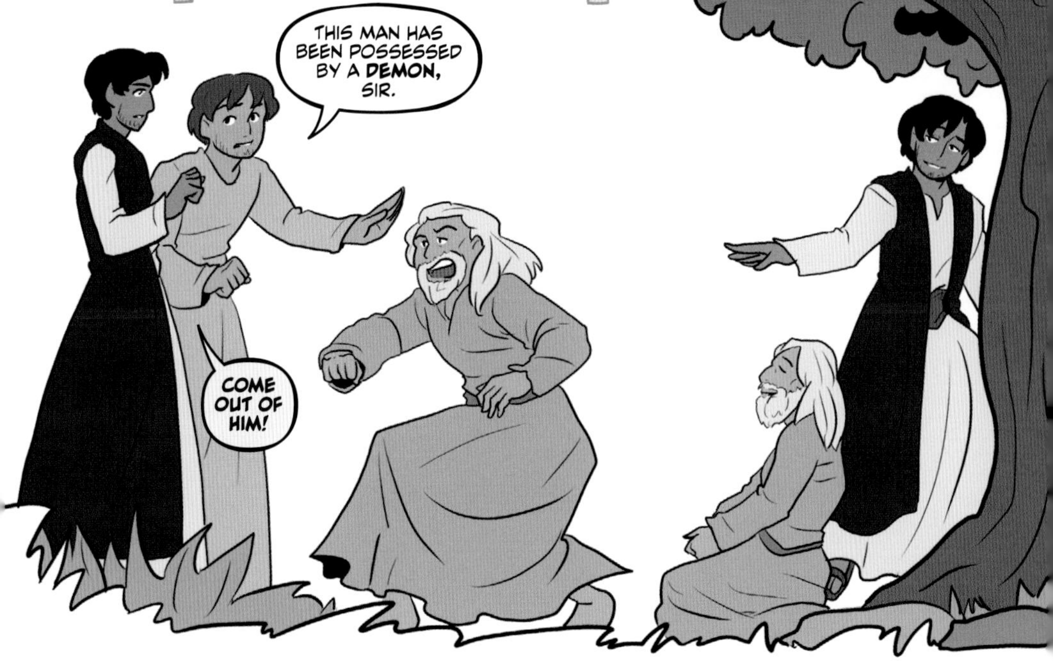
THIS MAN HAS BEEN POSSESSED BY A **DEMON,** SIR.
COME OUT OF HIM!

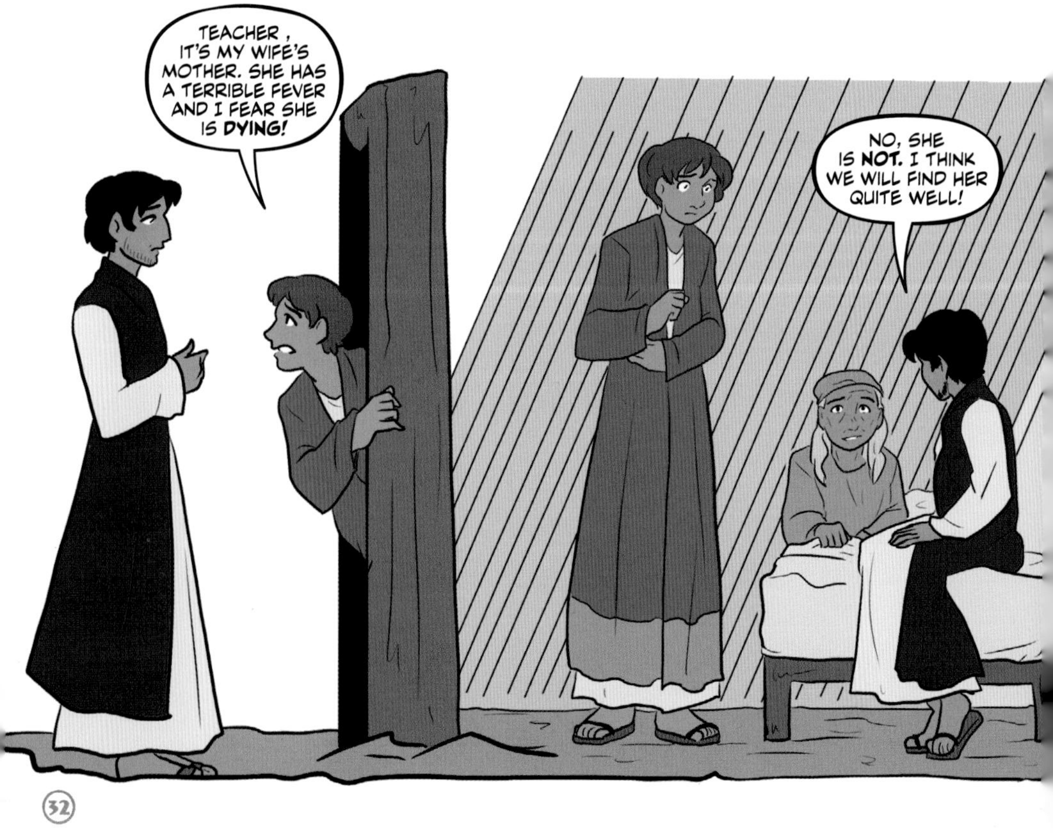
TEACHER , IT'S MY WIFE'S MOTHER. SHE HAS A TERRIBLE FEVER AND I FEAR SHE IS **DYING!**
NO, SHE IS **NOT.** I THINK WE WILL FIND HER QUITE WELL!

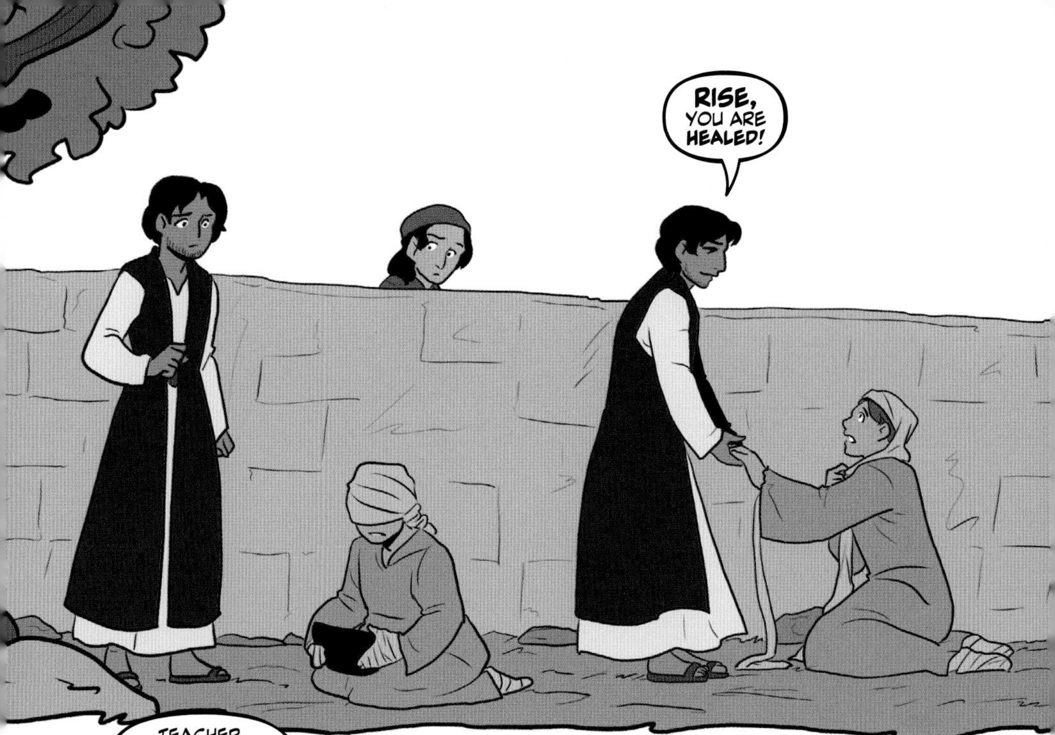
RISE, YOU ARE HEALED!

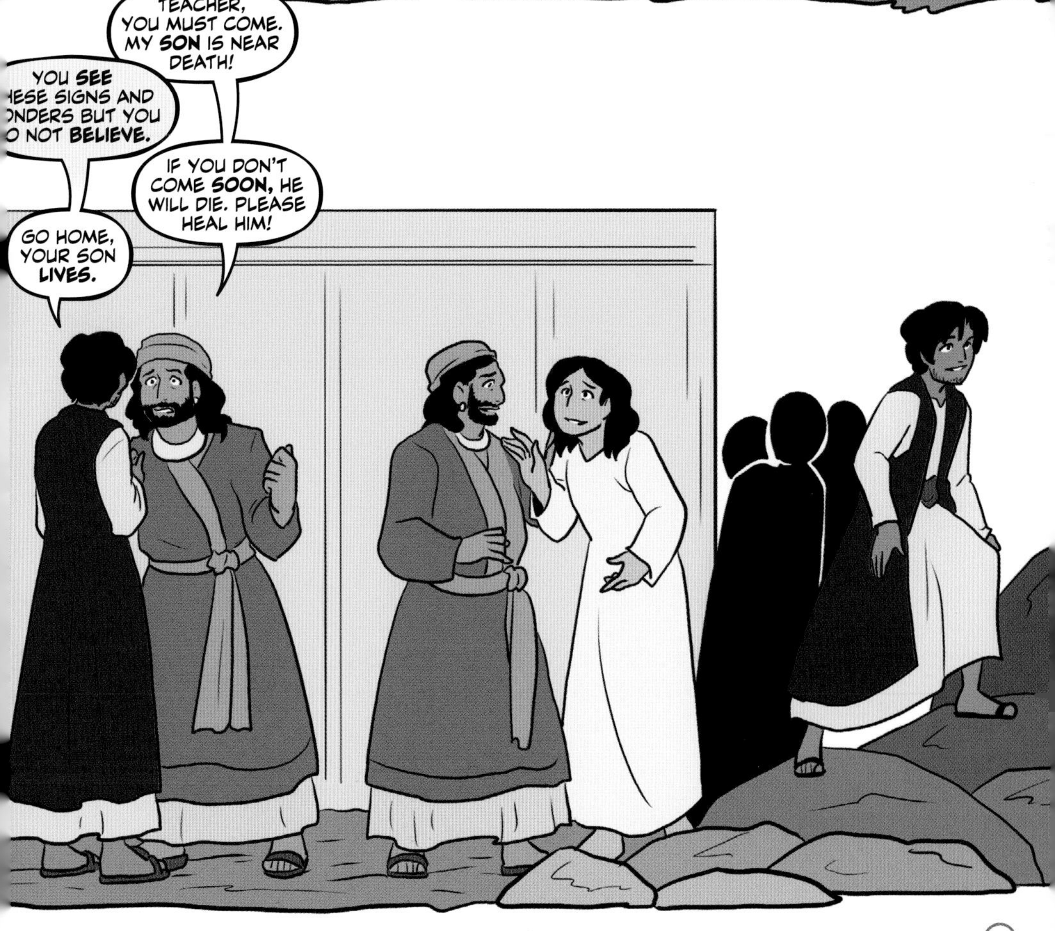
TEACHER, YOU MUST COME. MY SON IS NEAR DEATH!
YOU SEE HESE SIGNS AND ONDERS BUT YOU O NOT BELIEVE.
IF YOU DON'T COME SOON, HE WILL DIE. PLEASE HEAL HIM!
GO HOME, YOUR SON LIVES.

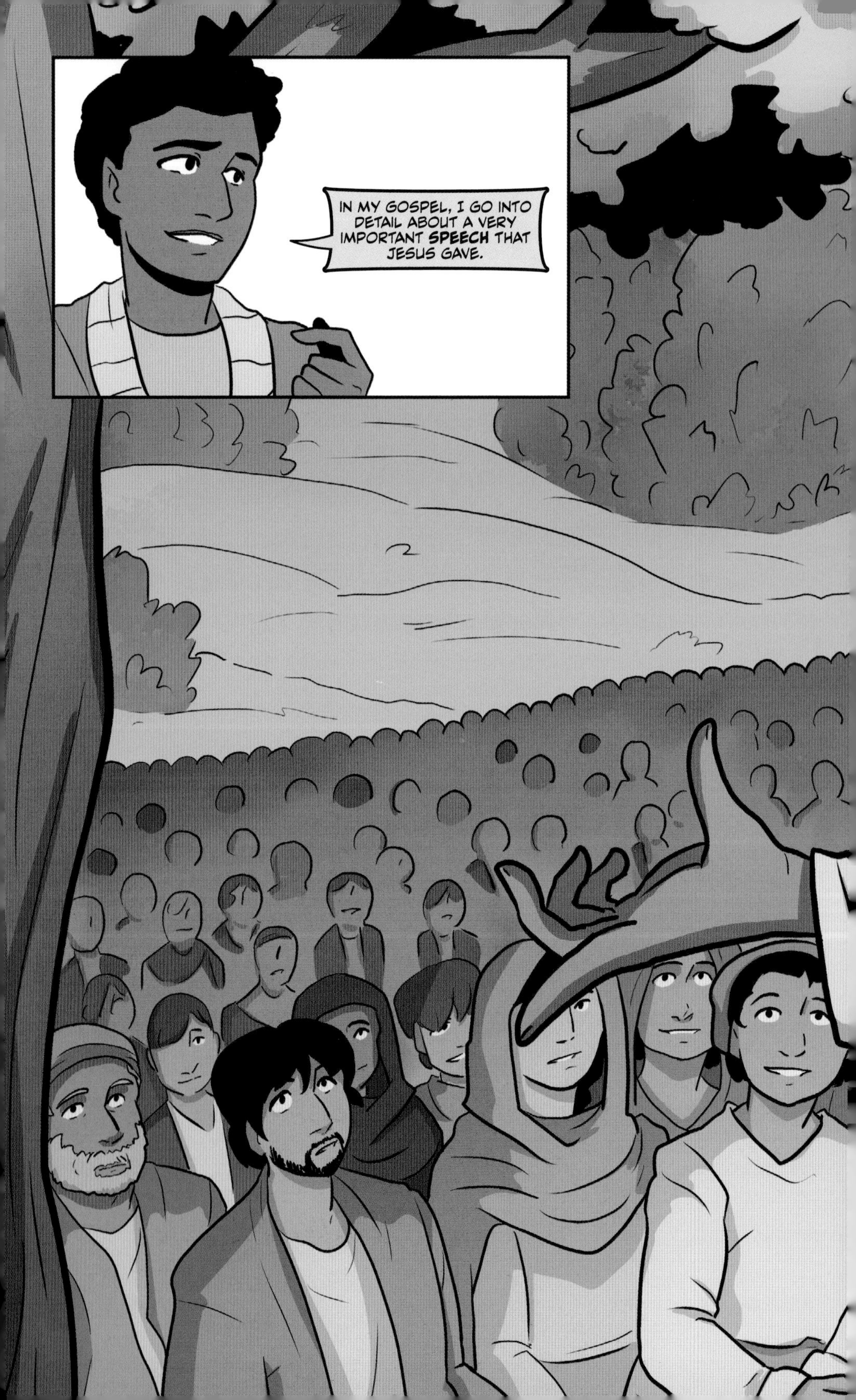
IN MY GOSPEL, I GO INTO DETAIL ABOUT A VERY IMPORTANT **SPEECH** THAT JESUS GAVE.

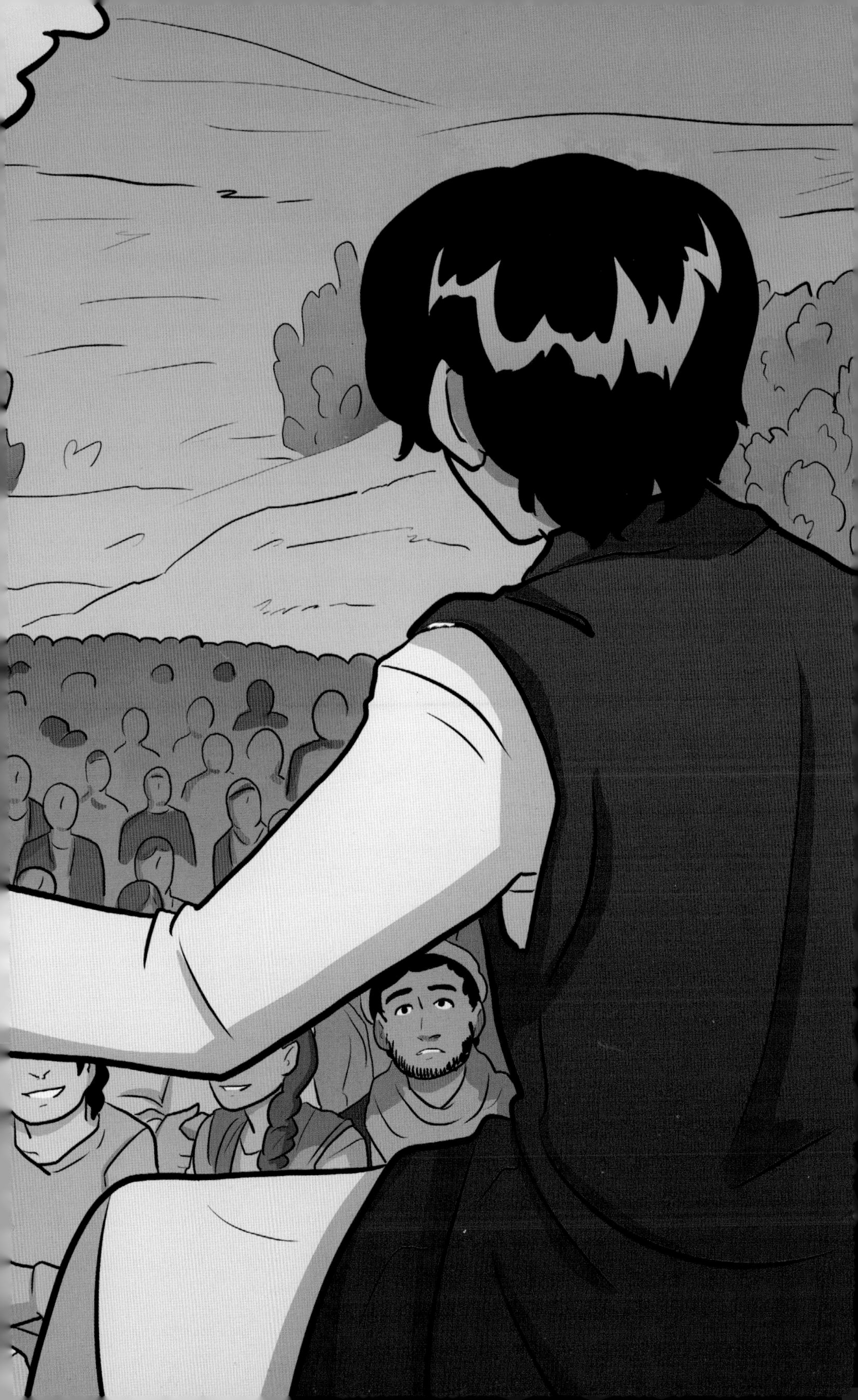

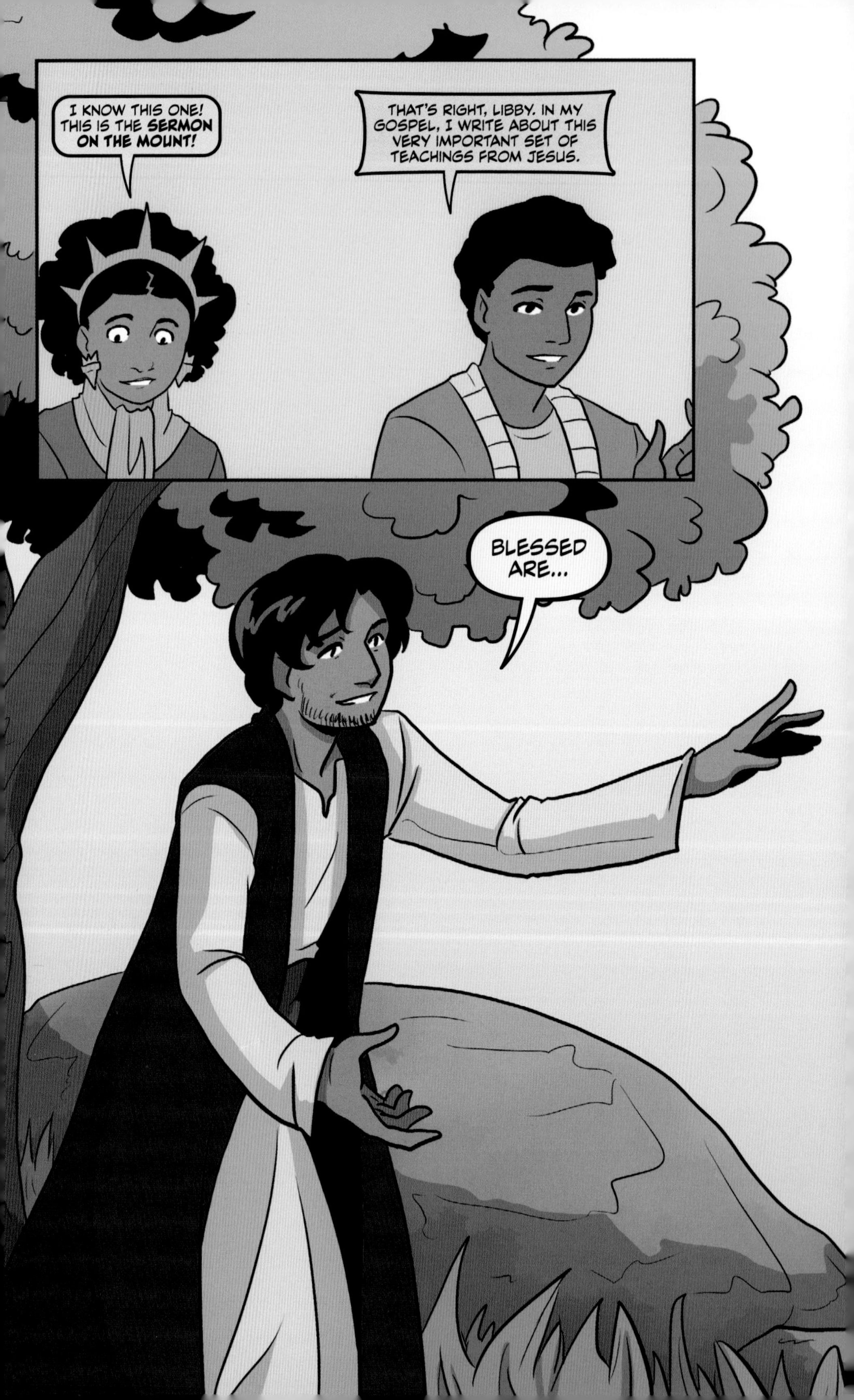
I KNOW THIS ONE! THIS IS THE **SERMON ON THE MOUNT!**
THAT'S RIGHT, LIBBY. IN MY GOSPEL, I WRITE ABOUT THIS VERY IMPORTANT SET OF TEACHINGS FROM JESUS.
BLESSED ARE...

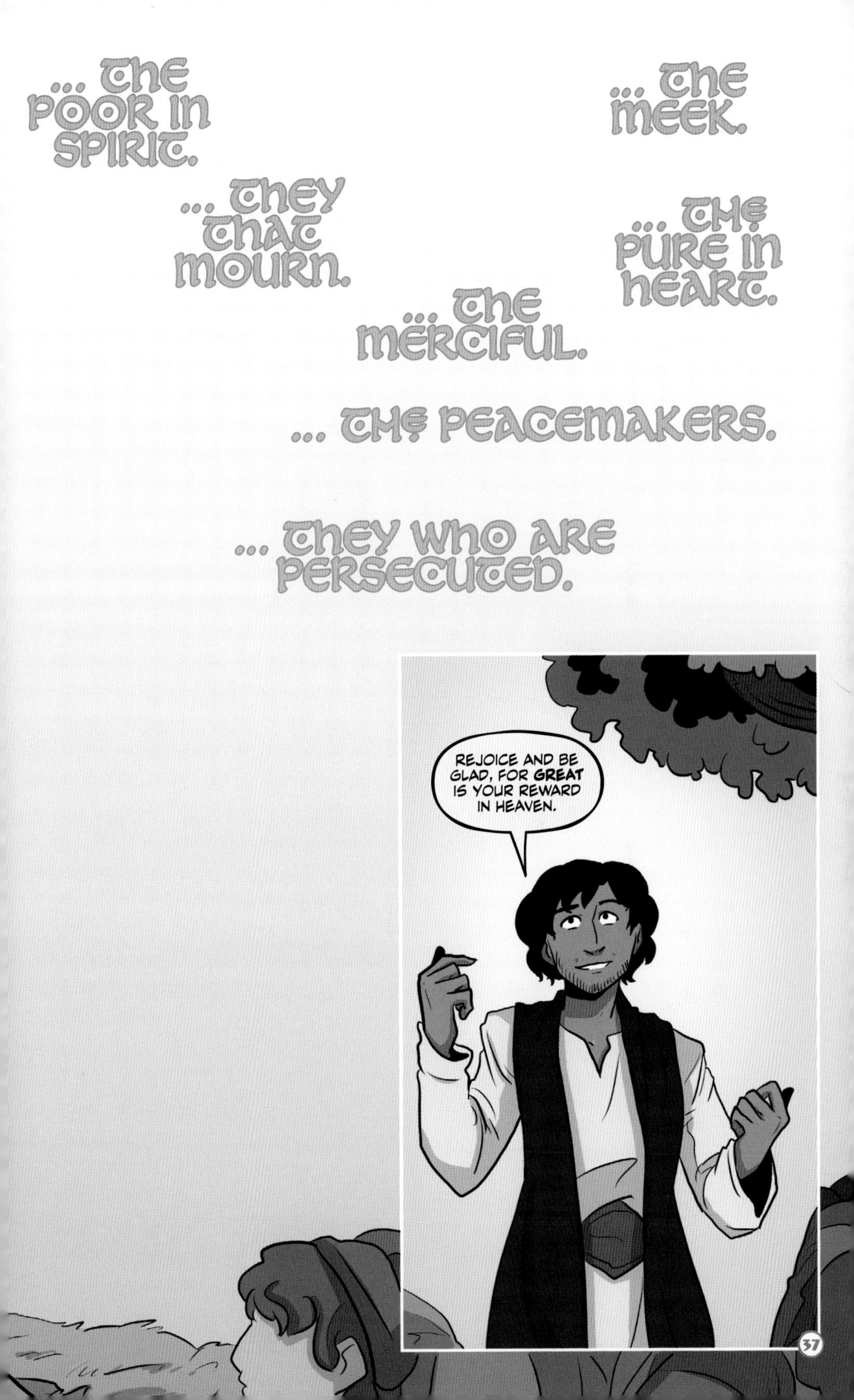
... THE POOR IN SPIRIT.
... THE MEEK.
... THEY THAT MOURN.
... THE PURE IN HEART.
... THE MERCIFUL.
... THE PEACEMAKERS.
... THEY WHO ARE PERSECUTED.
REJOICE AND BE GLAD, FOR **GREAT** IS YOUR REWARD IN HEAVEN.

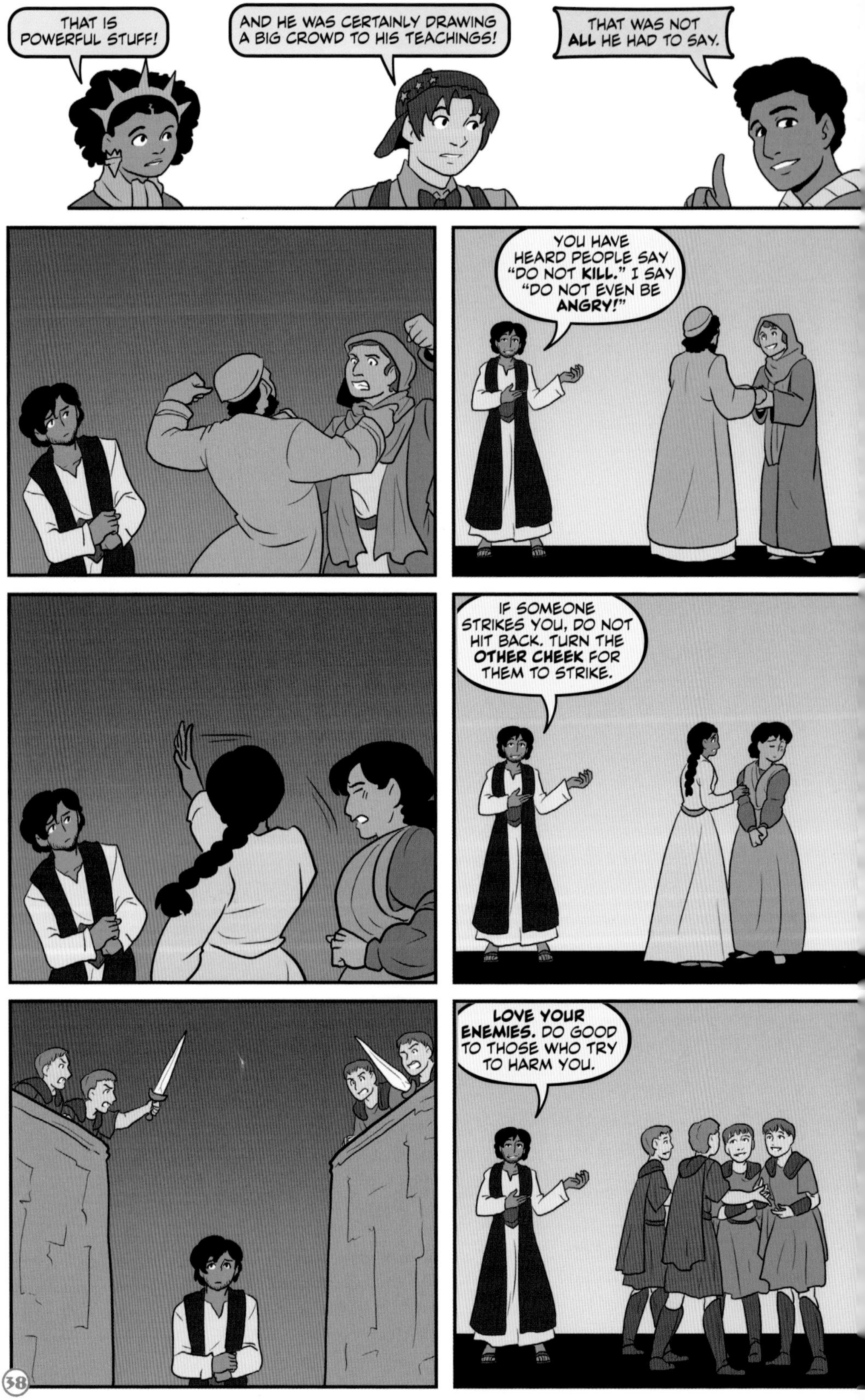
THAT IS POWERFUL STUFF!
AND HE WAS CERTAINLY DRAWING A BIG CROWD TO HIS TEACHINGS!
THAT WAS NOT **ALL** HE HAD TO SAY.
YOU HAVE HEARD PEOPLE SAY "DO NOT **KILL.**" I SAY "DO NOT EVEN BE **ANGRY!**"
IF SOMEONE STRIKES YOU, DO NOT HIT BACK. TURN THE **OTHER CHEEK** FOR THEM TO STRIKE.
LOVE YOUR ENEMIES. DO GOOD TO THOSE WHO TRY TO HARM YOU.

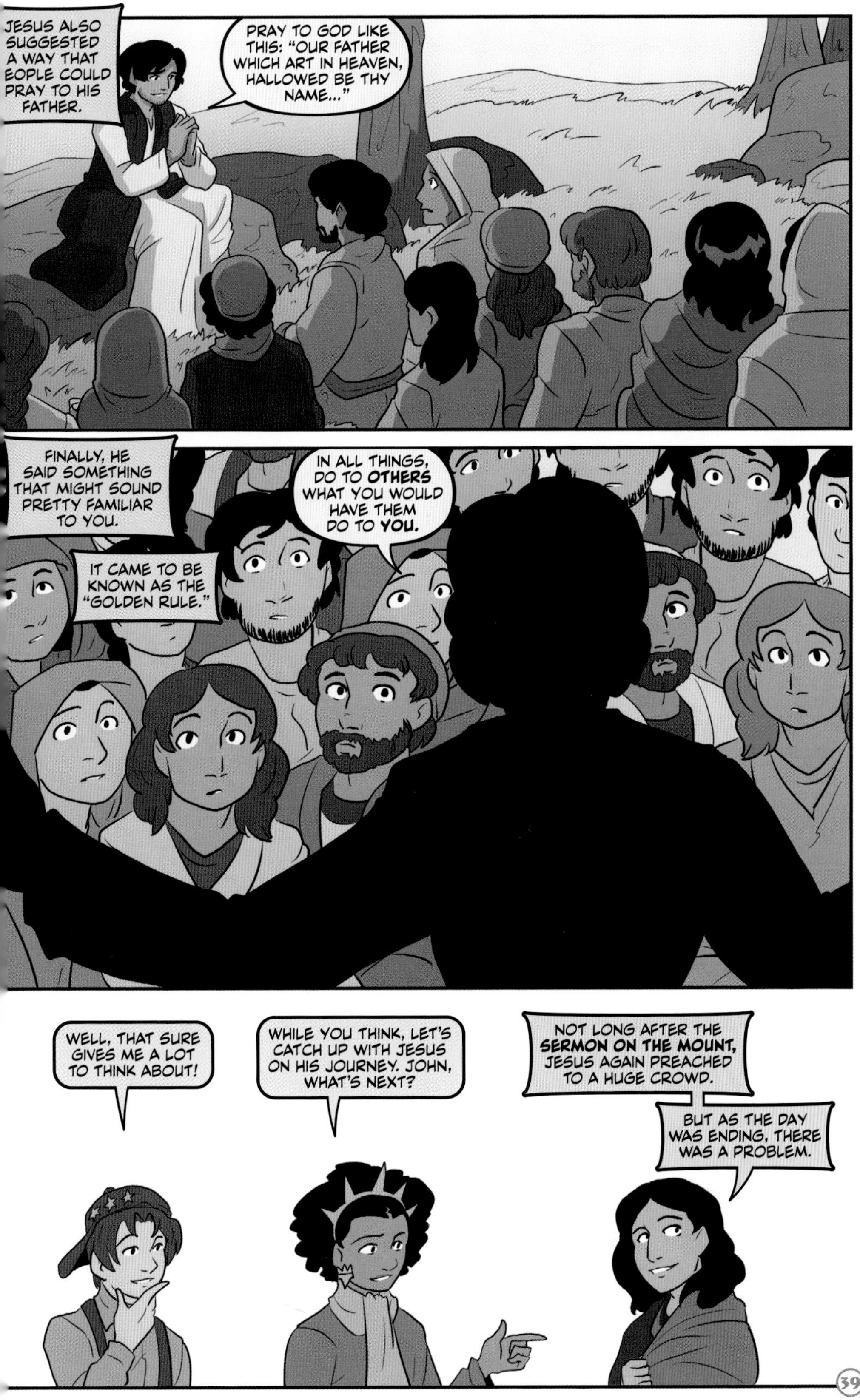
JESUS ALSO SUGGESTED A WAY THAT EOPLE COULD PRAY TO HIS FATHER.
PRAY TO GOD LIKE THIS: "OUR FATHER WHICH ART IN HEAVEN, HALLOWED BE THY NAME..."
FINALLY, HE SAID SOMETHING THAT MIGHT SOUND PRETTY FAMILIAR TO YOU.
IN ALL THINGS, DO TO **OTHERS** WHAT YOU WOULD HAVE THEM DO TO **YOU.**
IT CAME TO BE KNOWN AS THE "GOLDEN RULE."
WELL, THAT SURE GIVES ME A LOT TO THINK ABOUT!
WHILE YOU THINK, LET'S CATCH UP WITH JESUS ON HIS JOURNEY. JOHN, WHAT'S NEXT?
NOT LONG AFTER THE **SERMON ON THE MOUNT,** JESUS AGAIN PREACHED TO A HUGE CROWD.
BUT AS THE DAY WAS ENDING, THERE WAS A PROBLEM.

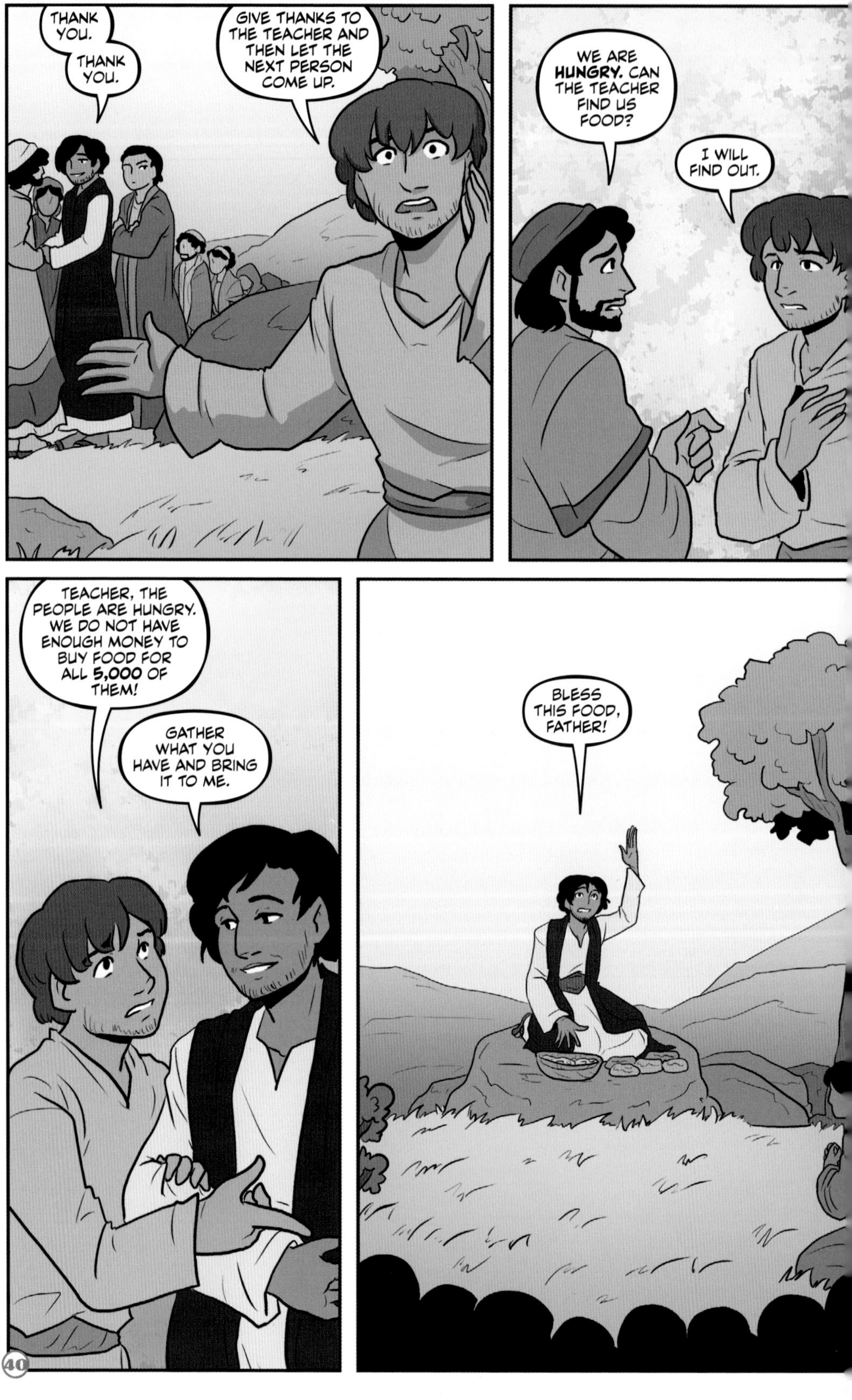
THANK YOU.
THANK YOU.
GIVE THANKS TO THE TEACHER AND THEN LET THE NEXT PERSON COME UP.
WE ARE **HUNGRY.** CAN THE TEACHER FIND US FOOD?
I WILL FIND OUT.
TEACHER, THE PEOPLE ARE HUNGRY. WE DO NOT HAVE ENOUGH MONEY TO BUY FOOD FOR ALL **5,000** OF THEM!
GATHER WHAT YOU HAVE AND BRING IT TO ME.
BLESS THIS FOOD, FATHER!

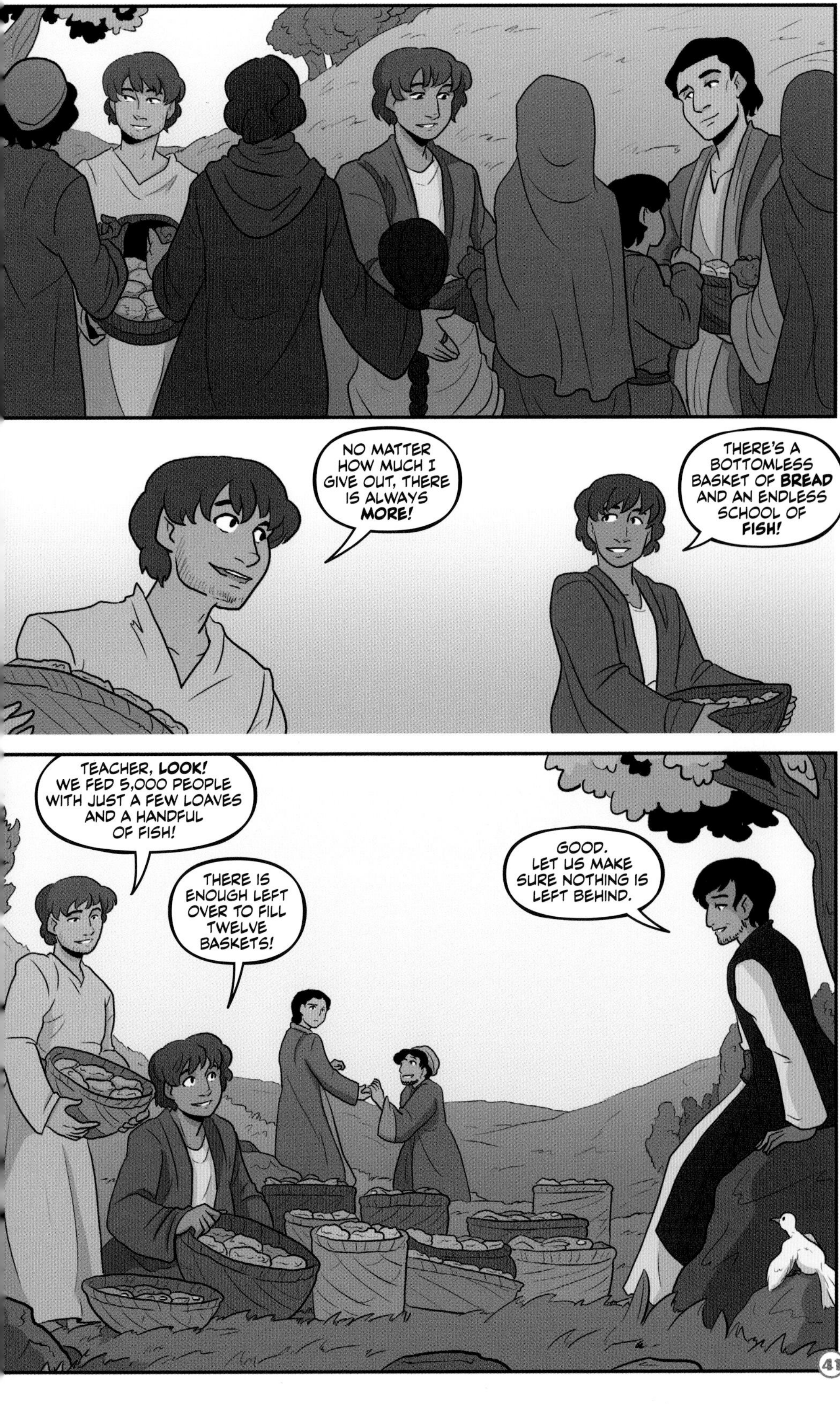
NO MATTER HOW MUCH I GIVE OUT, THERE IS ALWAYS **MORE!**
THERE'S A BOTTOMLESS BASKET OF **BREAD** AND AN ENDLESS SCHOOL OF **FISH!**
TEACHER, **LOOK!** WE FED 5,000 PEOPLE WITH JUST A FEW LOAVES AND A HANDFUL OF FISH!
THERE IS ENOUGH LEFT OVER TO FILL TWELVE BASKETS!
GOOD. LET US MAKE SURE NOTHING IS LEFT BEHIND.

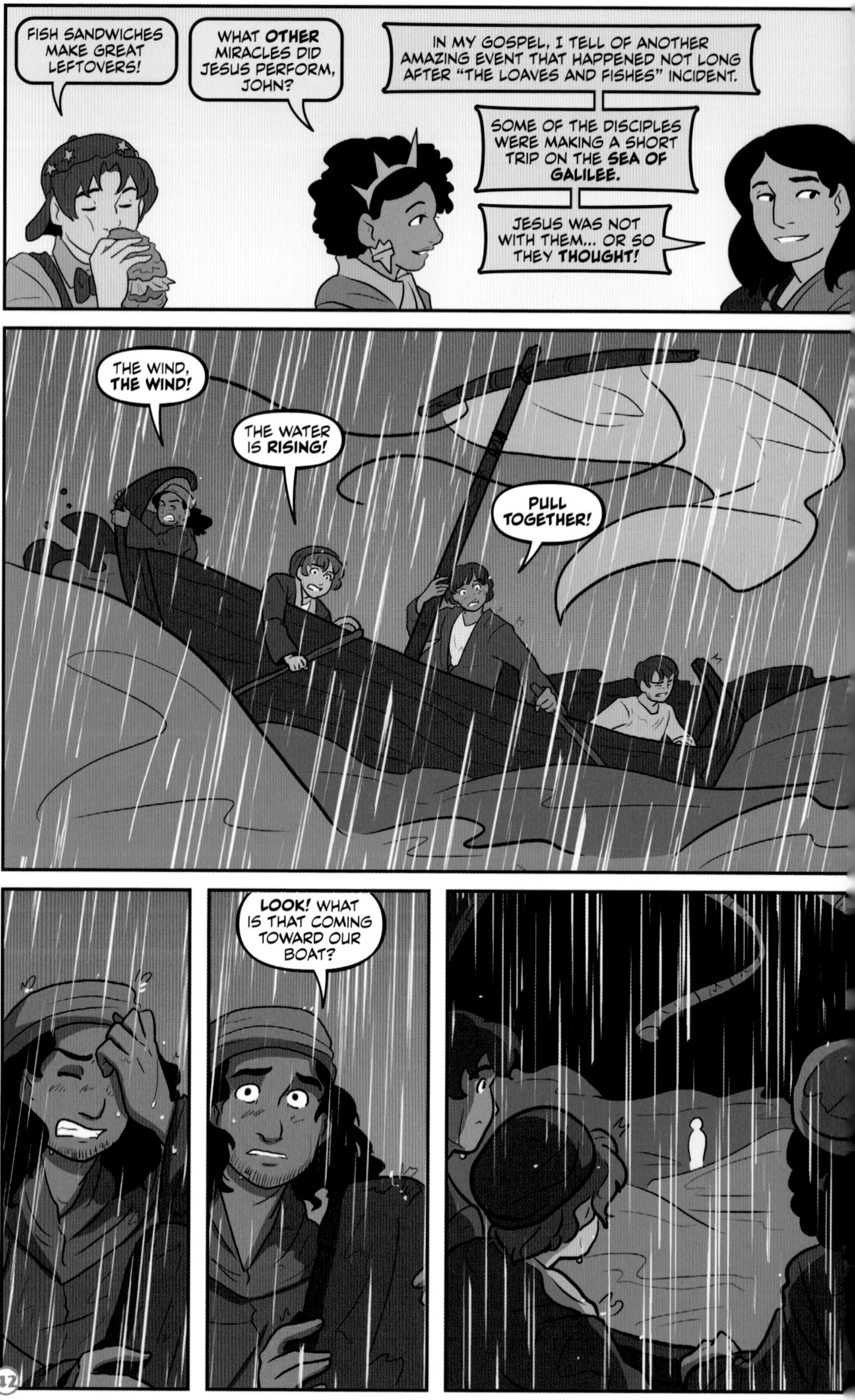
FISH SANDWICHES MAKE GREAT LEFTOVERS!
WHAT **OTHER** MIRACLES DID JESUS PERFORM, JOHN?
IN MY GOSPEL, I TELL OF ANOTHER AMAZING EVENT THAT HAPPENED NOT LONG AFTER "THE LOAVES AND FISHES" INCIDENT.
SOME OF THE DISCIPLES WERE MAKING A SHORT TRIP ON THE **SEA OF GALILEE.**
JESUS WAS NOT WITH THEM... OR SO THEY **THOUGHT!**
THE WIND, **THE WIND!**
THE WATER IS **RISING!**
PULL TOGETHER!
LOOK! WHAT IS THAT COMING TOWARD OUR BOAT?

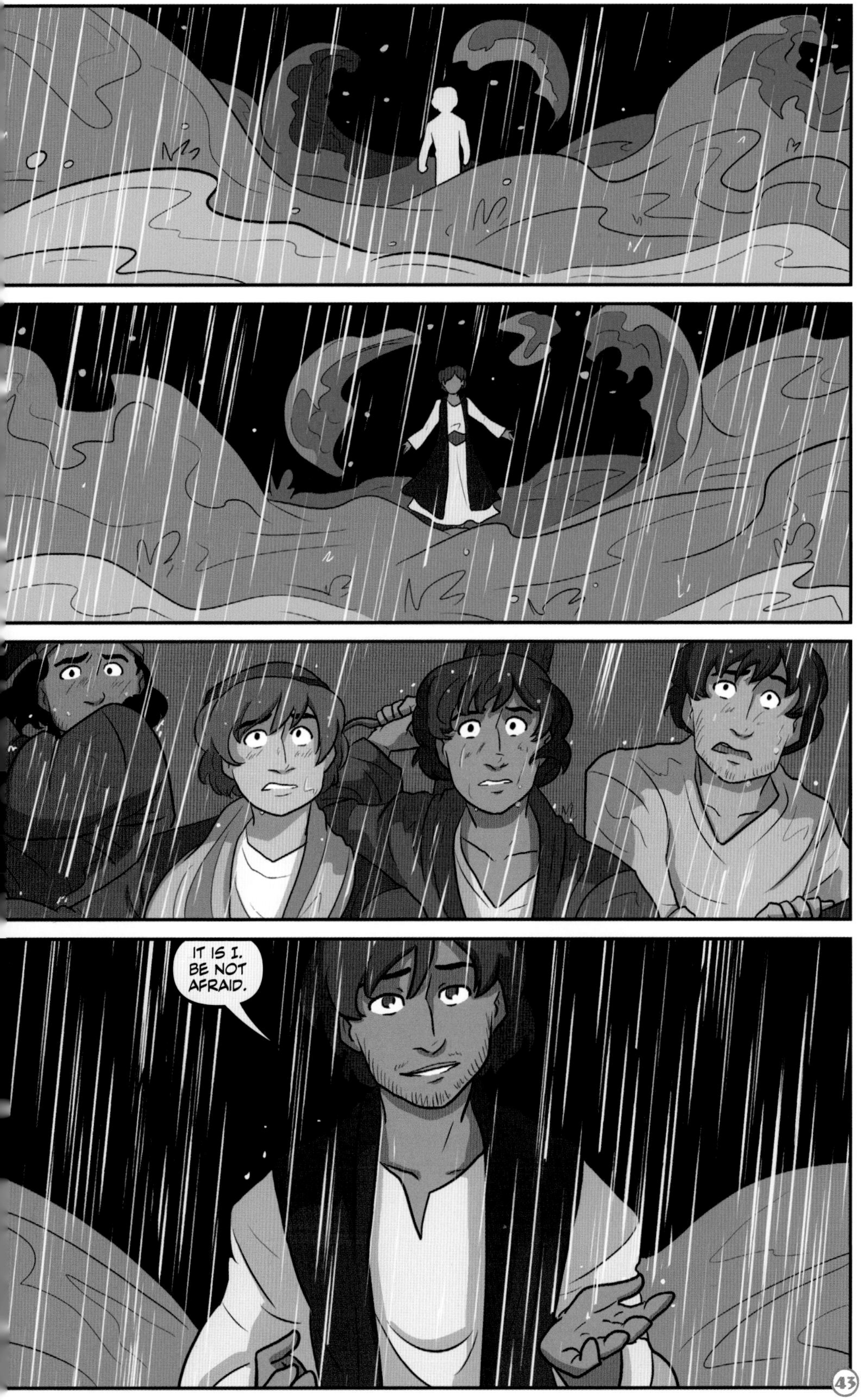
IT IS I. BE NOT AFRAID.

IF THAT IS **YOU**, LORD, TELL ME TO COME TO YOU ON THE WATER!

COME TO ME!

LORD, **SAVE** ME!

WHY DID YOU NOT HAVE **FAITH?** WHY DID YOU **DOUBT?**

THAT WAS AMAZING!

JESUS WAS SHOWING HIS DISCIPLES WHAT HE COULD DO WITH THE POWER OF GOD, HIS FATHER.

IN THIS TIME, HE MET AND TAUGHT THOUSANDS OF PEOPLE ALL OVER THE AREA. SEE?

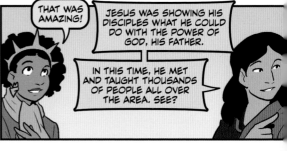

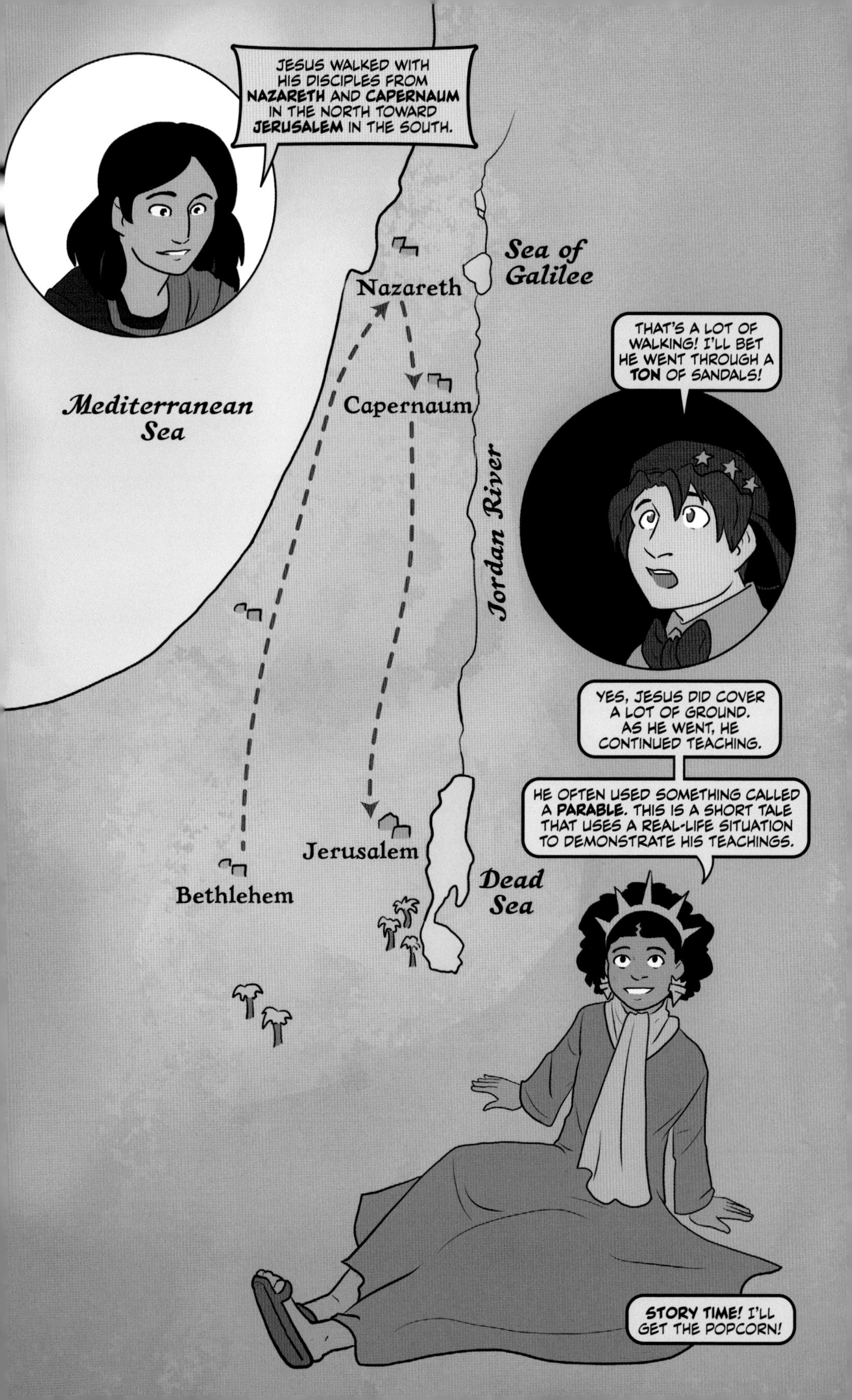
JESUS WALKED WITH HIS DISCIPLES FROM NAZARETH AND CAPERNAUM IN THE NORTH TOWARD JERUSALEM IN THE SOUTH.
Sea of Galilee
Nazareth
Mediterranean Sea
Capernaum
Jordan River
THAT'S A LOT OF WALKING! I'LL BET HE WENT THROUGH A TON OF SANDALS!
YES, JESUS DID COVER A LOT OF GROUND. AS HE WENT, HE CONTINUED TEACHING.
HE OFTEN USED SOMETHING CALLED A PARABLE. THIS IS A SHORT TALE THAT USES A REAL-LIFE SITUATION TO DEMONSTRATE HIS TEACHINGS.
Jerusalem
Bethlehem
Dead Sea
STORY TIME! I'LL GET THE POPCORN!

The Sower of Seeds

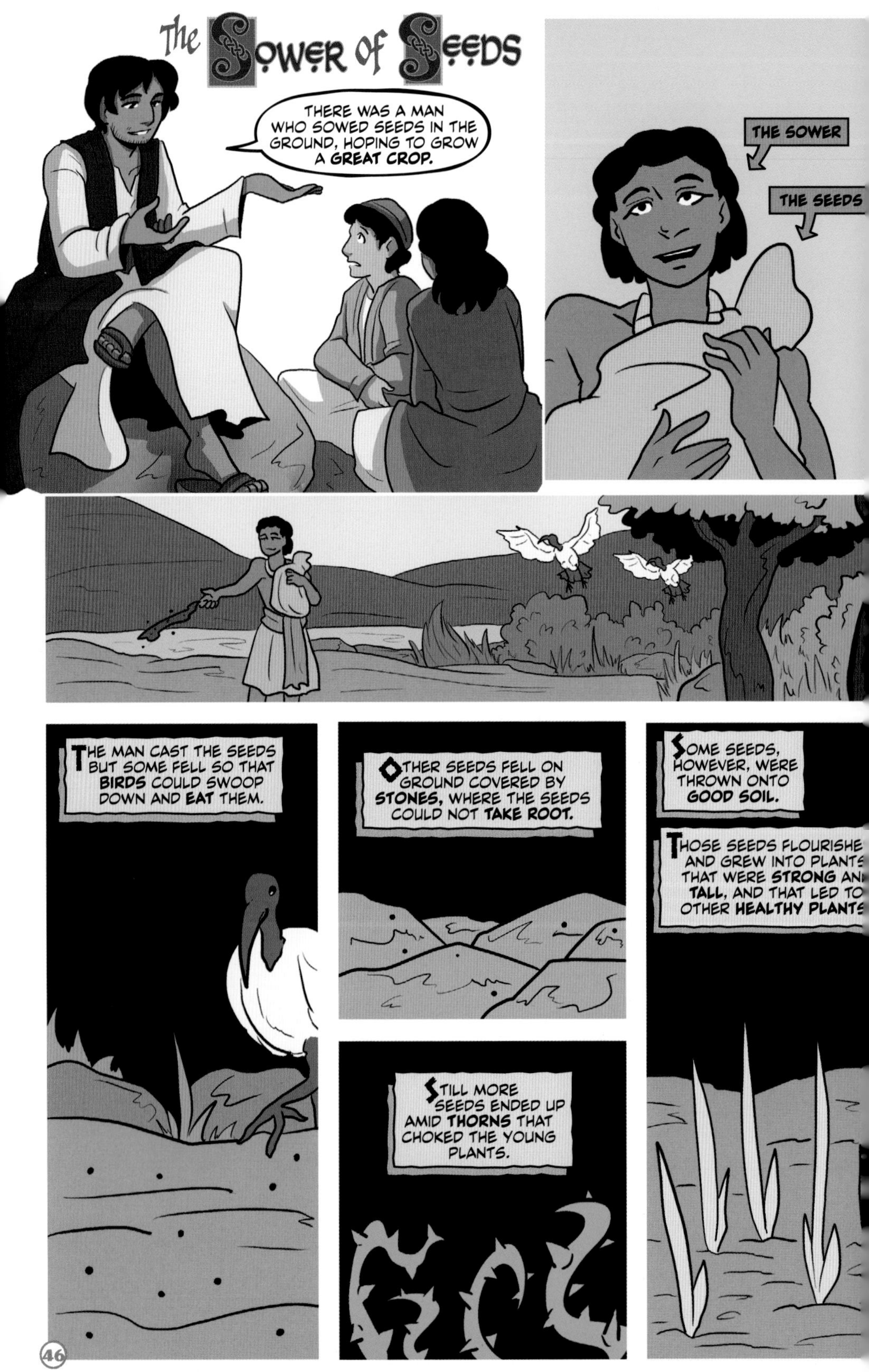

THERE WAS A MAN WHO SOWED SEEDS IN THE GROUND, HOPING TO GROW A **GREAT CROP.**
THE SOWER
THE SEEDS
THE MAN CAST THE SEEDS BUT SOME FELL SO THAT **BIRDS** COULD SWOOP DOWN AND **EAT** THEM.
OTHER SEEDS FELL ON GROUND COVERED BY **STONES,** WHERE THE SEEDS COULD NOT **TAKE ROOT.**
STILL MORE SEEDS ENDED UP AMID **THORNS** THAT CHOKED THE YOUNG PLANTS.
SOME SEEDS, HOWEVER, WERE THROWN ONTO **GOOD SOIL.**
THOSE SEEDS FLOURISHE AND GREW INTO PLANT THAT WERE **STRONG** AN **TALL**, AND THAT LED TO OTHER **HEALTHY PLANT**

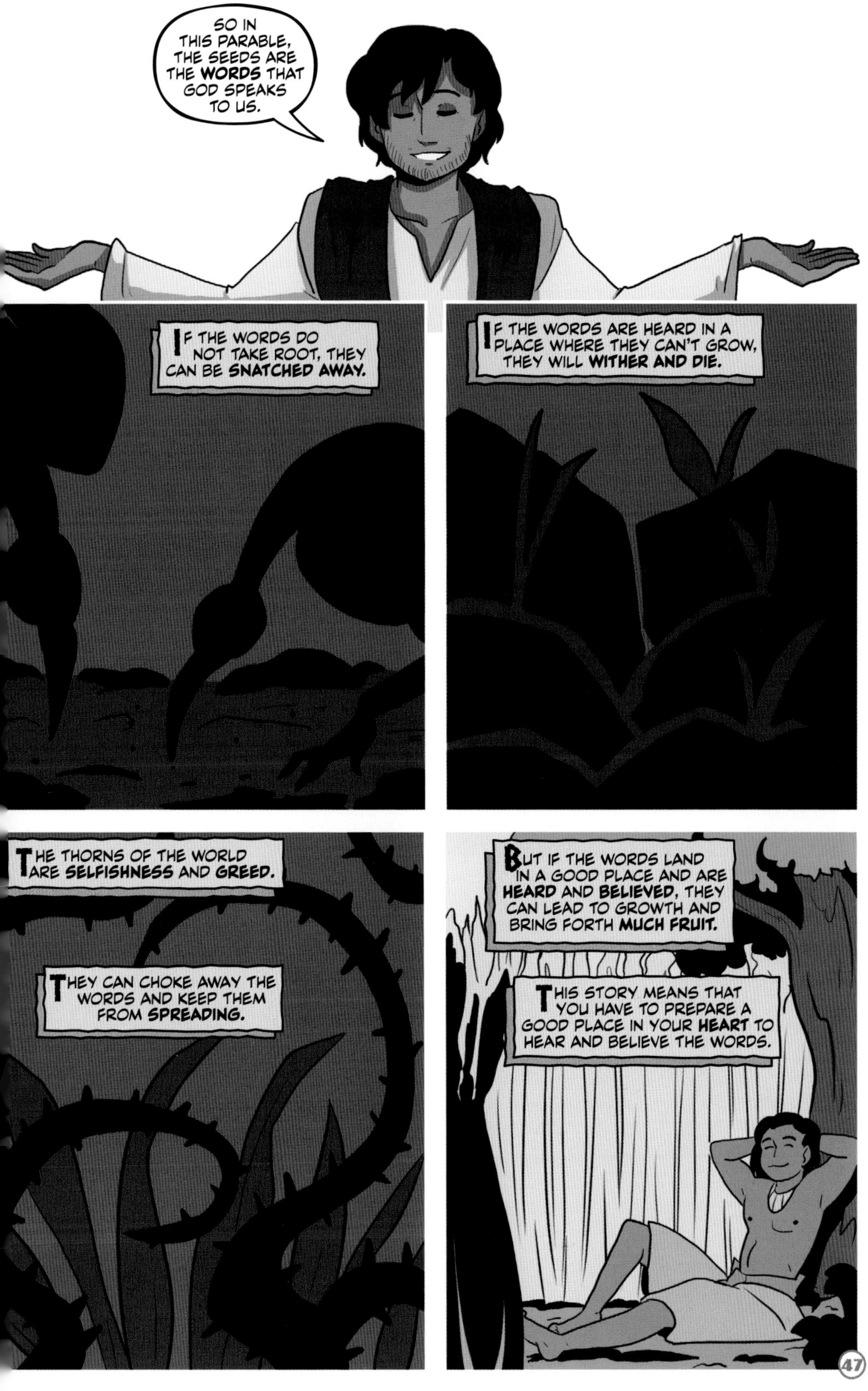
SO IN THIS PARABLE, THE SEEDS ARE THE WORDS THAT GOD SPEAKS TO US.
IF THE WORDS DO NOT TAKE ROOT, THEY CAN BE SNATCHED AWAY.
IF THE WORDS ARE HEARD IN A PLACE WHERE THEY CAN'T GROW, THEY WILL WITHER AND DIE.
THE THORNS OF THE WORLD ARE SELFISHNESS AND GREED.
THEY CAN CHOKE AWAY THE WORDS AND KEEP THEM FROM SPREADING.
BUT IF THE WORDS LAND IN A GOOD PLACE AND ARE HEARD AND BELIEVED, THEY CAN LEAD TO GROWTH AND BRING FORTH MUCH FRUIT.
THIS STORY MEANS THAT YOU HAVE TO PREPARE A GOOD PLACE IN YOUR HEART TO HEAR AND BELIEVE THE WORDS.

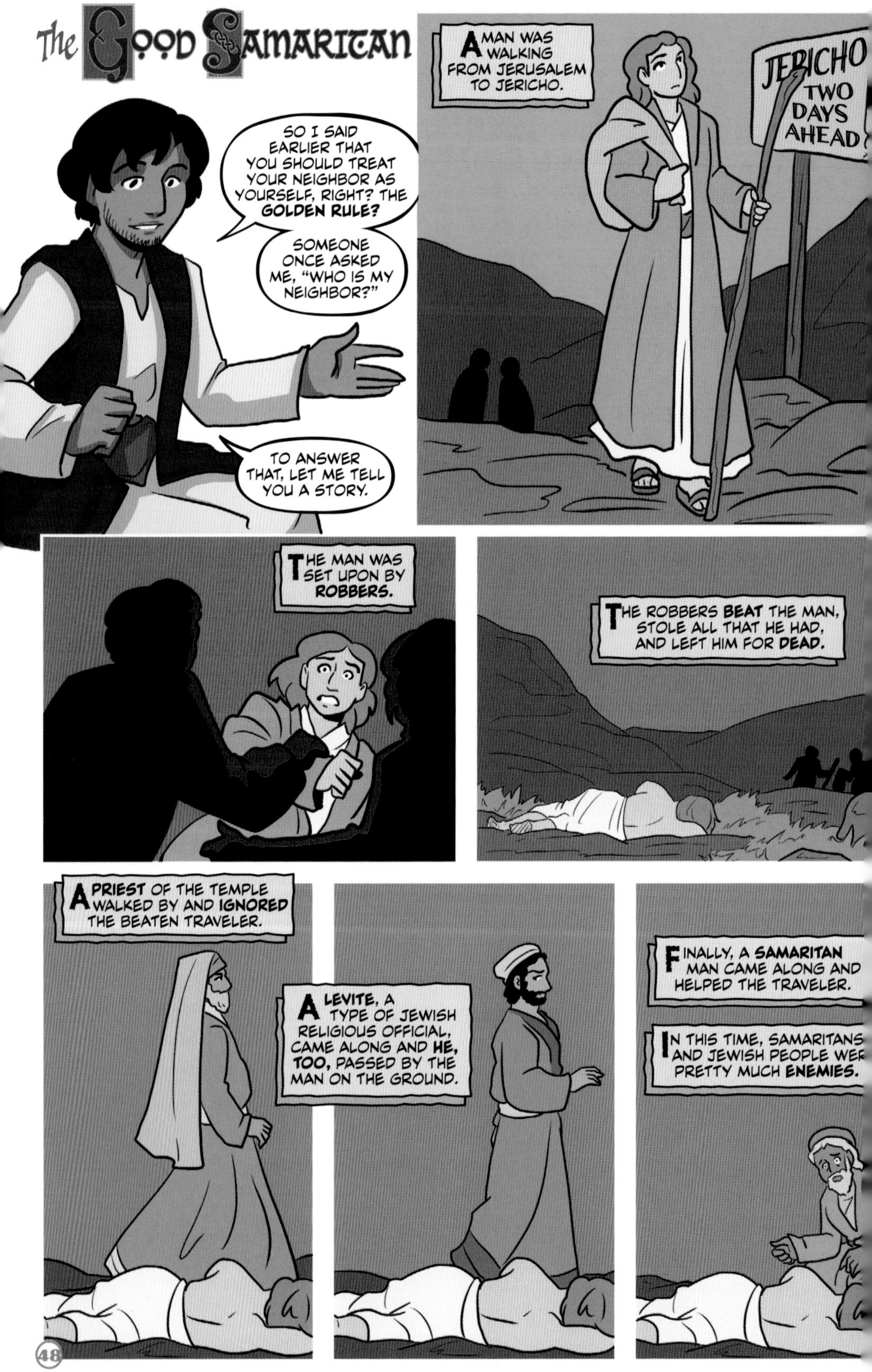
The Good Samaritan
SO I SAID EARLIER THAT YOU SHOULD TREAT YOUR NEIGHBOR AS YOURSELF, RIGHT? THE GOLDEN RULE?
SOMEONE ONCE ASKED ME, "WHO IS MY NEIGHBOR?"
TO ANSWER THAT, LET ME TELL YOU A STORY.
A MAN WAS WALKING FROM JERUSALEM TO JERICHO.
JERICHO TWO DAYS AHEAD
THE MAN WAS SET UPON BY ROBBERS.
THE ROBBERS BEAT THE MAN, STOLE ALL THAT HE HAD, AND LEFT HIM FOR DEAD.
A PRIEST OF THE TEMPLE WALKED BY AND IGNORED THE BEATEN TRAVELER.
A LEVITE, A TYPE OF JEWISH RELIGIOUS OFFICIAL, CAME ALONG AND HE, TOO, PASSED BY THE MAN ON THE GROUND.
FINALLY, A SAMARITAN MAN CAME ALONG AND HELPED THE TRAVELER.
IN THIS TIME, SAMARITANS AND JEWISH PEOPLE WER PRETTY MUCH ENEMIES.

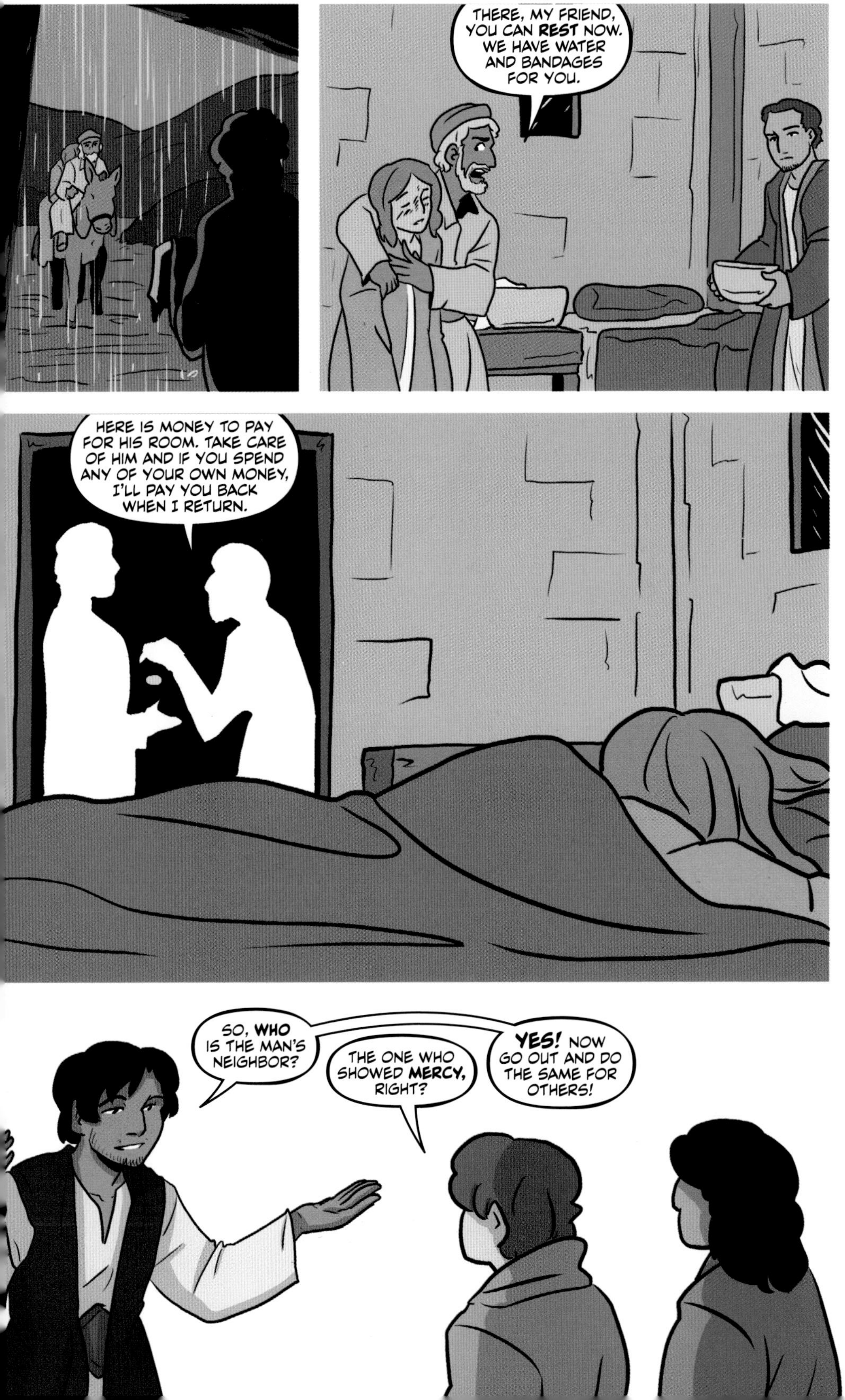
THERE, MY FRIEND, YOU CAN **REST** NOW. WE HAVE WATER AND BANDAGES FOR YOU.
HERE IS MONEY TO PAY FOR HIS ROOM. TAKE CARE OF HIM AND IF YOU SPEND ANY OF YOUR OWN MONEY, I'LL PAY YOU BACK WHEN I RETURN.
SO, **WHO** IS THE MAN'S NEIGHBOR?
THE ONE WHO SHOWED **MERCY**, RIGHT?
YES! NOW GO OUT AND DO THE SAME FOR OTHERS!

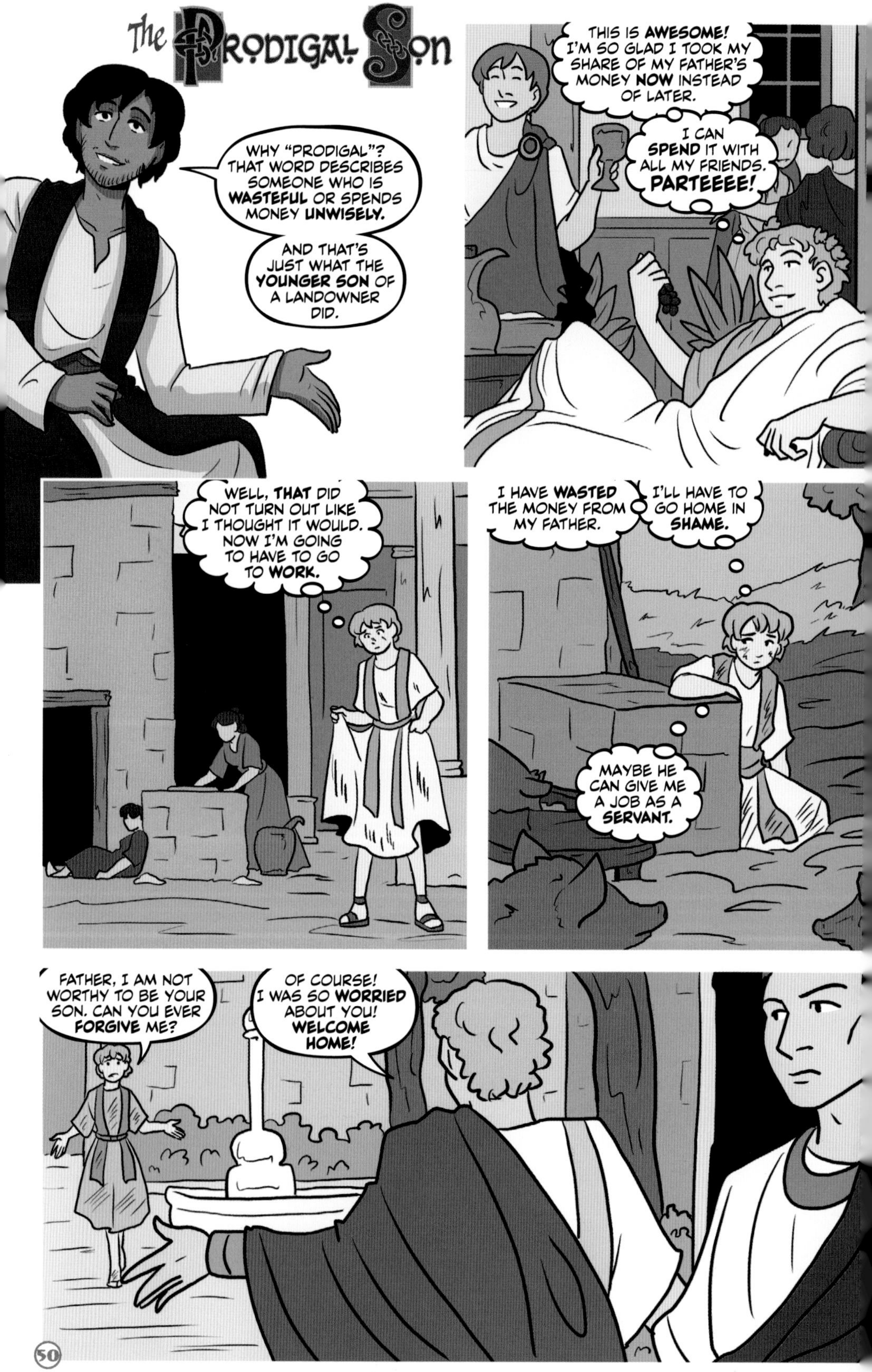
The Prodigal Son
WHY "PRODIGAL"? THAT WORD DESCRIBES SOMEONE WHO IS WASTEFUL OR SPENDS MONEY UNWISELY.
AND THAT'S JUST WHAT THE YOUNGER SON OF A LANDOWNER DID.
THIS IS AWESOME! I'M SO GLAD I TOOK MY SHARE OF MY FATHER'S MONEY NOW INSTEAD OF LATER.
I CAN SPEND IT WITH ALL MY FRIENDS. PARTEEEE!
WELL, THAT DID NOT TURN OUT LIKE I THOUGHT IT WOULD. NOW I'M GOING TO HAVE TO GO TO WORK.
I HAVE WASTED THE MONEY FROM MY FATHER.
I'LL HAVE TO GO HOME IN SHAME.
MAYBE HE CAN GIVE ME A JOB AS A SERVANT.
FATHER, I AM NOT WORTHY TO BE YOUR SON. CAN YOU EVER FORGIVE ME?
OF COURSE! I WAS SO WORRIED ABOUT YOU! WELCOME HOME!

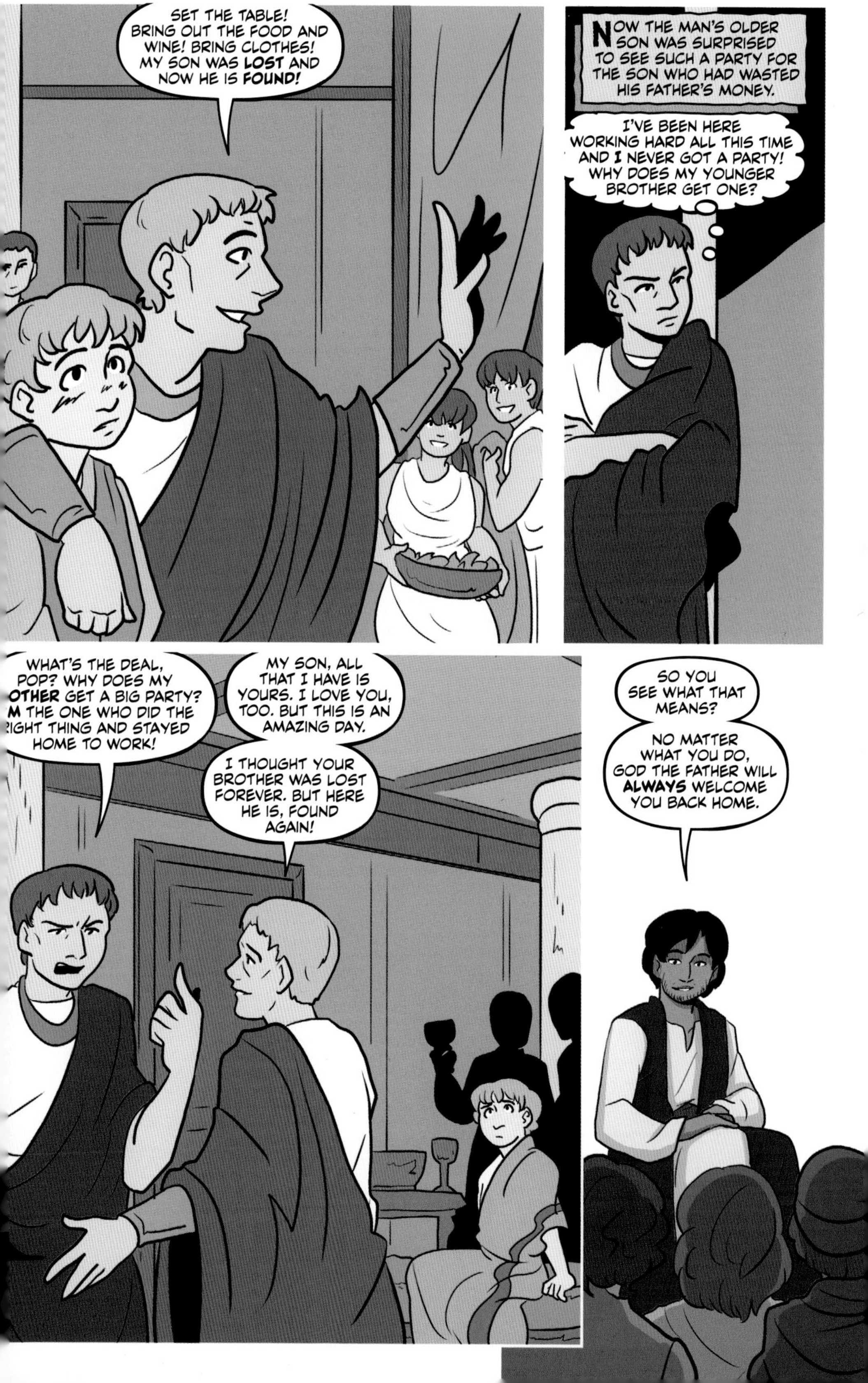
SET THE TABLE! BRING OUT THE FOOD AND WINE! BRING CLOTHES! MY SON WAS **LOST** AND NOW HE IS **FOUND!**
NOW THE MAN'S OLDER SON WAS SURPRISED TO SEE SUCH A PARTY FOR THE SON WHO HAD WASTED HIS FATHER'S MONEY.
I'VE BEEN HERE WORKING HARD ALL THIS TIME AND **I** NEVER GOT A PARTY! WHY DOES MY YOUNGER BROTHER GET ONE?
WHAT'S THE DEAL, POP? WHY DOES MY **OTHER** GET A BIG PARTY? **M** THE ONE WHO DID THE RIGHT THING AND STAYED HOME TO WORK!
MY SON, ALL THAT I HAVE IS YOURS. I LOVE YOU, TOO. BUT THIS IS AN AMAZING DAY.
I THOUGHT YOUR BROTHER WAS LOST FOREVER. BUT HERE HE IS, FOUND AGAIN!
SO YOU SEE WHAT THAT MEANS?
NO MATTER WHAT YOU DO, GOD THE FATHER WILL **ALWAYS** WELCOME YOU BACK HOME.

The Sheep and the Gate

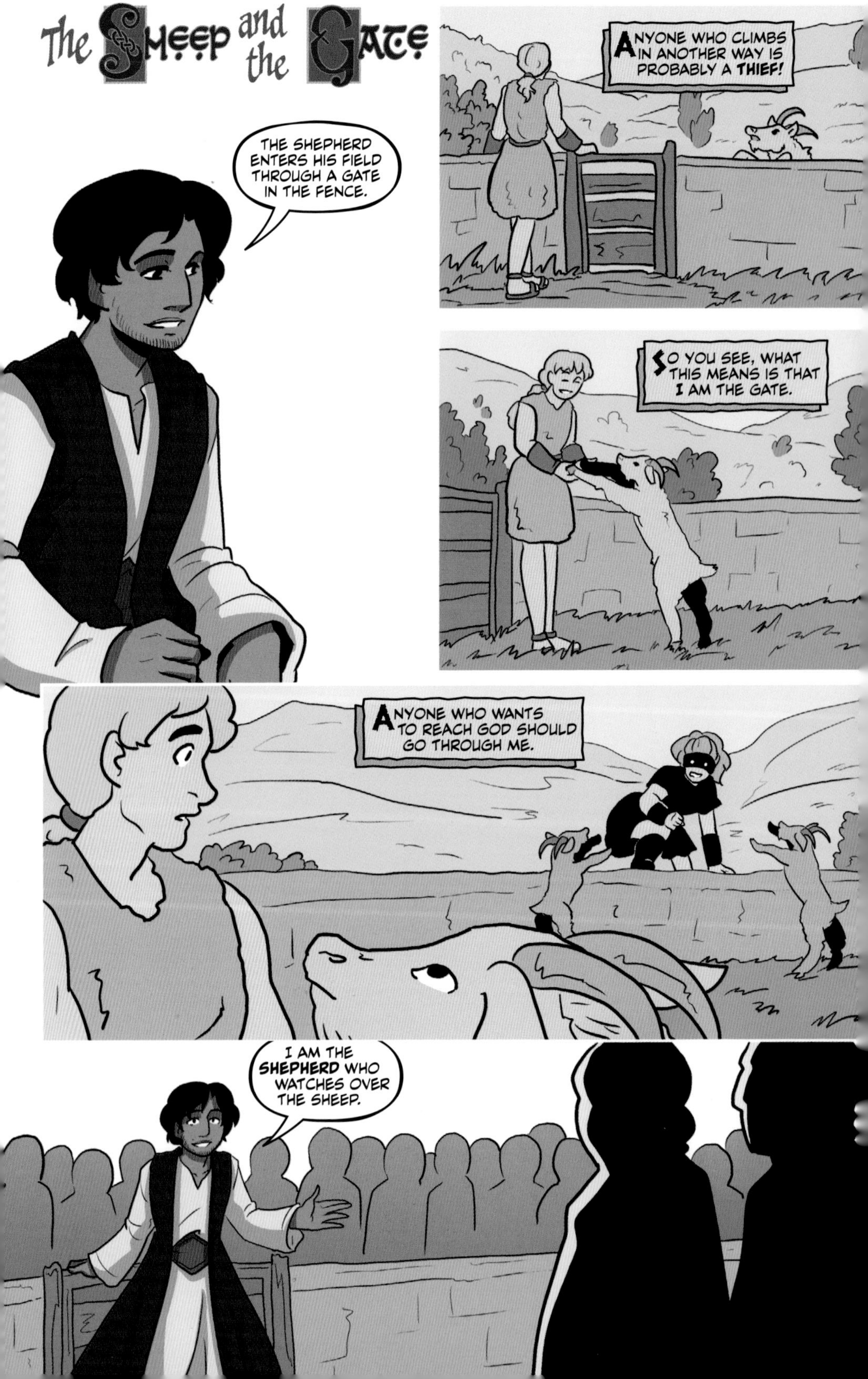
THE SHEPHERD ENTERS HIS FIELD THROUGH A GATE IN THE FENCE.
ANYONE WHO CLIMBS IN ANOTHER WAY IS PROBABLY A THIEF!
SO YOU SEE, WHAT THIS MEANS IS THAT I AM THE GATE.
ANYONE WHO WANTS TO REACH GOD SHOULD GO THROUGH ME.
I AM THE SHEPHERD WHO WATCHES OVER THE SHEEP.

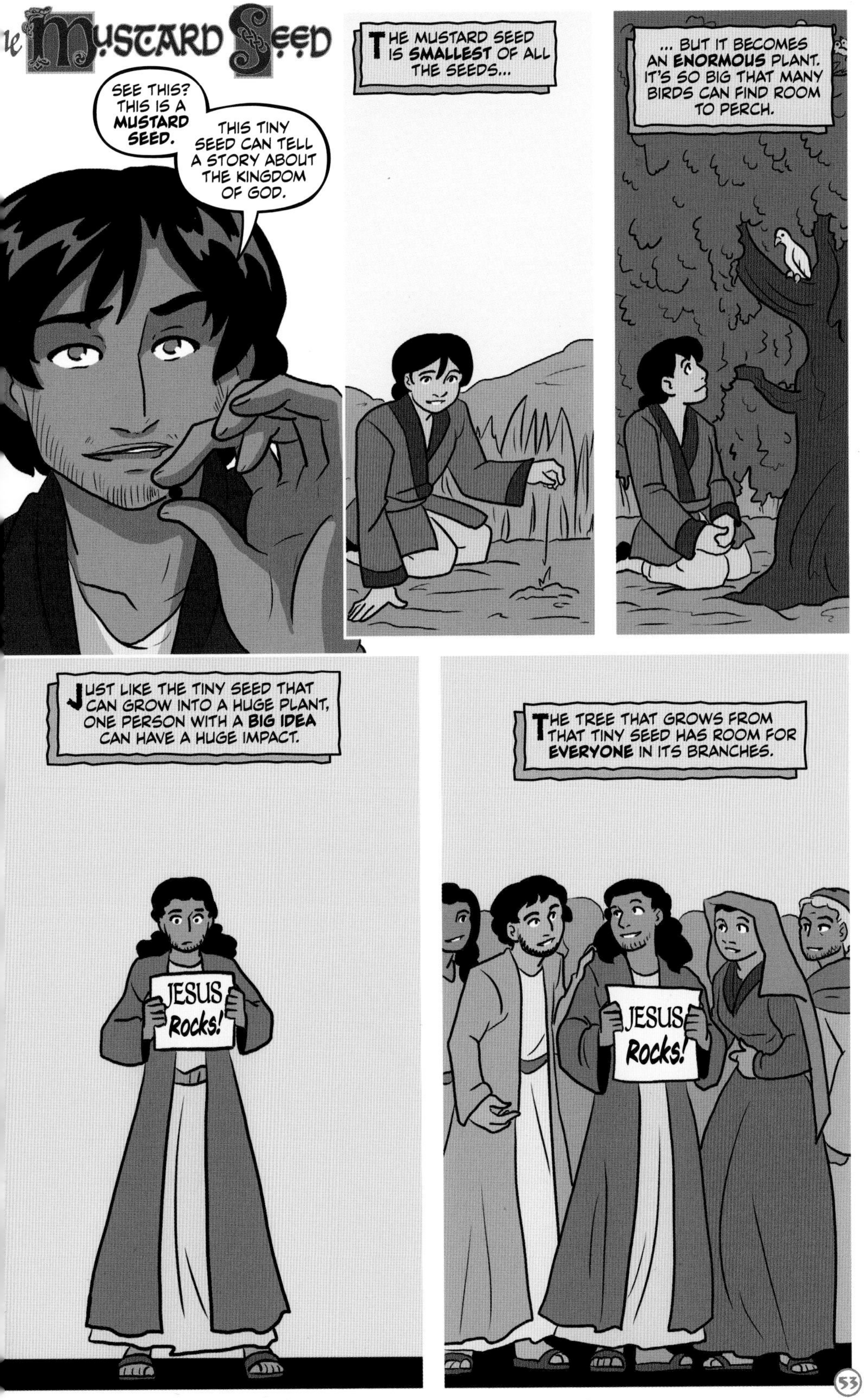

Mustard Seed
SEE THIS? THIS IS A MUSTARD SEED.
THIS TINY SEED CAN TELL A STORY ABOUT THE KINGDOM OF GOD.
THE MUSTARD SEED IS SMALLEST OF ALL THE SEEDS...
... BUT IT BECOMES AN ENORMOUS PLANT. IT'S SO BIG THAT MANY BIRDS CAN FIND ROOM TO PERCH.
JUST LIKE THE TINY SEED THAT CAN GROW INTO A HUGE PLANT, ONE PERSON WITH A BIG IDEA CAN HAVE A HUGE IMPACT.
JESUS Rocks!
THE TREE THAT GROWS FROM THAT TINY SEED HAS ROOM FOR EVERYONE IN ITS BRANCHES.
JESUS Rocks!

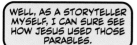

WELL, AS A STORYTELLER MYSELF, I CAN SURE SEE HOW JESUS USED THOSE PARABLES.

PLUS, THE POPCORN WAS DIVINE!

NOW, AS WE GET BACK TO OUR MAIN STORY, JESUS AND HIS DISCIPLES ARE MAKING THEIR WAY TOWARD **JERUSALEM** FOR PASSOVER.

AND THINGS ARE ABOUT TO GET **INTENSE!**

SO, PETER, YOU'VE BEEN FOLLOWING ME FOR A WHILE NOW. WHO DO YOU THINK I **AM?**

WELL, YOU'RE THE **CHRIST,** THE SON OF GOD.

YES, YES, THAT'S RIGHT. PETER, I'LL TELL YOU WHAT.

I'M GIVING YOU THE KEYS TO THE KINGDOM.

I WANT YOU TO BUILD MY **CHURCH** HERE ON EARTH.

AND YOU SHOULD KNOW WHAT I KNOW.

I'M GOING TO BE **ARRESTED** IN JERUSALEM AND WILL PROBABLY SUFFER GREATLY.

I THINK I WILL EVEN BE **KILLED** THERE.

NO! **NO!**

NO, TEACHER!

WE WILL NOT **LET** THEM!

NO, NO, IT'S ALL RIGHT.

ON THE THIRD DAY AFTER I AM KILLED, I WILL BE **RAISED** AGAIN.

NOW, LET'S KEEP MOVING.

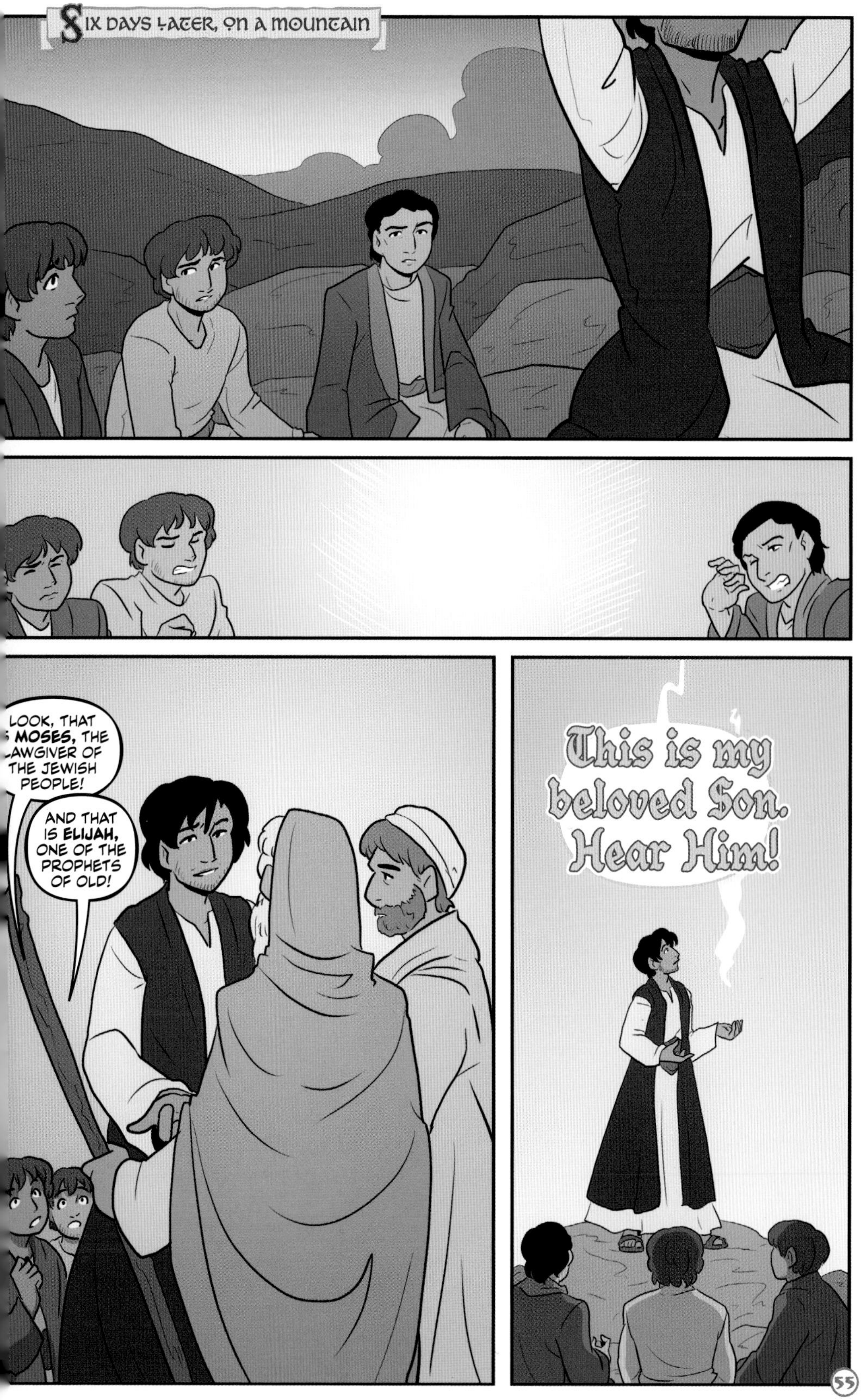
SIX DAYS LATER, ON A MOUNTAIN
LOOK, THAT S MOSES, THE AWGIVER OF THE JEWISH PEOPLE!
AND THAT IS ELIJAH, ONE OF THE PROPHETS OF OLD!
This is my beloved Son. Hear Him!

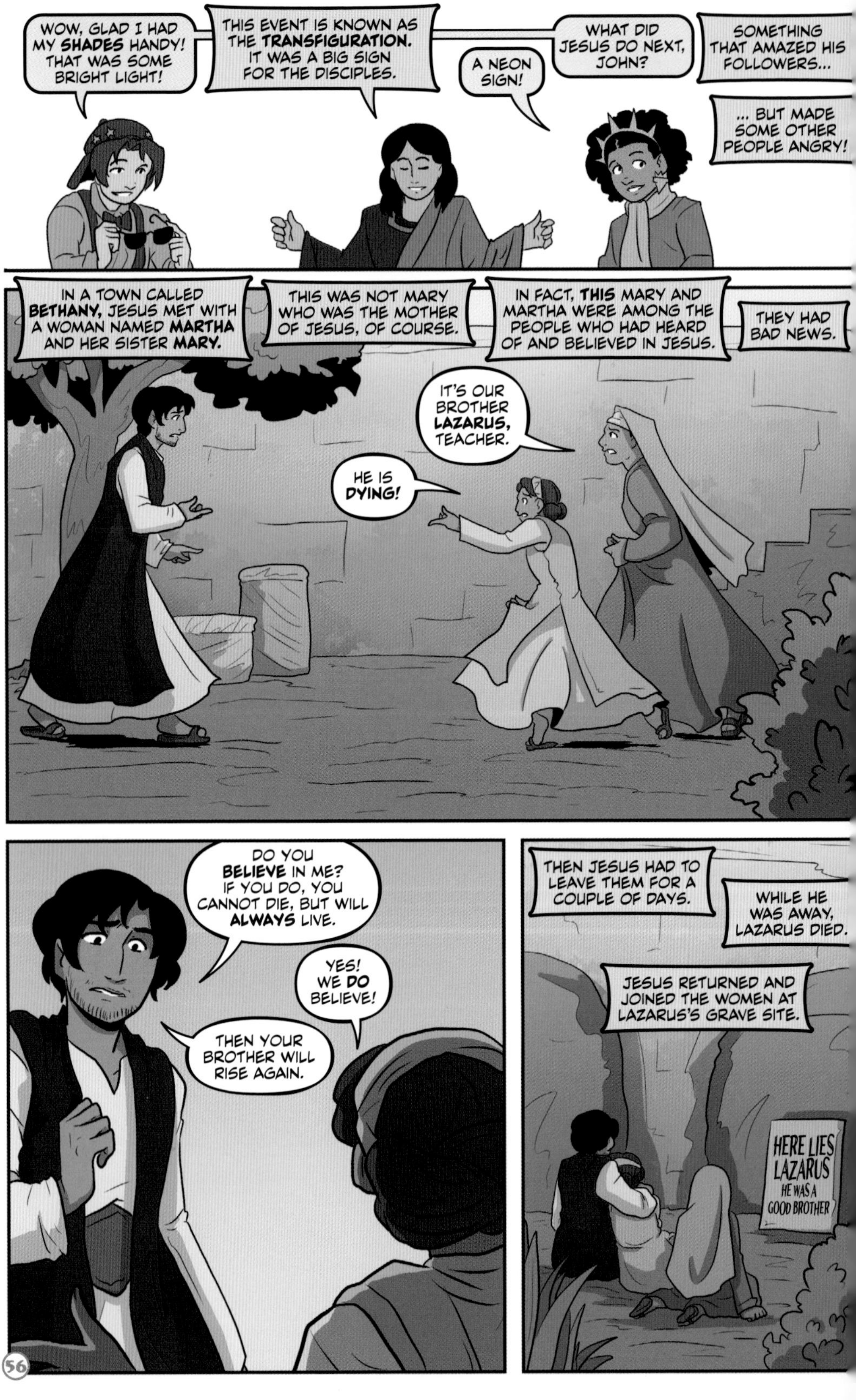

WOW, GLAD I HAD MY SHADES HANDY! THAT WAS SOME BRIGHT LIGHT!
THIS EVENT IS KNOWN AS THE TRANSFIGURATION. IT WAS A BIG SIGN FOR THE DISCIPLES.
A NEON SIGN!
WHAT DID JESUS DO NEXT, JOHN?
SOMETHING THAT AMAZED HIS FOLLOWERS...
... BUT MADE SOME OTHER PEOPLE ANGRY!
IN A TOWN CALLED BETHANY, JESUS MET WITH A WOMAN NAMED MARTHA AND HER SISTER MARY.
THIS WAS NOT MARY WHO WAS THE MOTHER OF JESUS, OF COURSE.
IN FACT, THIS MARY AND MARTHA WERE AMONG THE PEOPLE WHO HAD HEARD OF AND BELIEVED IN JESUS.
THEY HAD BAD NEWS.
IT'S OUR BROTHER LAZARUS, TEACHER.
HE IS DYING!
DO YOU BELIEVE IN ME? IF YOU DO, YOU CANNOT DIE, BUT WILL ALWAYS LIVE.
YES! WE DO BELIEVE!
THEN YOUR BROTHER WILL RISE AGAIN.
THEN JESUS HAD TO LEAVE THEM FOR A COUPLE OF DAYS.
WHILE HE WAS AWAY, LAZARUS DIED.
JESUS RETURNED AND JOINED THE WOMEN AT LAZARUS'S GRAVE SITE.
HERE LIES LAZARUS
HE WAS A GOOD BROTHER

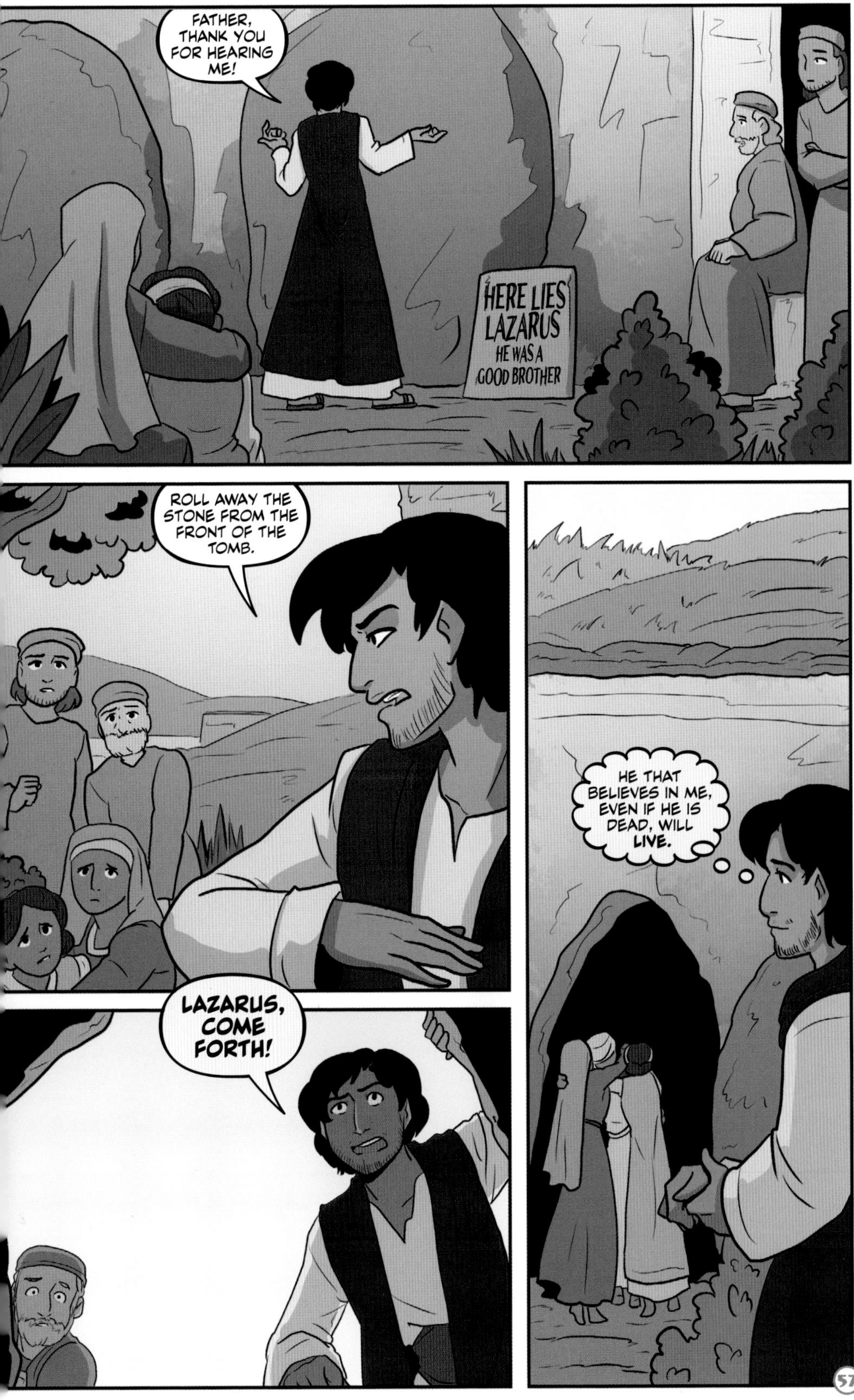
FATHER, THANK YOU FOR HEARING ME!
HERE LIES LAZARUS HE WAS A GOOD BROTHER
ROLL AWAY THE STONE FROM THE FRONT OF THE TOMB.
HE THAT BELIEVES IN ME, EVEN IF HE IS DEAD, WILL **LIVE.**
LAZARUS, COME FORTH!

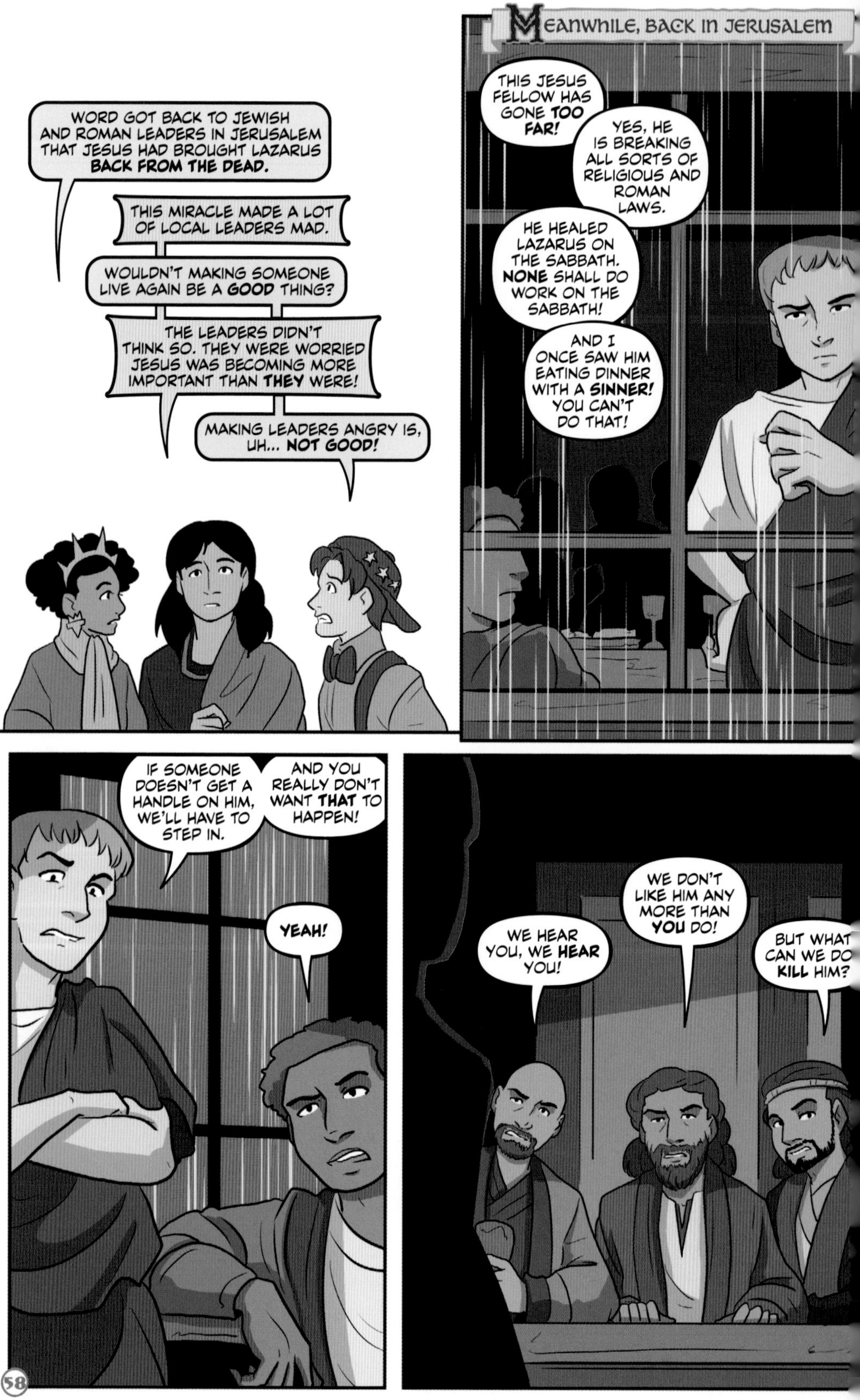
WORD GOT BACK TO JEWISH AND ROMAN LEADERS IN JERUSALEM THAT JESUS HAD BROUGHT LAZARUS BACK FROM THE DEAD.
THIS MIRACLE MADE A LOT OF LOCAL LEADERS MAD.
WOULDN'T MAKING SOMEONE LIVE AGAIN BE A GOOD THING?
THE LEADERS DIDN'T THINK SO. THEY WERE WORRIED JESUS WAS BECOMING MORE IMPORTANT THAN THEY WERE!
MAKING LEADERS ANGRY IS, UH... NOT GOOD!
MEANWHILE, BACK IN JERUSALEM
THIS JESUS FELLOW HAS GONE TOO FAR!
YES, HE IS BREAKING ALL SORTS OF RELIGIOUS AND ROMAN LAWS.
HE HEALED LAZARUS ON THE SABBATH. NONE SHALL DO WORK ON THE SABBATH!
AND I ONCE SAW HIM EATING DINNER WITH A SINNER! YOU CAN'T DO THAT!
IF SOMEONE DOESN'T GET A HANDLE ON HIM, WE'LL HAVE TO STEP IN.
AND YOU REALLY DON'T WANT THAT TO HAPPEN!
YEAH!
WE HEAR YOU, WE HEAR YOU!
WE DON'T LIKE HIM ANY MORE THAN YOU DO!
BUT WHAT CAN WE DO KILL HIM?

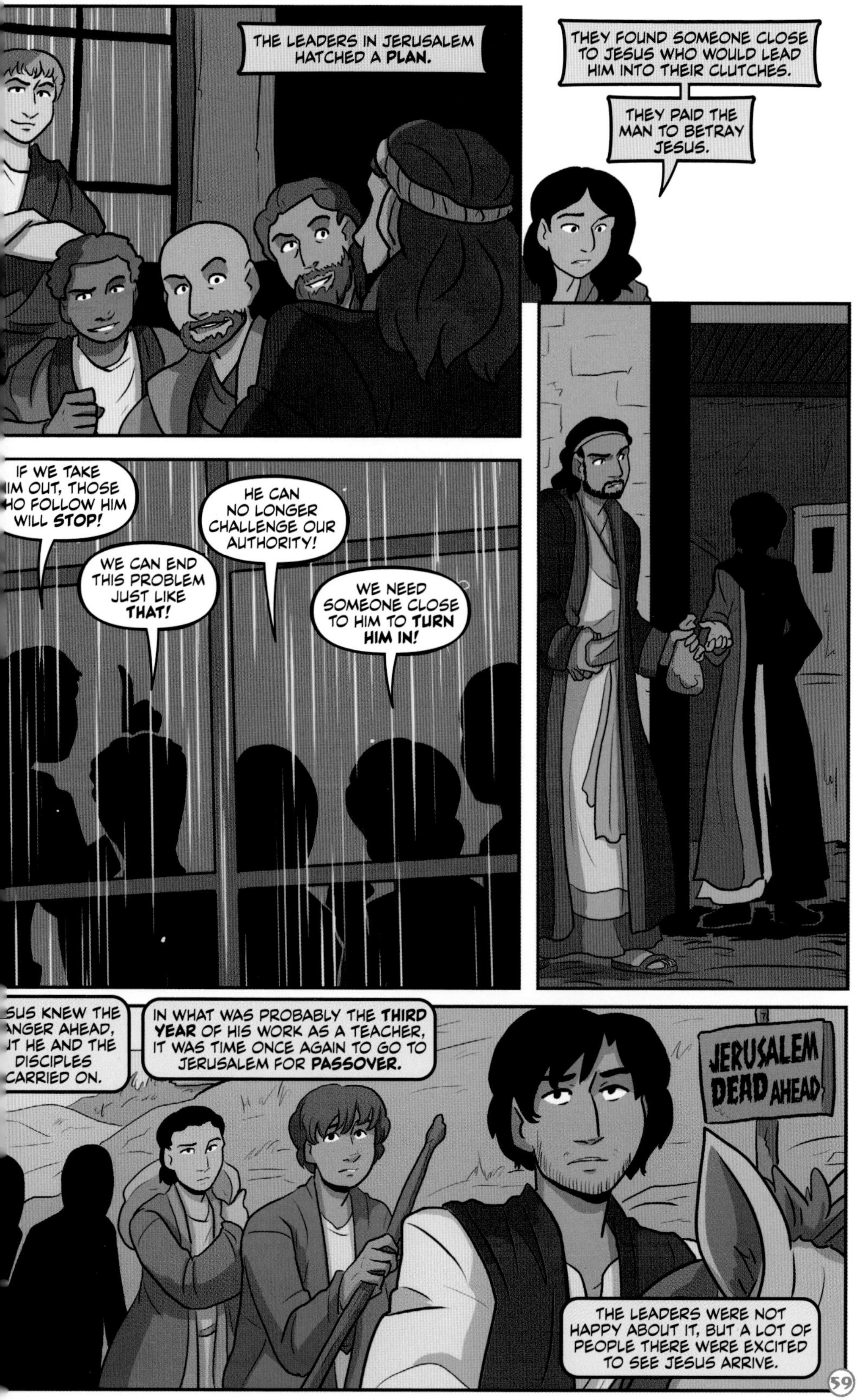
THE LEADERS IN JERUSALEM HATCHED A **PLAN.**
THEY FOUND SOMEONE CLOSE TO JESUS WHO WOULD LEAD HIM INTO THEIR CLUTCHES.
THEY PAID THE MAN TO BETRAY JESUS.
IF WE TAKE IM OUT, THOSE HO FOLLOW HIM WILL **STOP!**
WE CAN END THIS PROBLEM JUST LIKE **THAT!**
HE CAN NO LONGER CHALLENGE OUR AUTHORITY!
WE NEED SOMEONE CLOSE TO HIM TO **TURN HIM IN!**
SUS KNEW THE ANGER AHEAD, UT HE AND THE DISCIPLES CARRIED ON.
IN WHAT WAS PROBABLY THE **THIRD YEAR** OF HIS WORK AS A TEACHER, IT WAS TIME ONCE AGAIN TO GO TO JERUSALEM FOR **PASSOVER.**
JERUSALEM DEAD AHEAD
THE LEADERS WERE NOT HAPPY ABOUT IT, BUT A LOT OF PEOPLE THERE WERE EXCITED TO SEE JESUS ARRIVE.

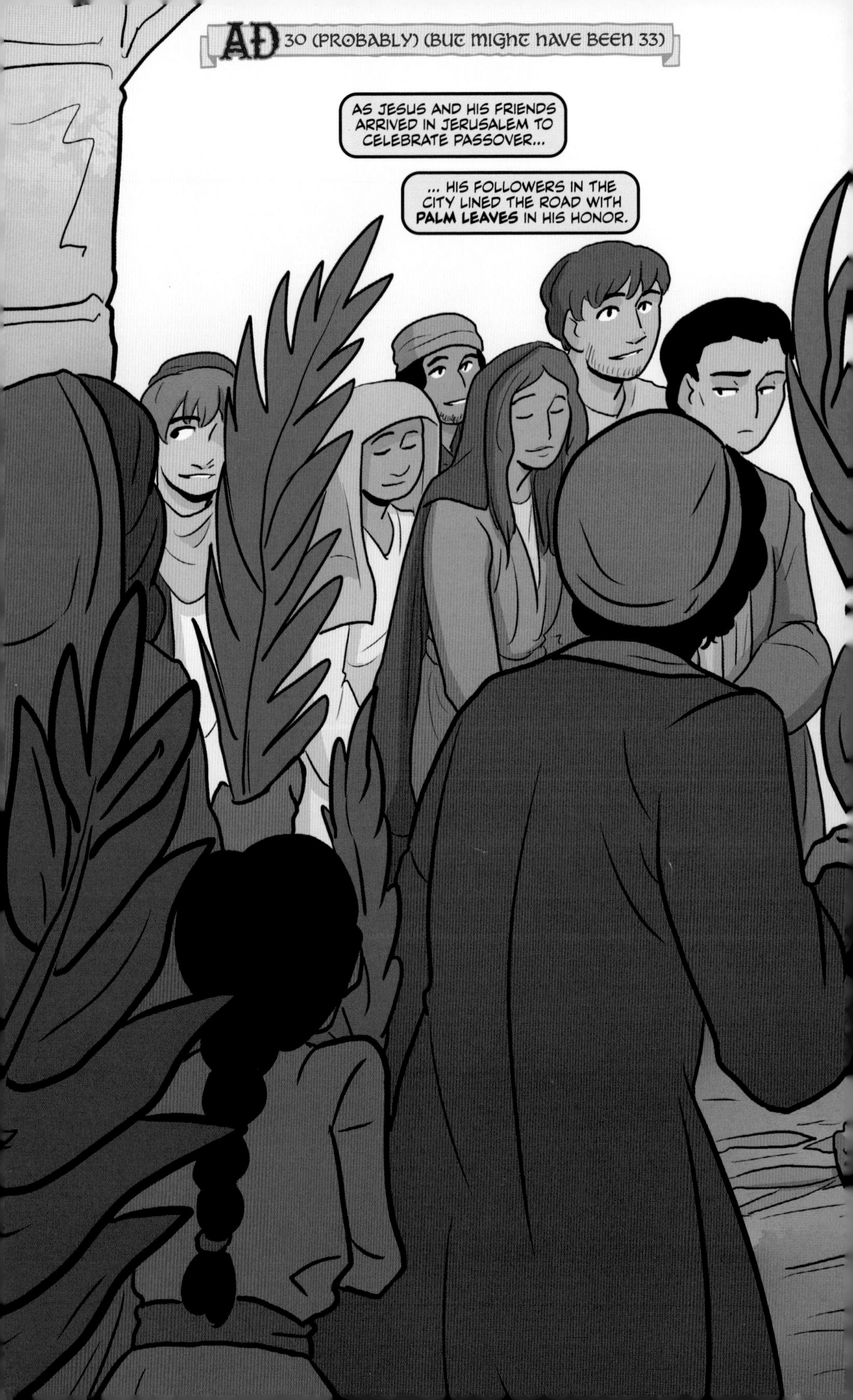
AD 30 (PROBABLY) (BUT MIGHT HAVE BEEN 33)
AS JESUS AND HIS FRIENDS ARRIVED IN JERUSALEM TO CELEBRATE PASSOVER...
... HIS FOLLOWERS IN THE CITY LINED THE ROAD WITH PALM LEAVES IN HIS HONOR.

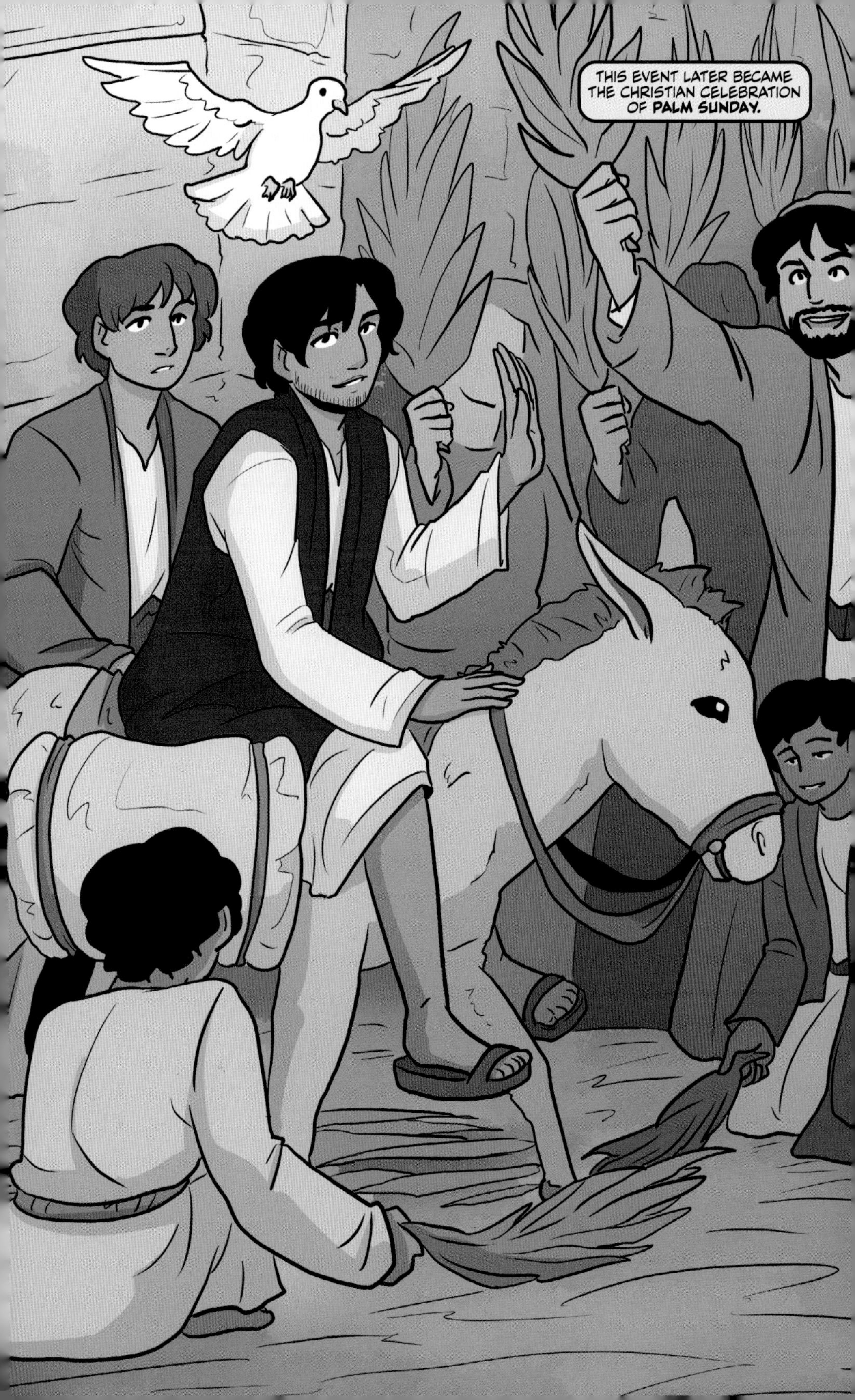
THIS EVENT LATER BECAME THE CHRISTIAN CELEBRATION OF **PALM SUNDAY.**

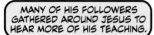

MANY OF HIS FOLLOWERS GATHERED AROUND JESUS TO HEAR MORE OF HIS TEACHING.

BUT THEY WERE NOT THE ONLY PEOPLE GATHERING.

THE LEADERS OF THE CITY SENT SPIES TO TRY TO TRICK JESUS INTO SAYING SOMETHING THEY COULD ARREST HIM FOR.

DO YOU THINK IT IS OKAY FOR JUDEANS TO PAY TAXES TO CAESAR, THE LEADER OF THE ROMANS?

SHOW ME A ROMAN COIN.

WHO IS THIS ON THIS COIN?

THE ROMAN EMPEROR, CAESAR!

WHY DO THEY TRY TO TEMPT ME?

GIVE CAESAR WHAT BELONGS TO CAESAR. BUT GIVE GOD ALL THAT BELONGS TO GOD.

FOILED!

IT'S LIKE HE CAN SEE US COMING!

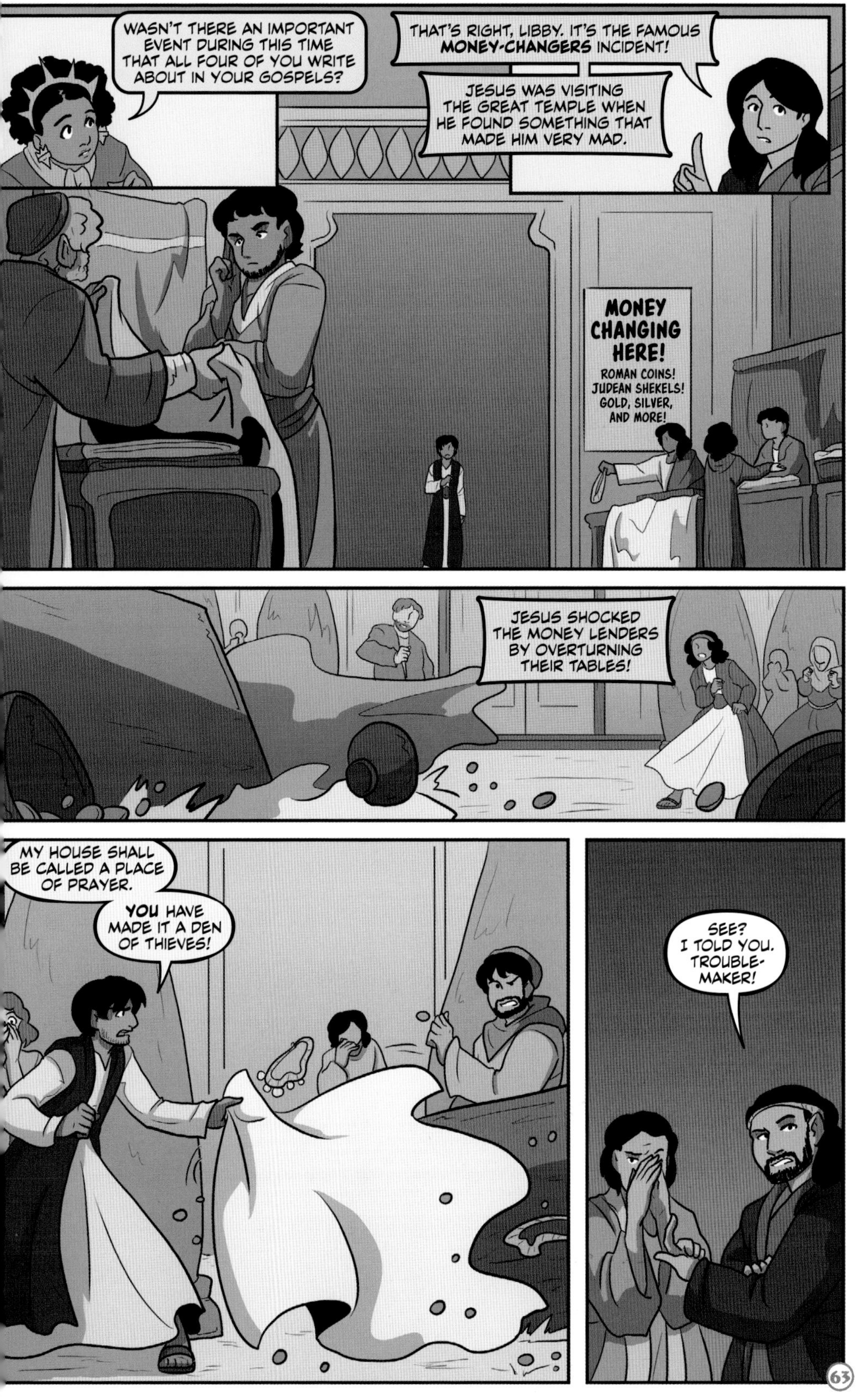

WASN'T THERE AN IMPORTANT EVENT DURING THIS TIME THAT ALL FOUR OF YOU WRITE ABOUT IN YOUR GOSPELS?
THAT'S RIGHT, LIBBY. IT'S THE FAMOUS MONEY-CHANGERS INCIDENT!
JESUS WAS VISITING THE GREAT TEMPLE WHEN HE FOUND SOMETHING THAT MADE HIM VERY MAD.
MONEY CHANGING HERE!
ROMAN COINS! JUDEAN SHEKELS! GOLD, SILVER, AND MORE!
JESUS SHOCKED THE MONEY LENDERS BY OVERTURNING THEIR TABLES!
MY HOUSE SHALL BE CALLED A PLACE OF PRAYER.
YOU HAVE MADE IT A DEN OF THIEVES!
SEE? I TOLD YOU. TROUBLE-MAKER!

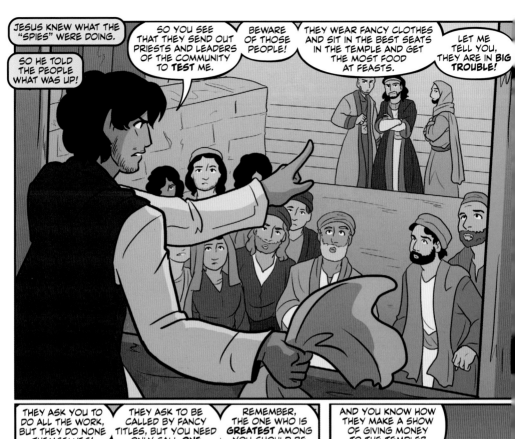

JESUS KNEW WHAT THE "SPIES" WERE DOING.

SO HE TOLD THE PEOPLE WHAT WAS UP!

SO YOU SEE THAT THEY SEND OUT PRIESTS AND LEADERS OF THE COMMUNITY TO **TEST** ME.

BEWARE OF THOSE PEOPLE!

THEY WEAR FANCY CLOTHES AND SIT IN THE BEST SEATS IN THE TEMPLE AND GET THE MOST FOOD AT FEASTS.

LET ME TELL YOU, THEY ARE IN **BIG TROUBLE!**

THEY ASK YOU TO DO ALL THE WORK, BUT THEY DO NONE THEMSELVES!

THEY ASK TO BE CALLED BY FANCY TITLES, BUT YOU NEED ONLY CALL **ONE** MAN **"FATHER."**

REMEMBER, THE ONE WHO IS **GREATEST** AMONG YOU SHOULD BE A SERVANT.

AND YOU KNOW HOW THEY MAKE A SHOW OF GIVING MONEY TO THE TEMPLE? LET ME TELL YOU A STORY.

YOU SEE HOW THE LEADERS AND THE PRIESTS DONATE IN FRONT OF EVERYON TO SHOW HOW MUCH THEY GAVE?

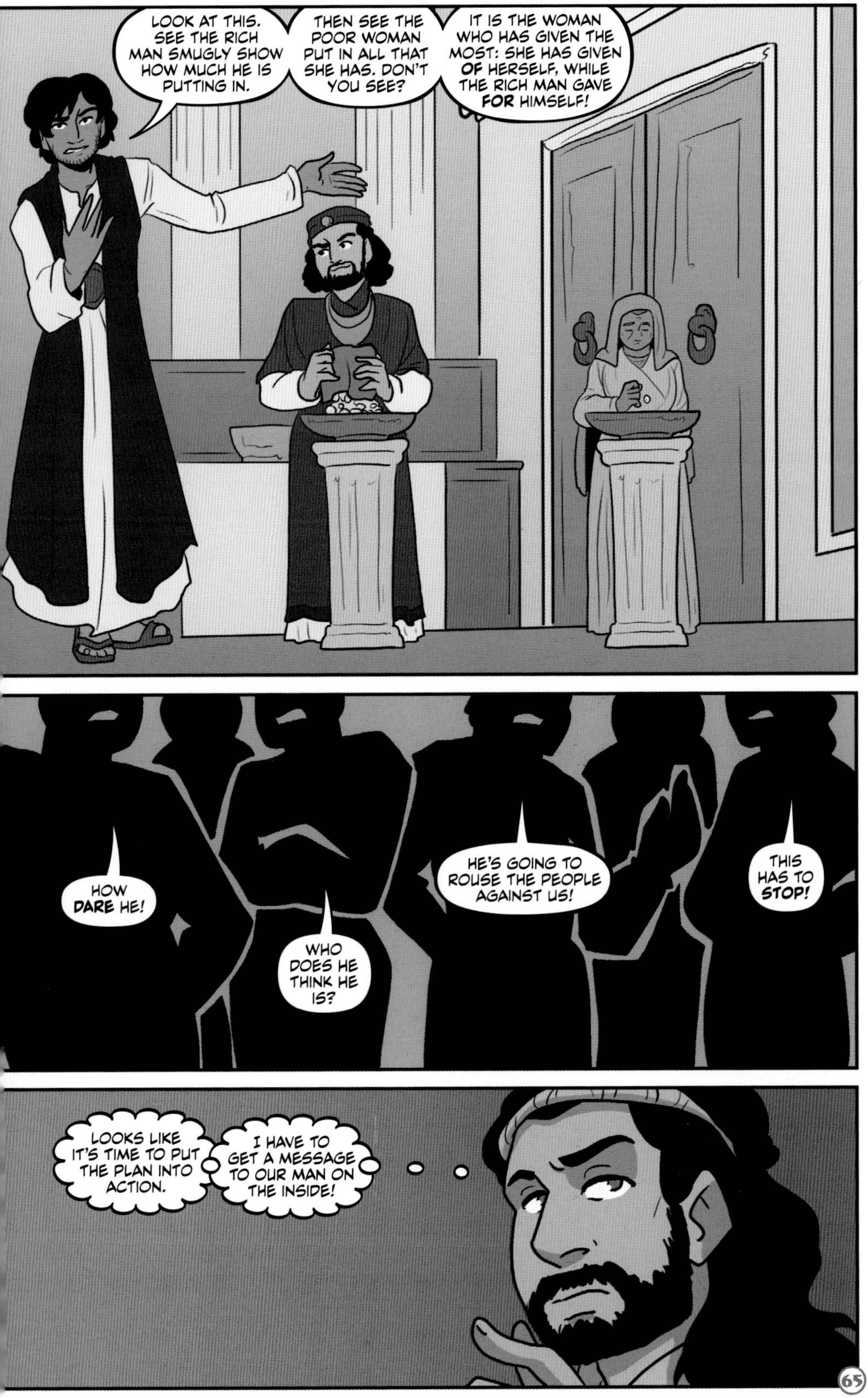
LOOK AT THIS. SEE THE RICH MAN SMUGLY SHOW HOW MUCH HE IS PUTTING IN.
THEN SEE THE POOR WOMAN PUT IN ALL THAT SHE HAS. DON'T YOU SEE?
IT IS THE WOMAN WHO HAS GIVEN THE MOST: SHE HAS GIVEN **OF** HERSELF, WHILE THE RICH MAN GAVE **FOR** HIMSELF!
HOW **DARE** HE!
WHO DOES HE THINK HE IS?
HE'S GOING TO ROUSE THE PEOPLE AGAINST US!
THIS HAS TO **STOP!**
LOOKS LIKE IT'S TIME TO PUT THE PLAN INTO ACTION.
I HAVE TO GET A MESSAGE TO OUR MAN ON THE INSIDE!

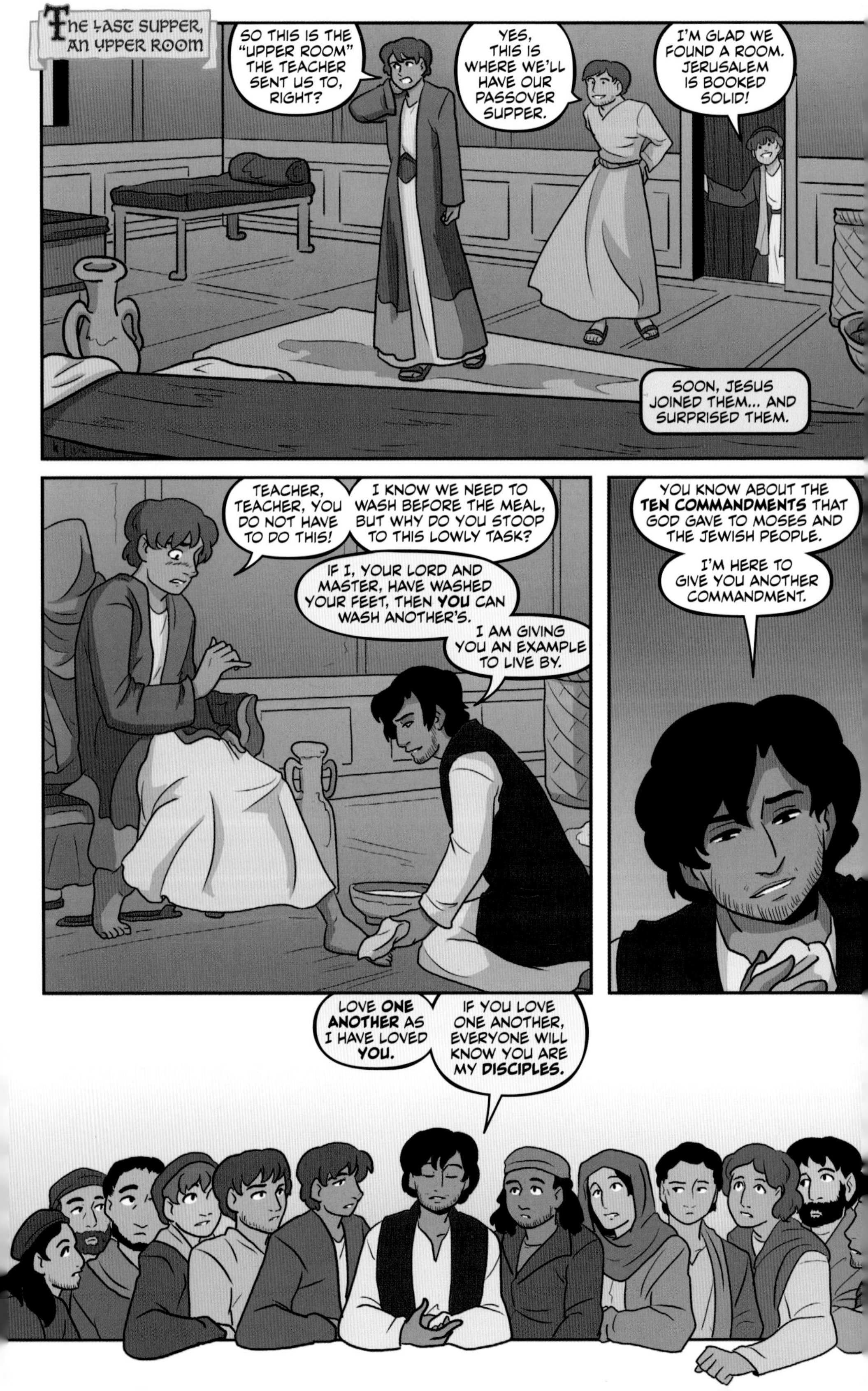
THE LAST SUPPER, AN UPPER ROOM
SO THIS IS THE "UPPER ROOM" THE TEACHER SENT US TO, RIGHT?
YES, THIS IS WHERE WE'LL HAVE OUR PASSOVER SUPPER.
I'M GLAD WE FOUND A ROOM. JERUSALEM IS BOOKED SOLID!
SOON, JESUS JOINED THEM... AND SURPRISED THEM.
TEACHER, TEACHER, YOU DO NOT HAVE TO DO THIS!
I KNOW WE NEED TO WASH BEFORE THE MEAL, BUT WHY DO YOU STOOP TO THIS LOWLY TASK?
IF I, YOUR LORD AND MASTER, HAVE WASHED YOUR FEET, THEN **YOU** CAN WASH ANOTHER'S.
I AM GIVING YOU AN EXAMPLE TO LIVE BY.
YOU KNOW ABOUT THE **TEN COMMANDMENTS** THAT GOD GAVE TO MOSES AND THE JEWISH PEOPLE.
I'M HERE TO GIVE YOU ANOTHER COMMANDMENT.
LOVE **ONE ANOTHER** AS I HAVE LOVED **YOU.**
IF YOU LOVE ONE ANOTHER, EVERYONE WILL KNOW YOU ARE MY **DISCIPLES.**

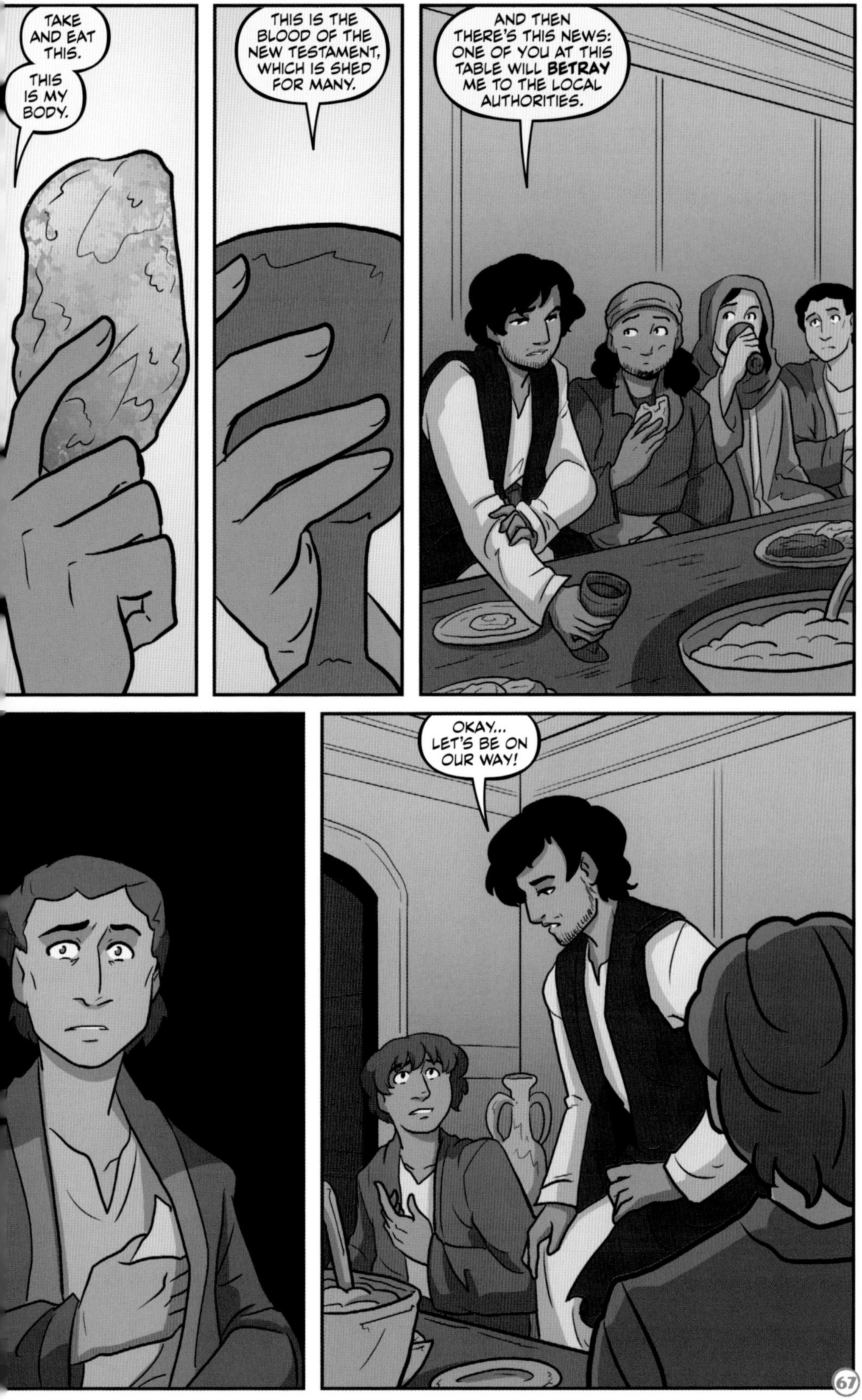
TAKE AND EAT THIS.
THIS IS MY BODY.
THIS IS THE BLOOD OF THE NEW TESTAMENT, WHICH IS SHED FOR MANY.
AND THEN THERE'S THIS NEWS: ONE OF YOU AT THIS TABLE WILL **BETRAY** ME TO THE LOCAL AUTHORITIES.
OKAY... LET'S BE ON OUR WAY!

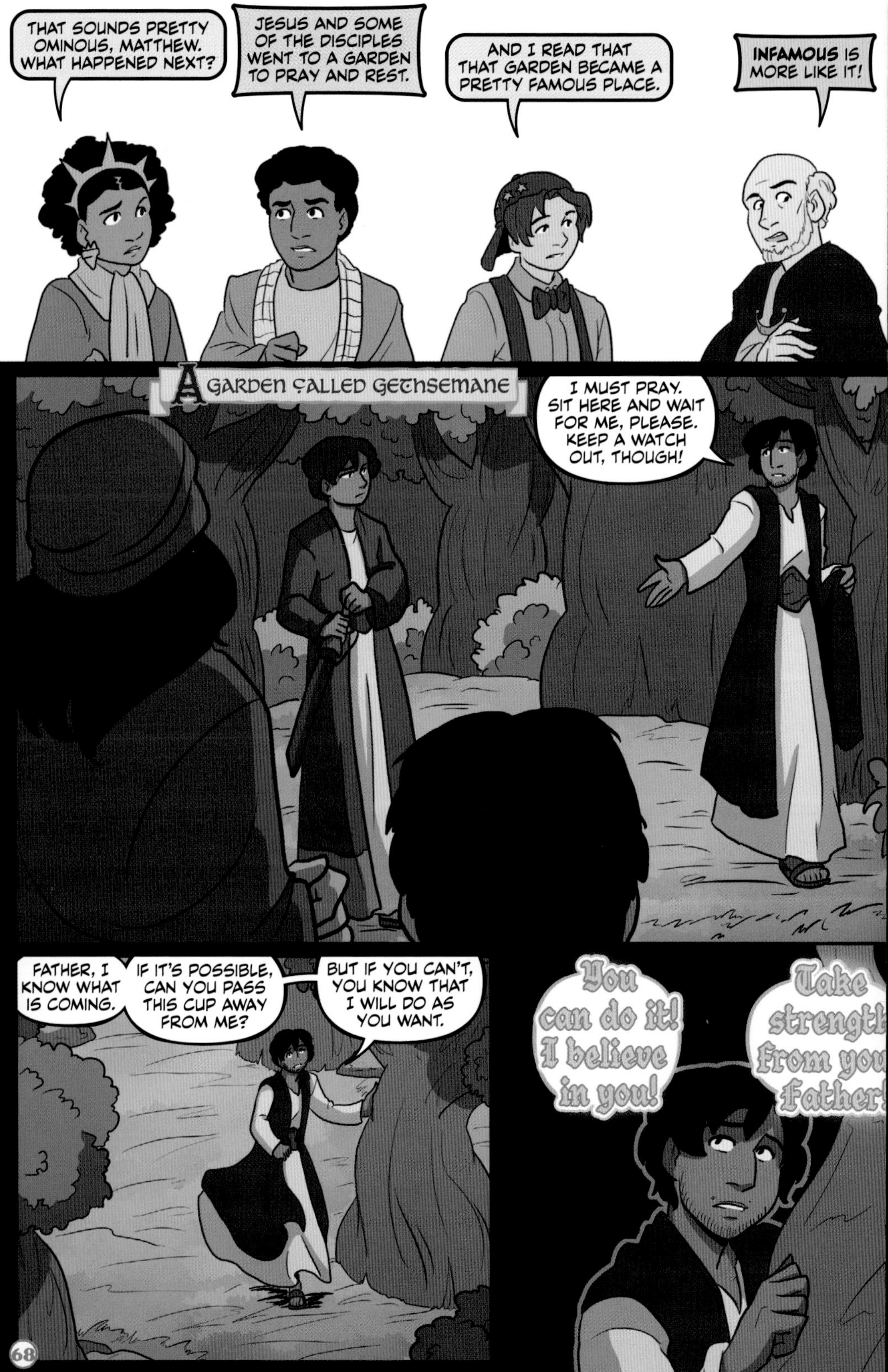
THAT SOUNDS PRETTY OMINOUS, MATTHEW. WHAT HAPPENED NEXT?
JESUS AND SOME OF THE DISCIPLES WENT TO A GARDEN TO PRAY AND REST.
AND I READ THAT THAT GARDEN BECAME A PRETTY FAMOUS PLACE.
INFAMOUS IS MORE LIKE IT!
A GARDEN CALLED GETHSEMANE
I MUST PRAY. SIT HERE AND WAIT FOR ME, PLEASE. KEEP A WATCH OUT, THOUGH!
FATHER, I KNOW WHAT IS COMING.
IF IT'S POSSIBLE, CAN YOU PASS THIS CUP AWAY FROM ME?
BUT IF YOU CAN'T, YOU KNOW THAT I WILL DO AS YOU WANT.
You can do it! I believe in you!

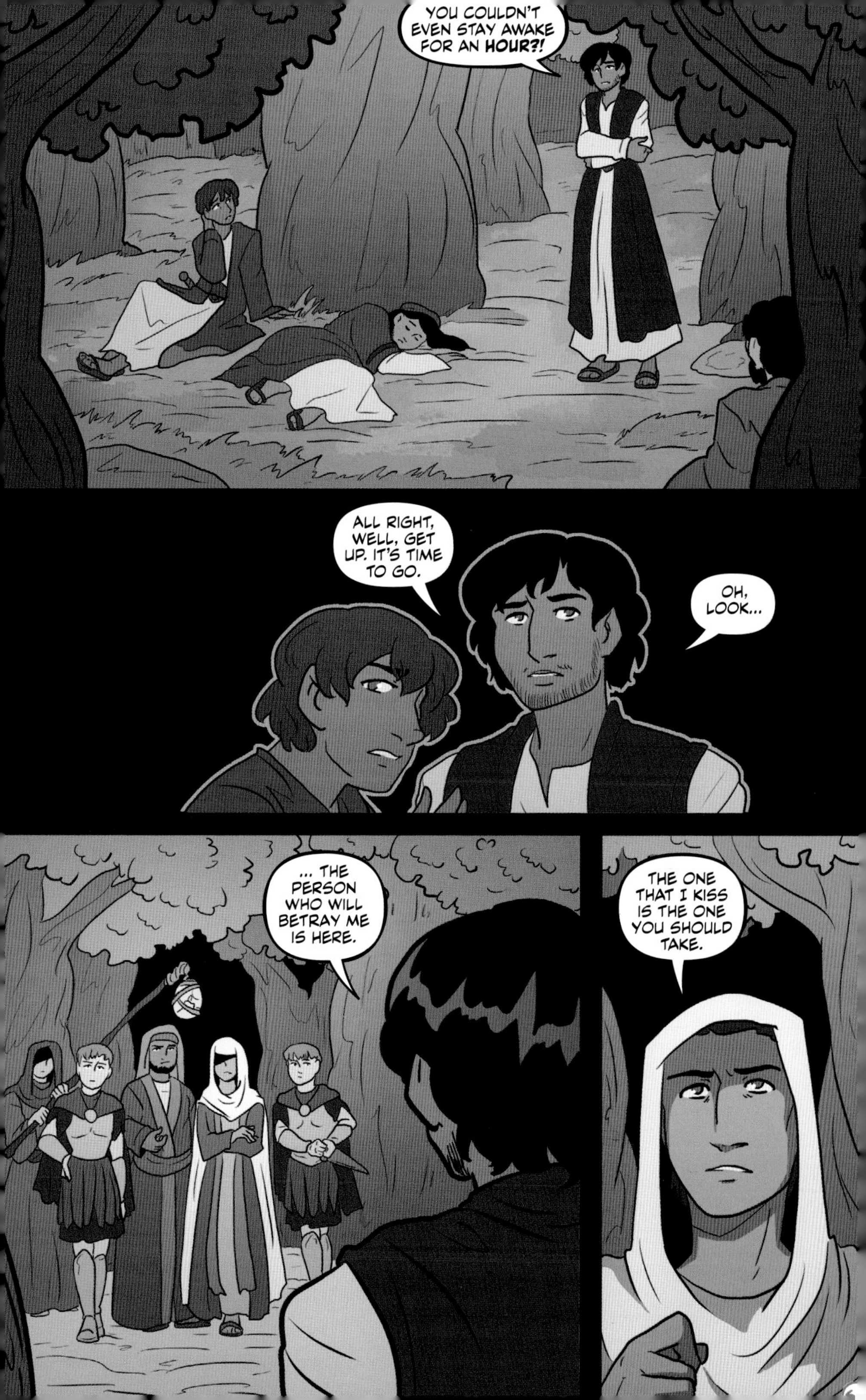
YOU COULDN'T EVEN STAY AWAKE FOR AN HOUR?!
ALL RIGHT, WELL, GET UP. IT'S TIME TO GO.
OH, LOOK...
... THE PERSON WHO WILL BETRAY ME IS HERE.
THE ONE THAT I KISS IS THE ONE YOU SHOULD TAKE.

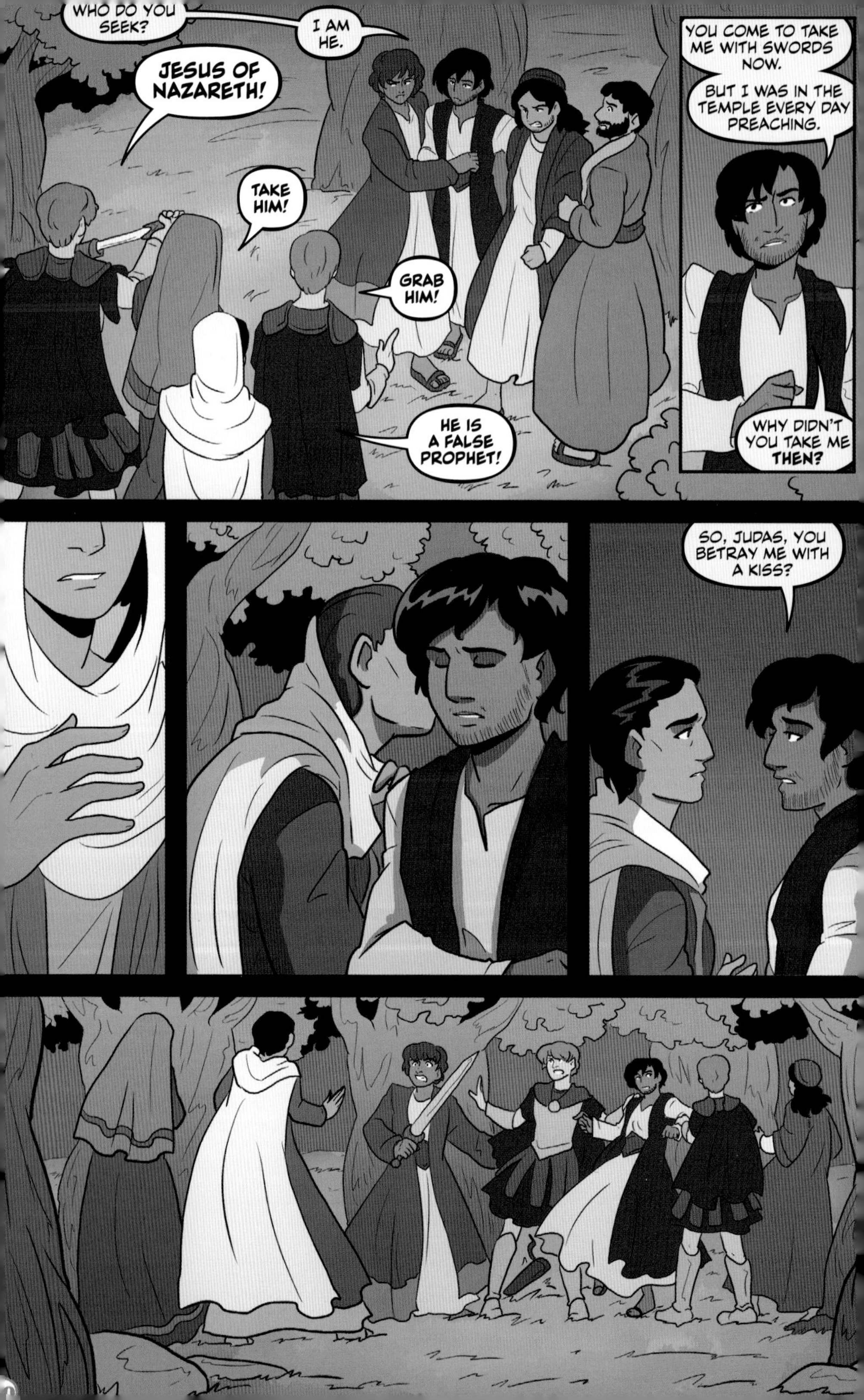
WHO DO YOU SEEK?
I AM HE.
JESUS OF NAZARETH!
TAKE HIM!
GRAB HIM!
HE IS A FALSE PROPHET!
YOU COME TO TAKE ME WITH SWORDS NOW.
BUT I WAS IN THE TEMPLE EVERY DAY PREACHING.
WHY DIDN'T YOU TAKE ME THEN?
SO, JUDAS, YOU BETRAY ME WITH A KISS?

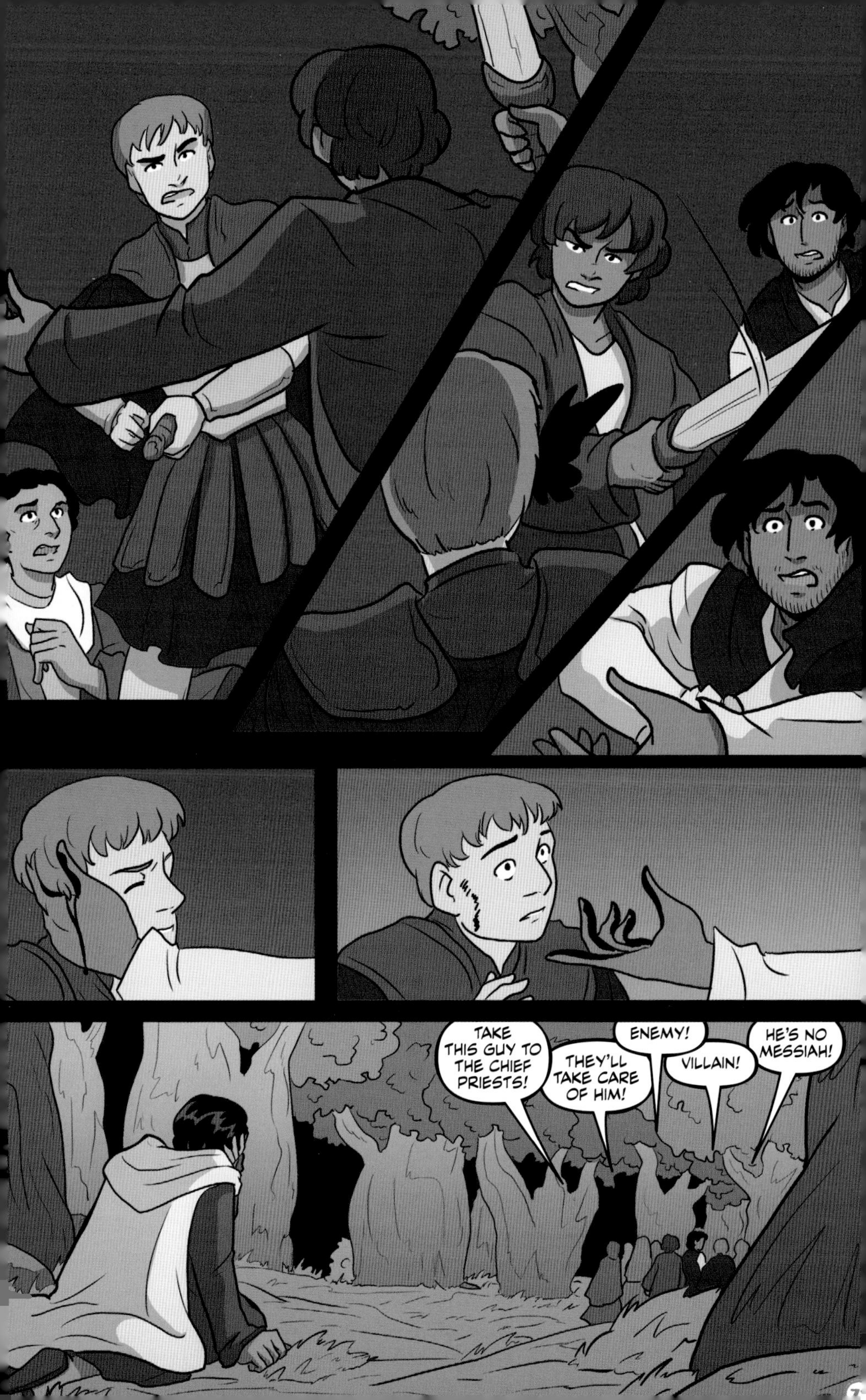
TAKE THIS GUY TO THE CHIEF PRIESTS!
THEY'LL TAKE CARE OF HIM!
ENEMY!
VILLAIN!
HE'S NO MESSIAH!

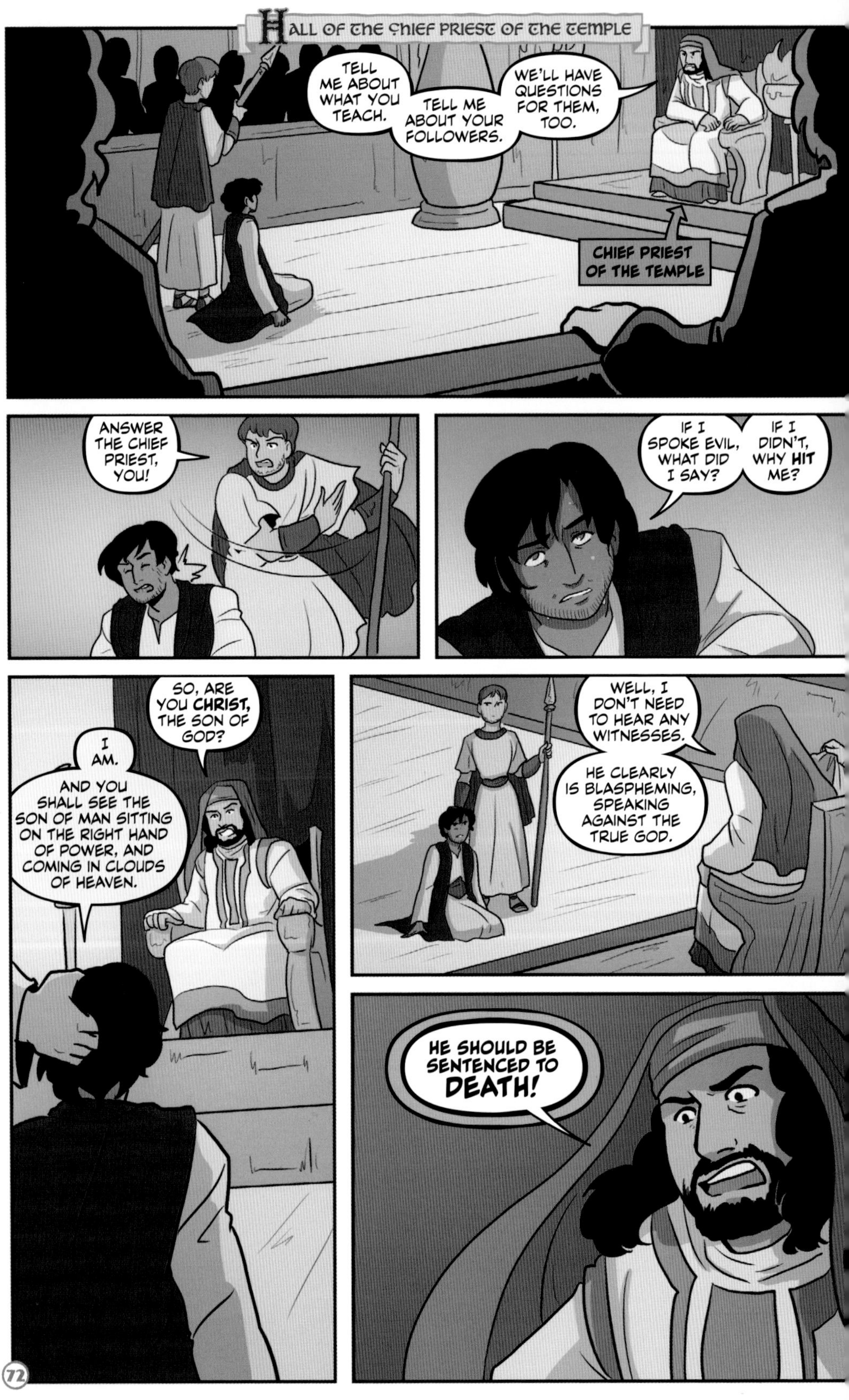
HALL OF THE CHIEF PRIEST OF THE TEMPLE
TELL ME ABOUT WHAT YOU TEACH.
TELL ME ABOUT YOUR FOLLOWERS.
WE'LL HAVE QUESTIONS FOR THEM, TOO.
CHIEF PRIEST OF THE TEMPLE
ANSWER THE CHIEF PRIEST, YOU!
IF I SPOKE EVIL, WHAT DID I SAY?
IF I DIDN'T, WHY HIT ME?
SO, ARE YOU CHRIST, THE SON OF GOD?
I AM.
AND YOU SHALL SEE THE SON OF MAN SITTING ON THE RIGHT HAND OF POWER, AND COMING IN CLOUDS OF HEAVEN.
WELL, I DON'T NEED TO HEAR ANY WITNESSES.
HE CLEARLY IS BLASPHEMING, SPEAKING AGAINST THE TRUE GOD.
HE SHOULD BE SENTENCED TO DEATH!

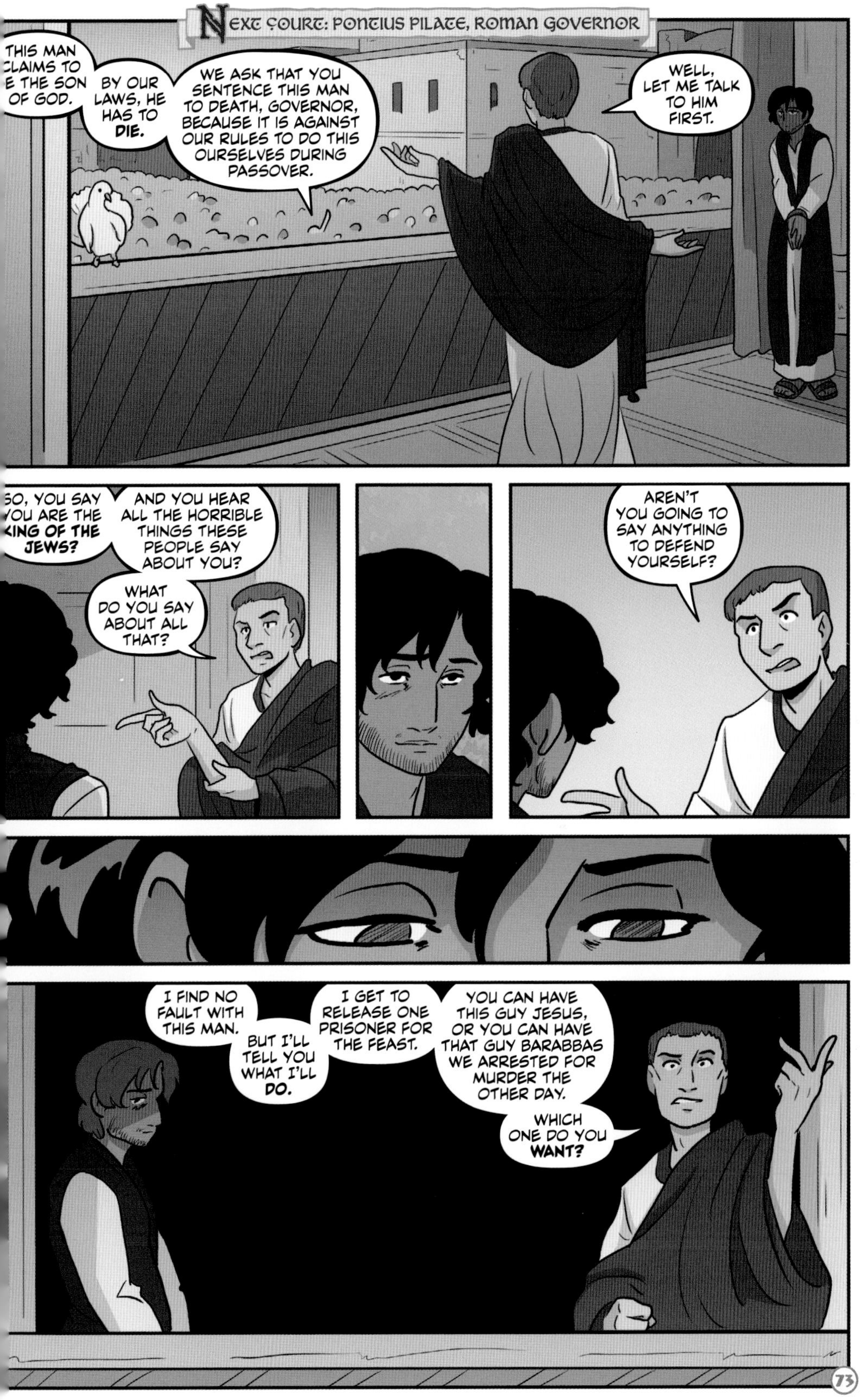
NEXT COURT: PONTIUS PILATE, ROMAN GOVERNOR
THIS MAN CLAIMS TO E THE SON OF GOD.
BY OUR LAWS, HE HAS TO **DIE.**
WE ASK THAT YOU SENTENCE THIS MAN TO DEATH, GOVERNOR, BECAUSE IT IS AGAINST OUR RULES TO DO THIS OURSELVES DURING PASSOVER.
WELL, LET ME TALK TO HIM FIRST.
SO, YOU SAY YOU ARE THE **KING OF THE JEWS?**
AND YOU HEAR ALL THE HORRIBLE THINGS THESE PEOPLE SAY ABOUT YOU?
WHAT DO YOU SAY ABOUT ALL THAT?
AREN'T YOU GOING TO SAY ANYTHING TO DEFEND YOURSELF?
I FIND NO FAULT WITH THIS MAN.
BUT I'LL TELL YOU WHAT I'LL **DO.**
I GET TO RELEASE ONE PRISONER FOR THE FEAST.
YOU CAN HAVE THIS GUY JESUS, OR YOU CAN HAVE THAT GUY BARABBAS WE ARRESTED FOR MURDER THE OTHER DAY.
WHICH ONE DO YOU **WANT?**

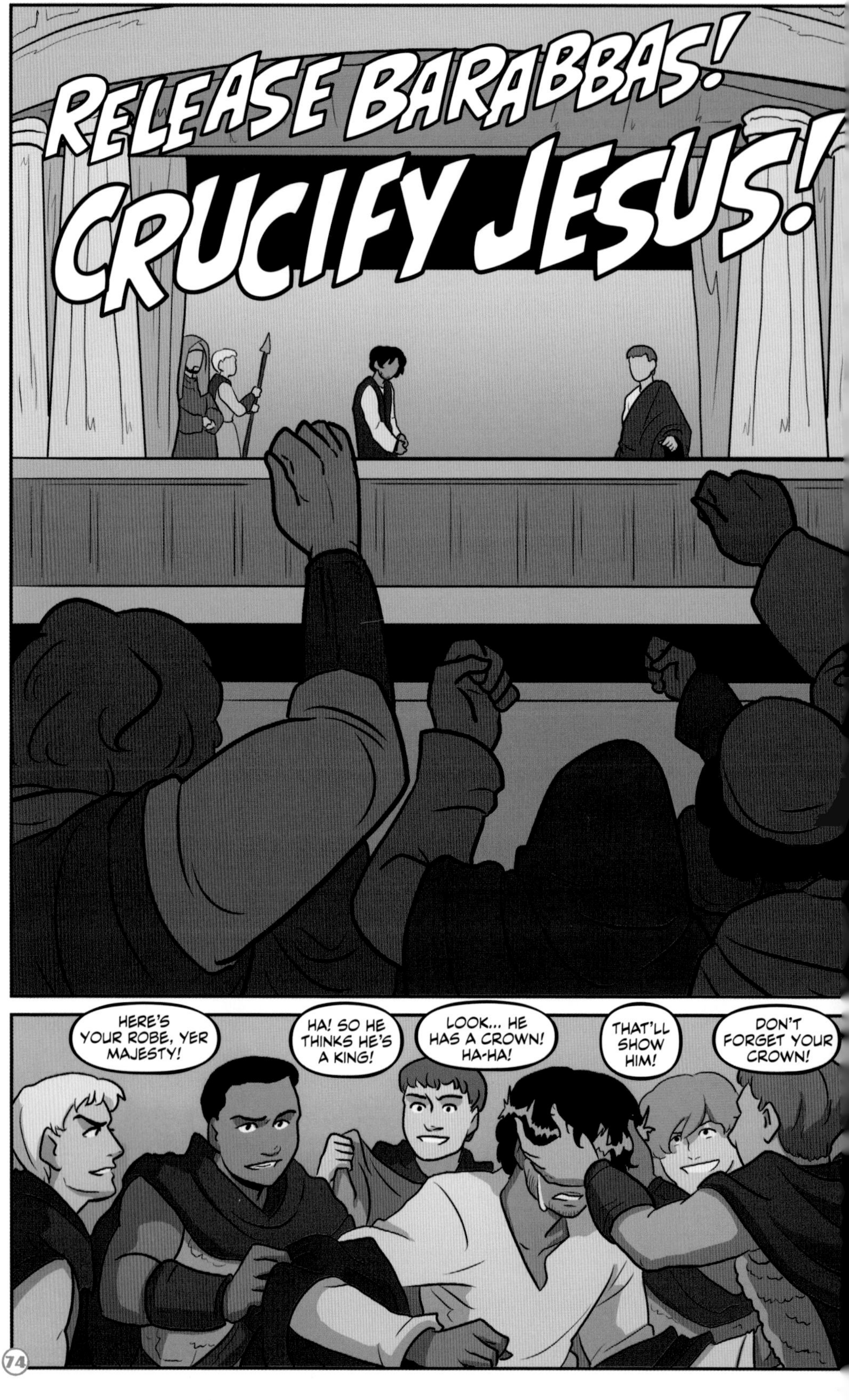
RELEASE BARABBAS!
CRUCIFY JESUS!
HERE'S YOUR ROBE, YER MAJESTY!
HA! SO HE THINKS HE'S A KING!
LOOK... HE HAS A CROWN! HA-HA!
THAT'LL SHOW HIM!
DON'T FORGET YOUR CROWN!

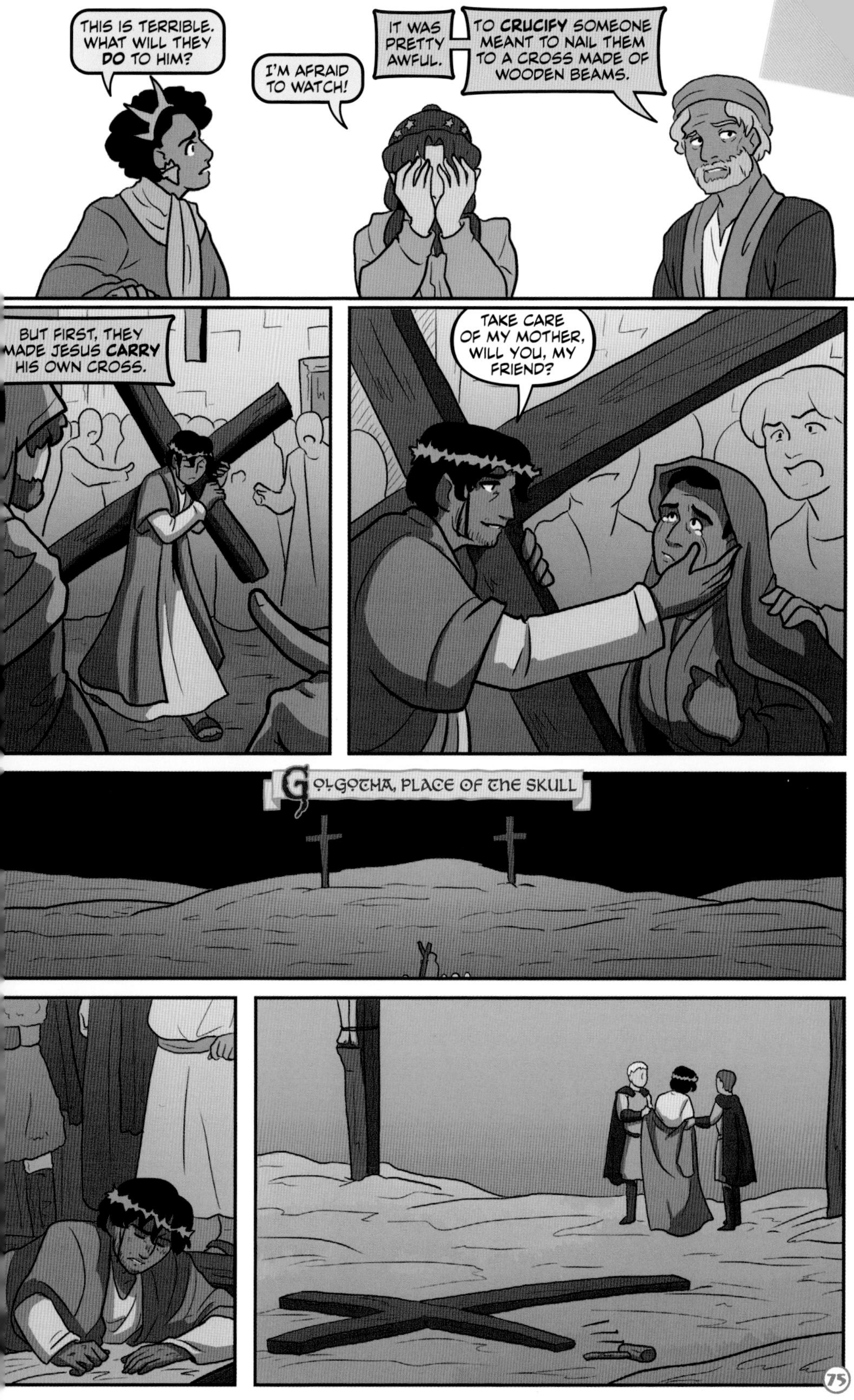
THIS IS TERRIBLE. WHAT WILL THEY DO TO HIM?
I'M AFRAID TO WATCH!
IT WAS PRETTY AWFUL.
TO CRUCIFY SOMEONE MEANT TO NAIL THEM TO A CROSS MADE OF WOODEN BEAMS.
BUT FIRST, THEY MADE JESUS CARRY HIS OWN CROSS.
TAKE CARE OF MY MOTHER, WILL YOU, MY FRIEND?
GOLGOTHA, PLACE OF THE SKULL

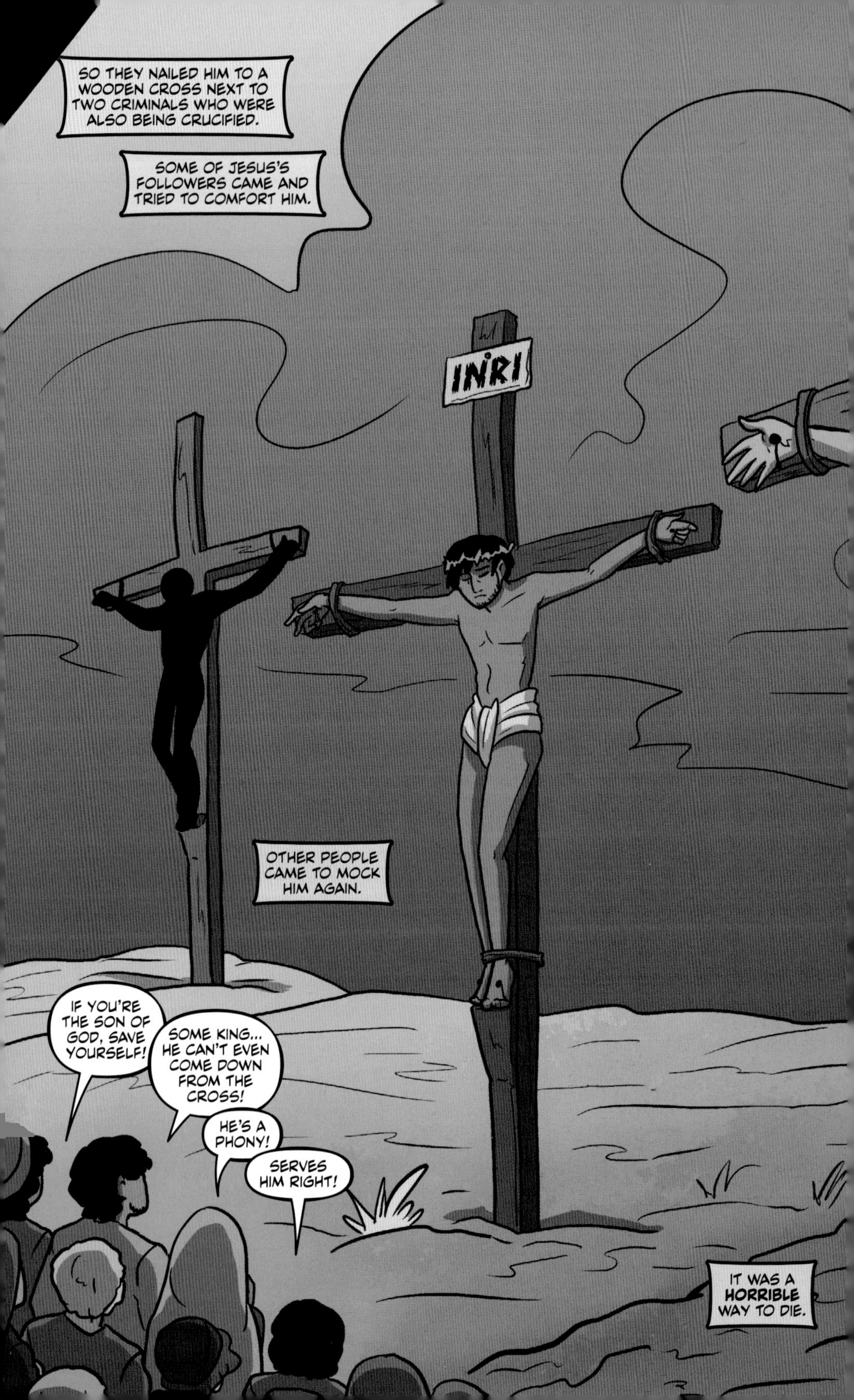
SO THEY NAILED HIM TO A WOODEN CROSS NEXT TO TWO CRIMINALS WHO WERE ALSO BEING CRUCIFIED.
SOME OF JESUS'S FOLLOWERS CAME AND TRIED TO COMFORT HIM.
INRI
OTHER PEOPLE CAME TO MOCK HIM AGAIN.
IF YOU'RE THE SON OF GOD, SAVE YOURSELF!
SOME KING... HE CAN'T EVEN COME DOWN FROM THE CROSS!
HE'S A PHONY!
SERVES HIM RIGHT!
IT WAS A **HORRIBLE** WAY TO DIE.

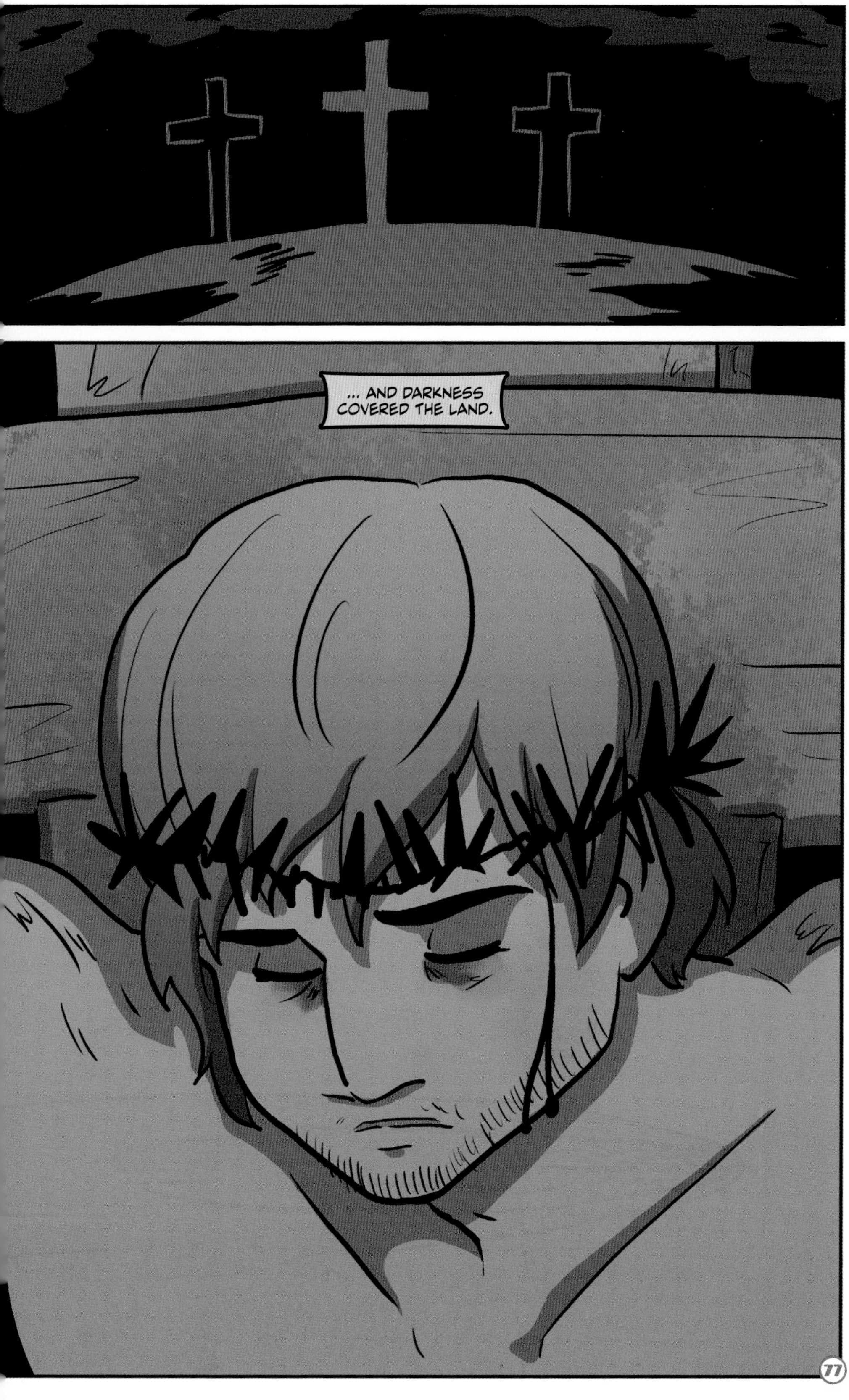
... AND DARKNESS
COVERED THE LAND.

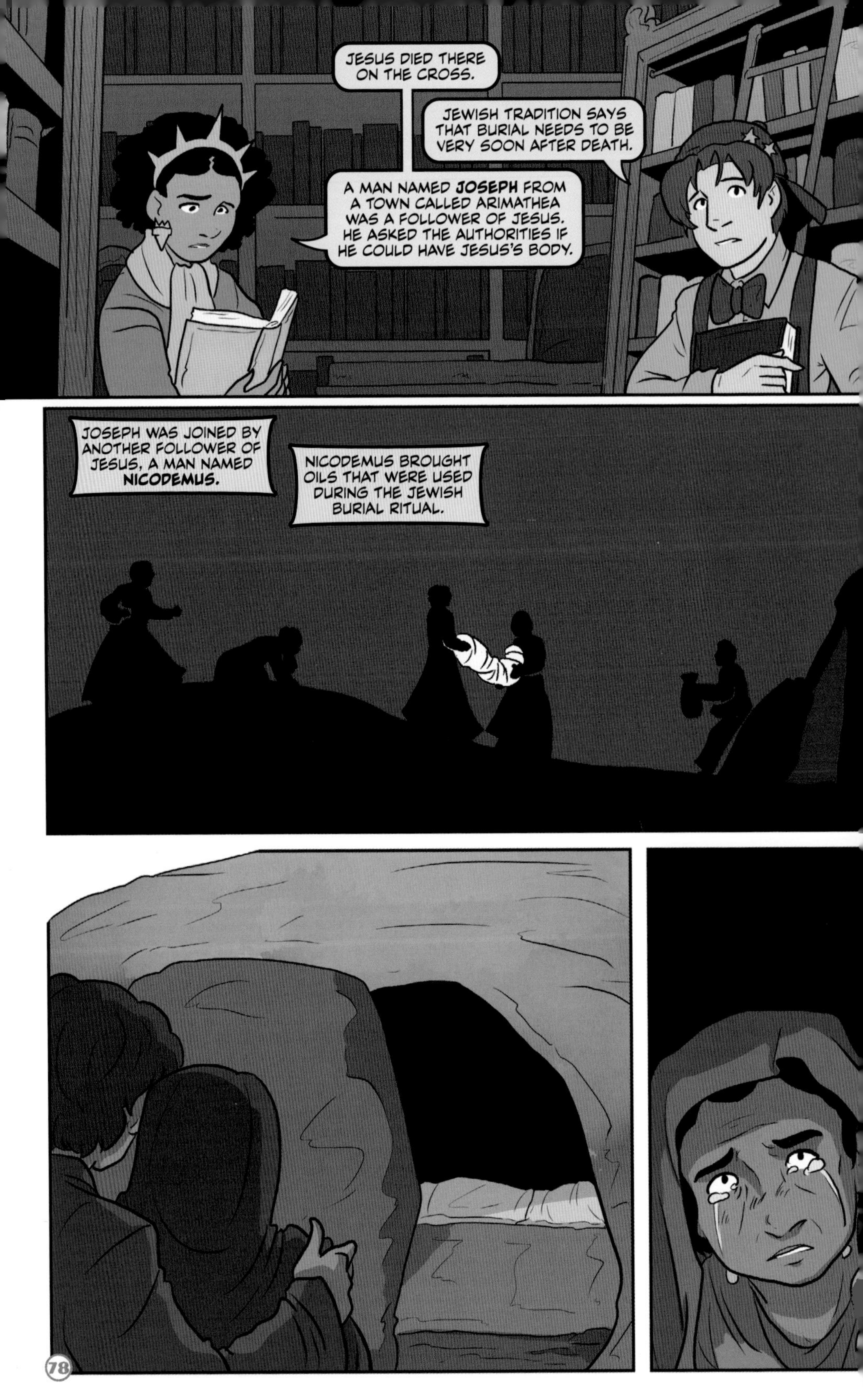

JESUS DIED THERE ON THE CROSS.
JEWISH TRADITION SAYS THAT BURIAL NEEDS TO BE VERY SOON AFTER DEATH.
A MAN NAMED **JOSEPH** FROM A TOWN CALLED ARIMATHEA WAS A FOLLOWER OF JESUS. HE ASKED THE AUTHORITIES IF HE COULD HAVE JESUS'S BODY.
JOSEPH WAS JOINED BY ANOTHER FOLLOWER OF JESUS, A MAN NAMED **NICODEMUS.**
NICODEMUS BROUGHT OILS THAT WERE USED DURING THE JEWISH BURIAL RITUAL.

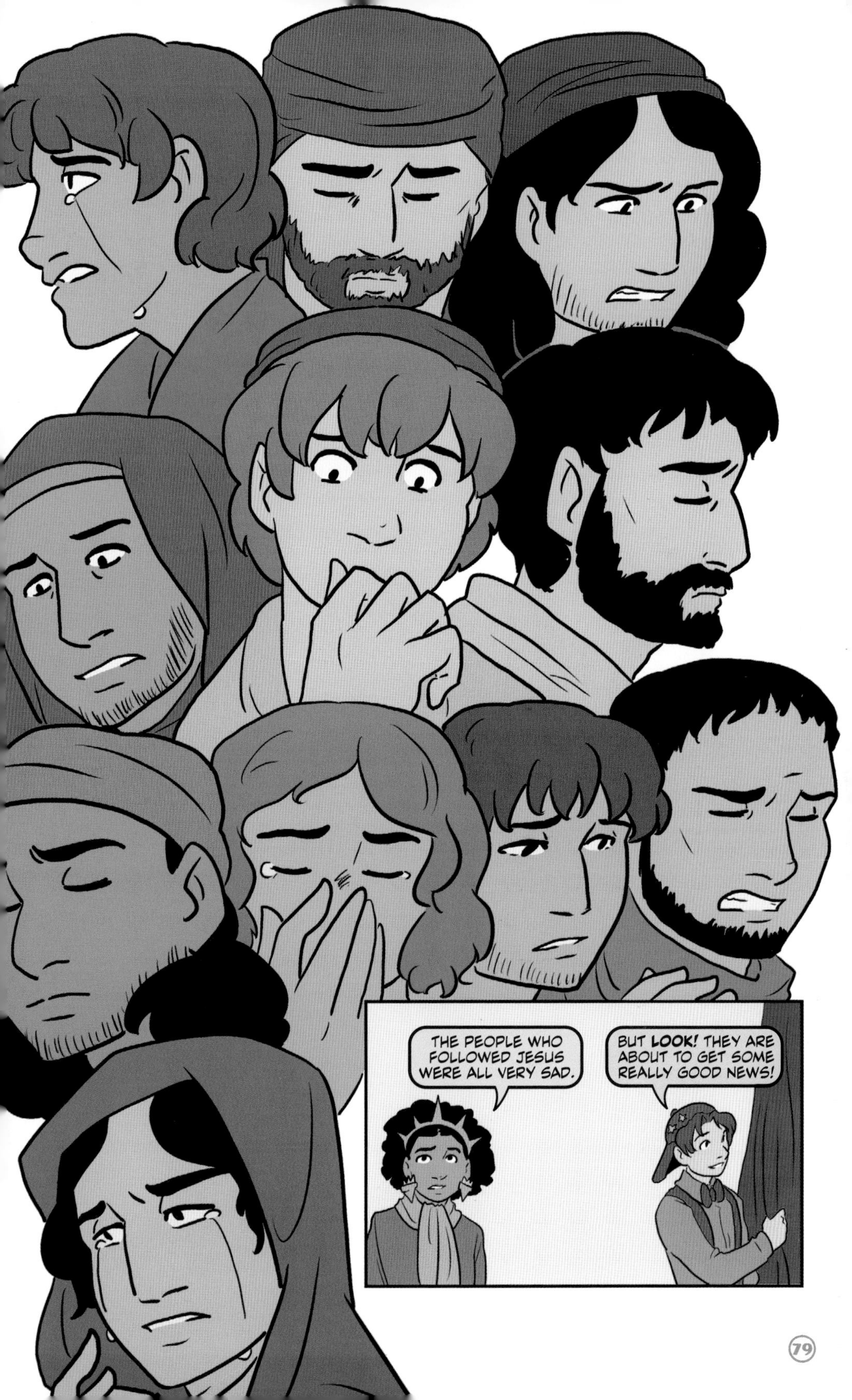
THE PEOPLE WHO FOLLOWED JESUS WERE ALL VERY SAD.
BUT **LOOK!** THEY ARE ABOUT TO GET SOME REALLY GOOD NEWS!

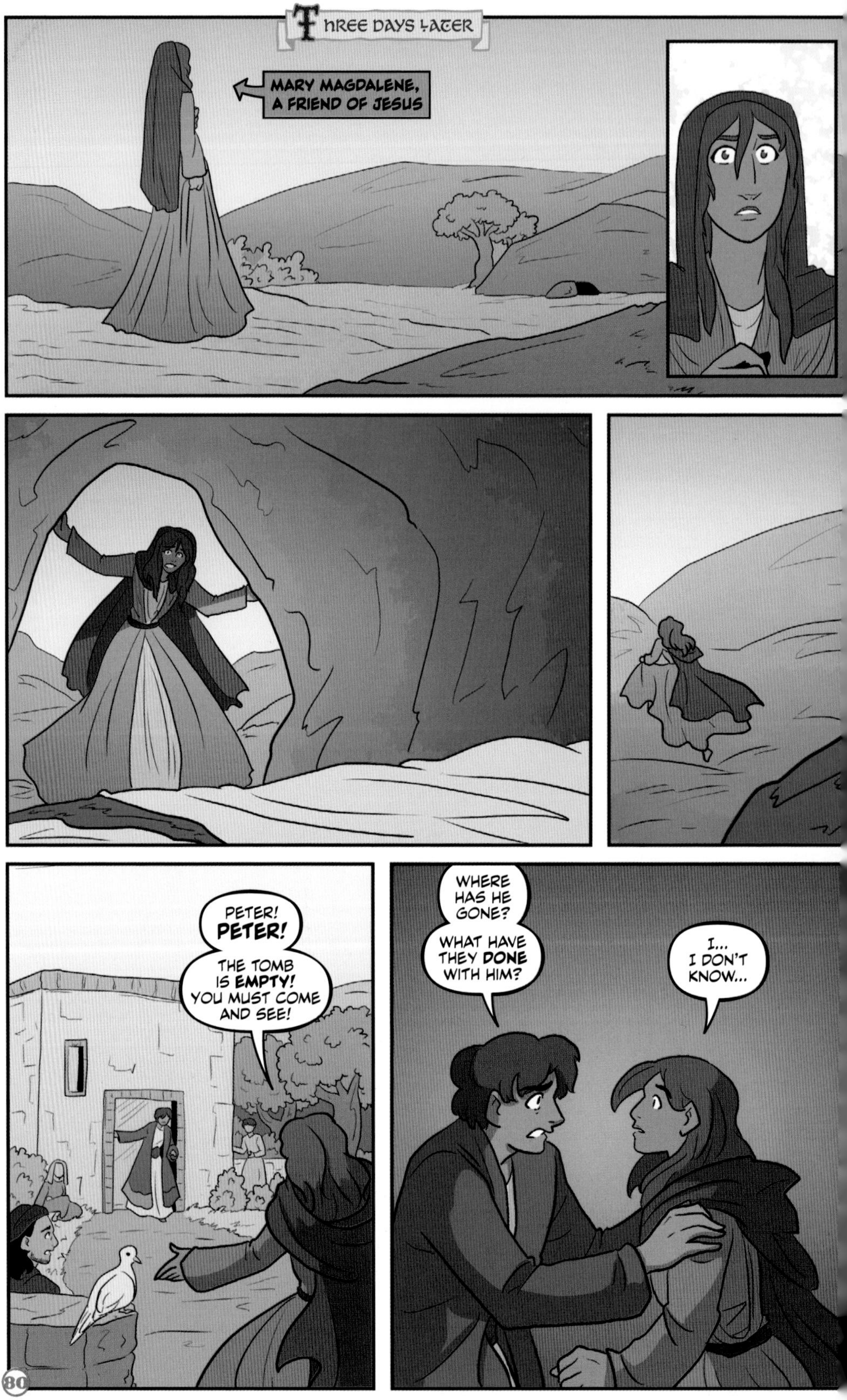
THREE DAYS LATER
MARY MAGDALENE, A FRIEND OF JESUS
PETER! PETER!
THE TOMB IS EMPTY! YOU MUST COME AND SEE!
WHERE HAS HE GONE?
WHAT HAVE THEY DONE WITH HIM?
I... I DON'T KNOW...

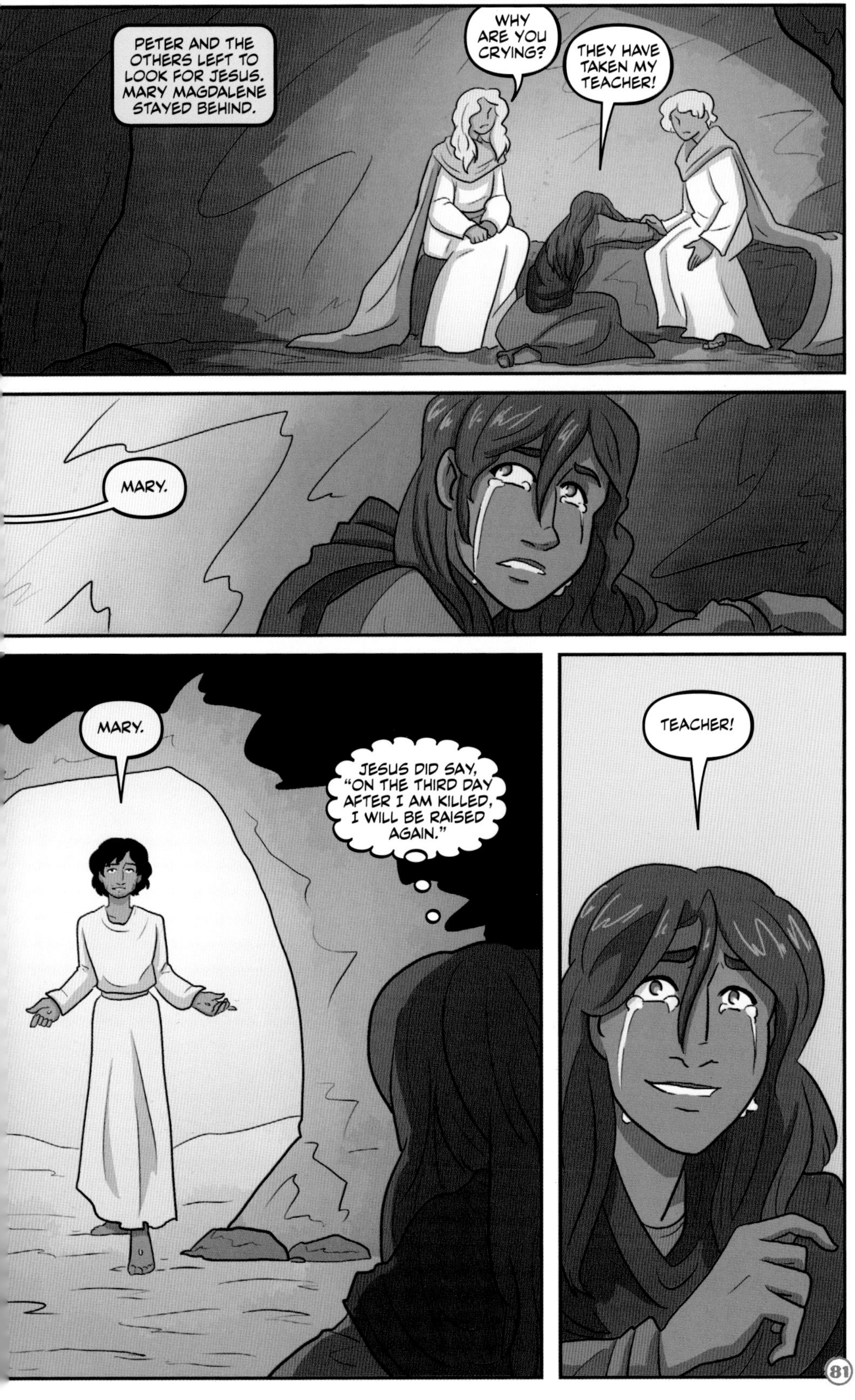
PETER AND THE OTHERS LEFT TO LOOK FOR JESUS. MARY MAGDALENE STAYED BEHIND.
WHY ARE YOU CRYING?
THEY HAVE TAKEN MY TEACHER!
MARY.
MARY.
JESUS DID SAY, "ON THE THIRD DAY AFTER I AM KILLED, I WILL BE RAISED AGAIN."
TEACHER!

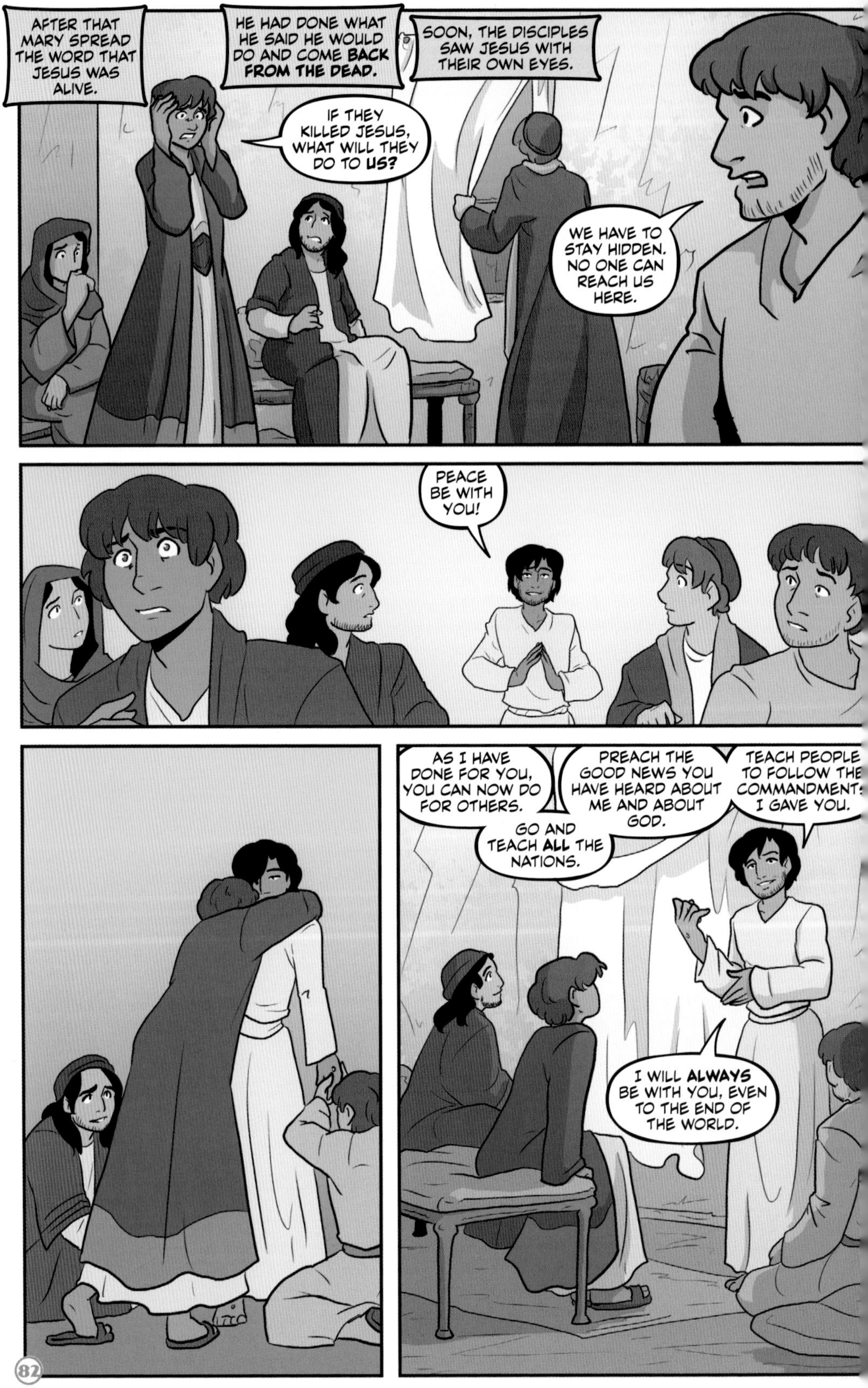
AFTER THAT MARY SPREAD THE WORD THAT JESUS WAS ALIVE.
HE HAD DONE WHAT HE SAID HE WOULD DO AND COME **BACK FROM THE DEAD.**
SOON, THE DISCIPLES SAW JESUS WITH THEIR OWN EYES.
IF THEY KILLED JESUS, WHAT WILL THEY DO TO **US?**
WE HAVE TO STAY HIDDEN. NO ONE CAN REACH US HERE.
PEACE BE WITH YOU!
AS I HAVE DONE FOR YOU, YOU CAN NOW DO FOR OTHERS.
GO AND TEACH **ALL** THE NATIONS.
PREACH THE GOOD NEWS YOU HAVE HEARD ABOUT ME AND ABOUT GOD.
TEACH PEOPLE TO FOLLOW THE COMMANDMENTS I GAVE YOU.
I WILL **ALWAYS** BE WITH YOU, EVEN TO THE END OF THE WORLD.

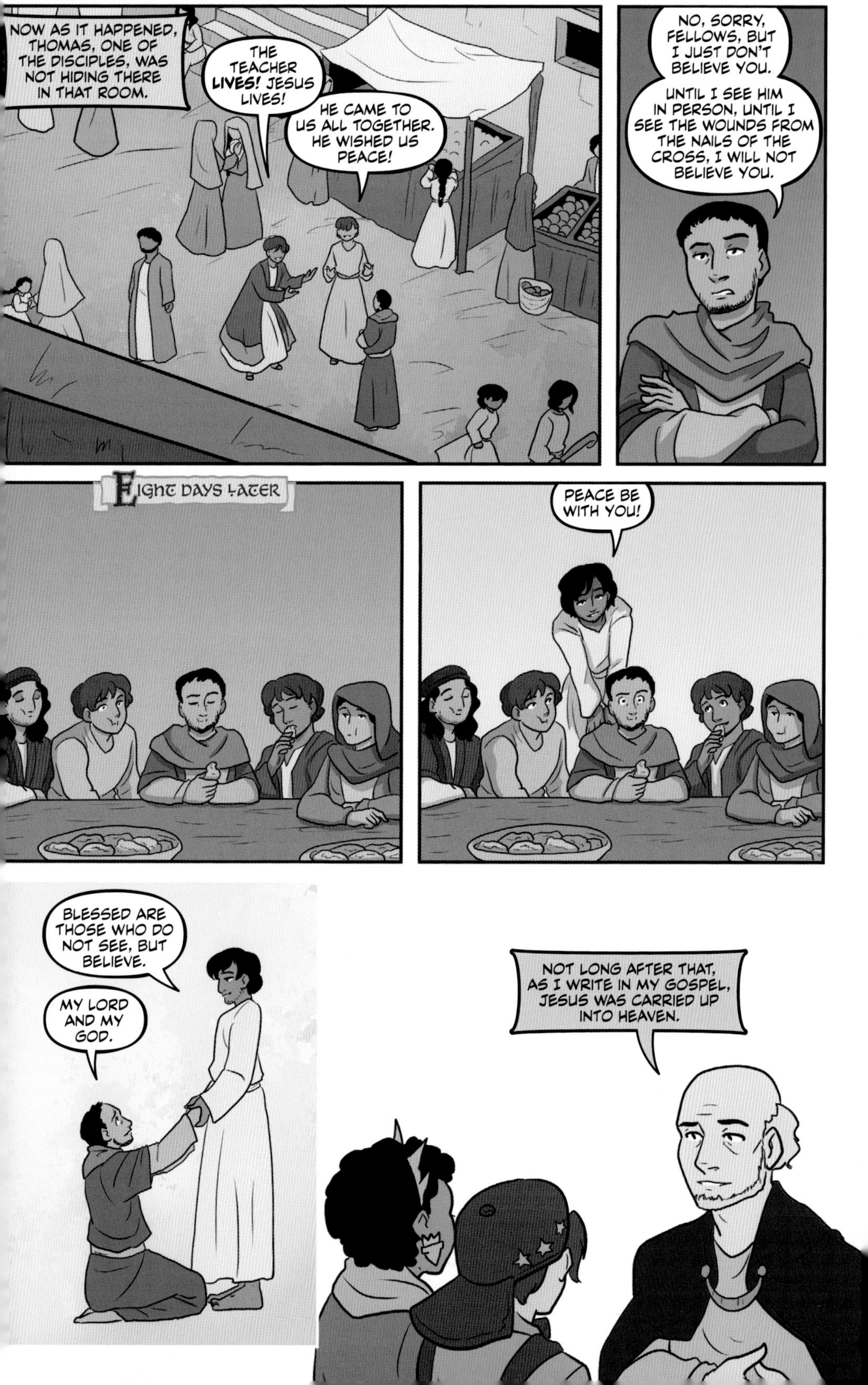

NOW AS IT HAPPENED, THOMAS, ONE OF THE DISCIPLES, WAS NOT HIDING THERE IN THAT ROOM.
THE TEACHER LIVES! JESUS LIVES!
HE CAME TO US ALL TOGETHER. HE WISHED US PEACE!
NO, SORRY, FELLOWS, BUT I JUST DON'T BELIEVE YOU.
UNTIL I SEE HIM IN PERSON, UNTIL I SEE THE WOUNDS FROM THE NAILS OF THE CROSS, I WILL NOT BELIEVE YOU.
EIGHT DAYS LATER
PEACE BE WITH YOU!
BLESSED ARE THOSE WHO DO NOT SEE, BUT BELIEVE.
MY LORD AND MY GOD.
NOT LONG AFTER THAT, AS I WRITE IN MY GOSPEL, JESUS WAS CARRIED UP INTO HEAVEN.

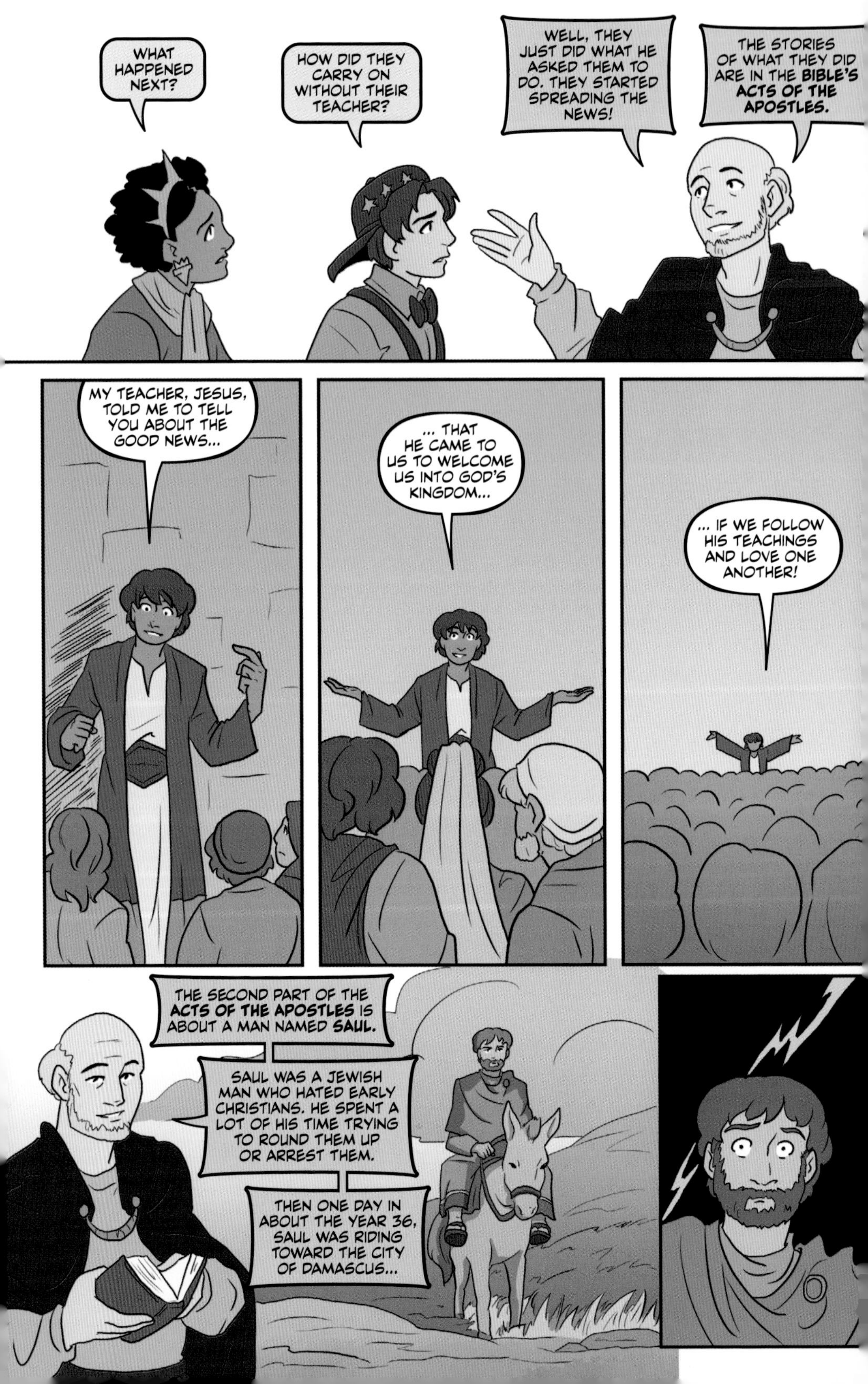
WHAT HAPPENED NEXT?
HOW DID THEY CARRY ON WITHOUT THEIR TEACHER?
WELL, THEY JUST DID WHAT HE ASKED THEM TO DO. THEY STARTED SPREADING THE NEWS!
THE STORIES OF WHAT THEY DID ARE IN THE **BIBLE'S ACTS OF THE APOSTLES.**
MY TEACHER, JESUS, TOLD ME TO TELL YOU ABOUT THE GOOD NEWS...
... THAT HE CAME TO US TO WELCOME US INTO GOD'S KINGDOM...
... IF WE FOLLOW HIS TEACHINGS AND LOVE ONE ANOTHER!
THE SECOND PART OF THE **ACTS OF THE APOSTLES** IS ABOUT A MAN NAMED **SAUL.**
SAUL WAS A JEWISH MAN WHO HATED EARLY CHRISTIANS. HE SPENT A LOT OF HIS TIME TRYING TO ROUND THEM UP OR ARREST THEM.
THEN ONE DAY IN ABOUT THE YEAR 36, SAUL WAS RIDING TOWARD THE CITY OF DAMASCUS...

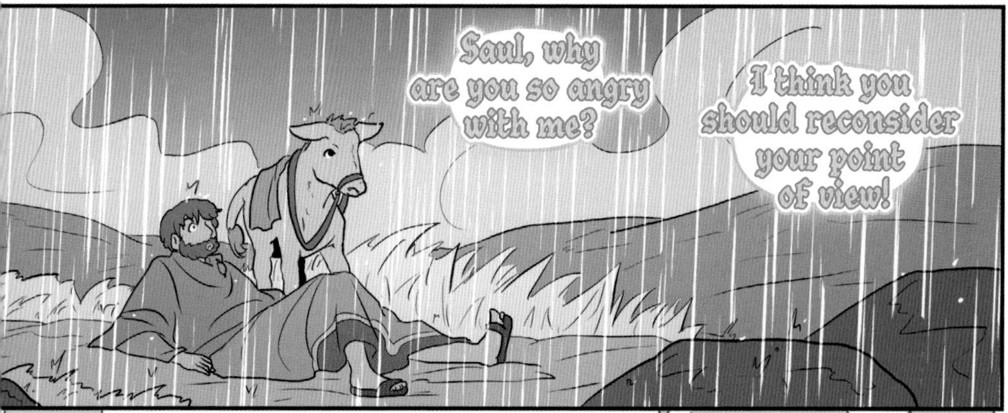
Saul, why are you so angry with me?
I think you should reconsider your point of view!

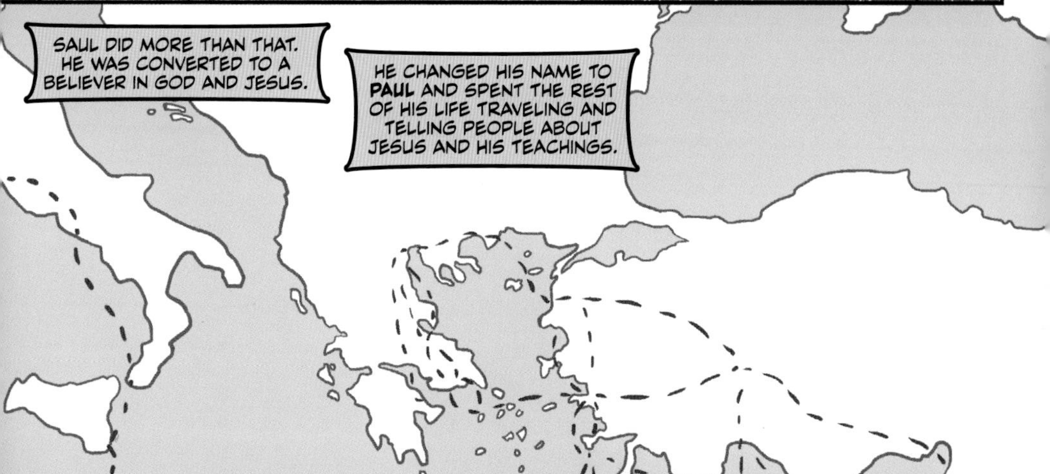
SAUL DID MORE THAN THAT. HE WAS CONVERTED TO A BELIEVER IN GOD AND JESUS.
HE CHANGED HIS NAME TO PAUL AND SPENT THE REST OF HIS LIFE TRAVELING AND TELLING PEOPLE ABOUT JESUS AND HIS TEACHINGS.
Mediterranean Sea
HE WAS A MAN ON THE MOVE!

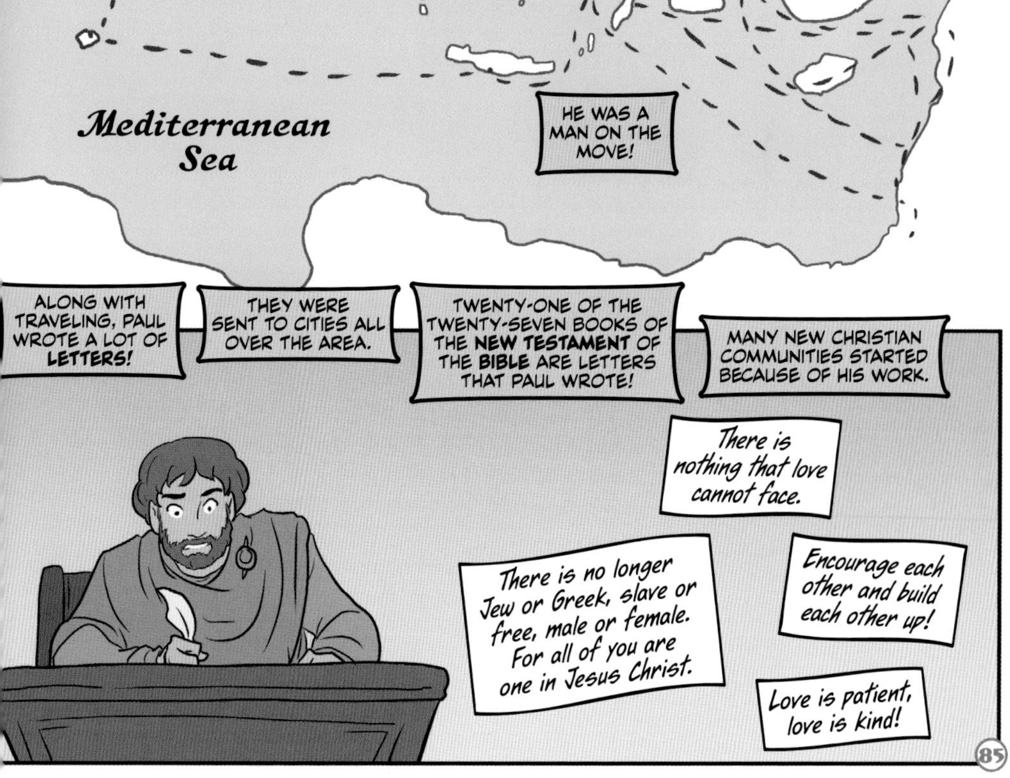
ALONG WITH TRAVELING, PAUL WROTE A LOT OF LETTERS!
THEY WERE SENT TO CITIES ALL OVER THE AREA.
TWENTY-ONE OF THE TWENTY-SEVEN BOOKS OF THE NEW TESTAMENT OF THE BIBLE ARE LETTERS THAT PAUL WROTE!
MANY NEW CHRISTIAN COMMUNITIES STARTED BECAUSE OF HIS WORK.
There is nothing that love cannot face.
There is no longer Jew or Greek, slave or free, male or female. For all of you are one in Jesus Christ.
Encourage each other and build each other up!
Love is patient, love is kind!

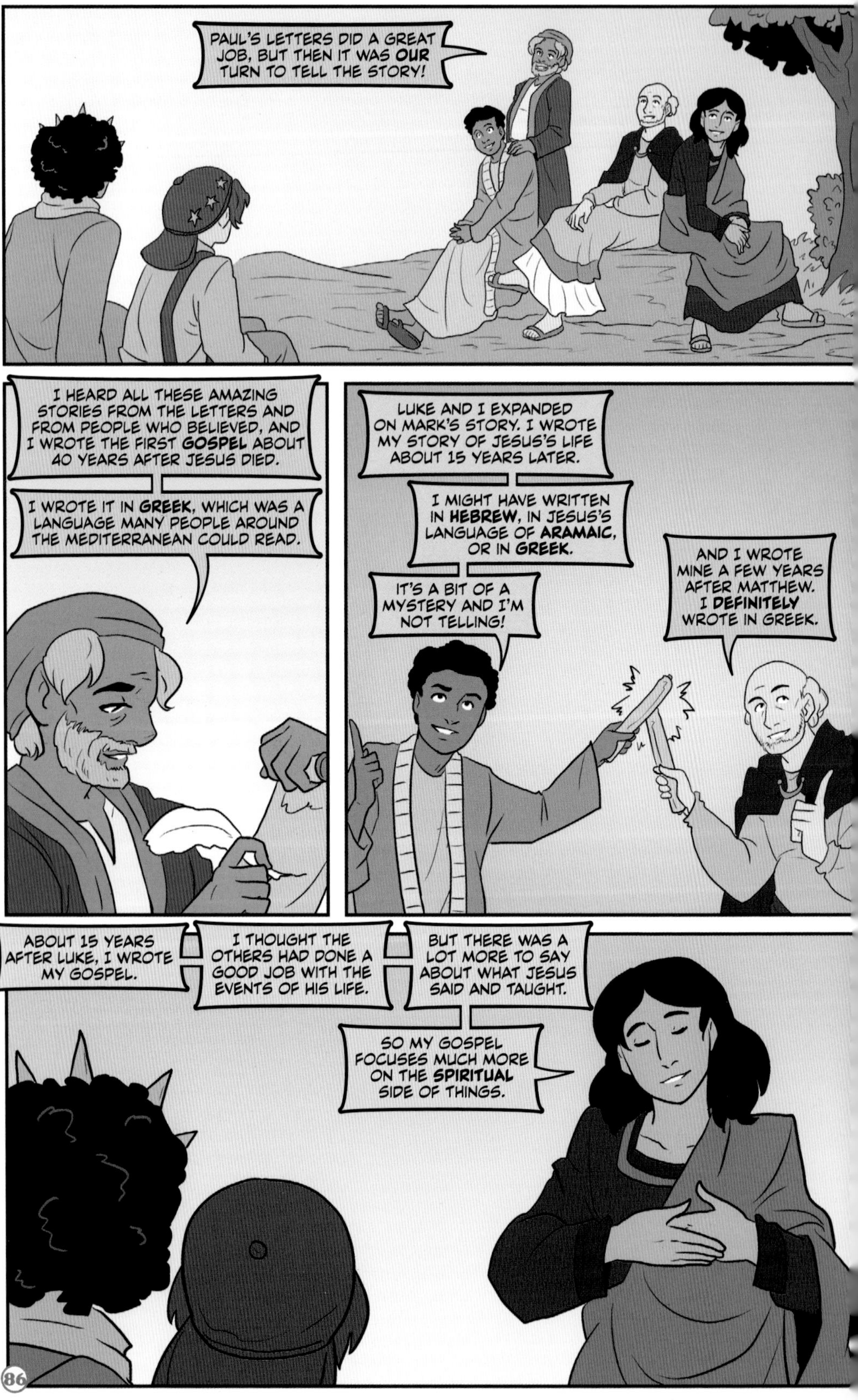

PAUL'S LETTERS DID A GREAT JOB, BUT THEN IT WAS **OUR** TURN TO TELL THE STORY!
I HEARD ALL THESE AMAZING STORIES FROM THE LETTERS AND FROM PEOPLE WHO BELIEVED, AND I WROTE THE FIRST **GOSPEL** ABOUT 40 YEARS AFTER JESUS DIED.
I WROTE IT IN **GREEK**, WHICH WAS A LANGUAGE MANY PEOPLE AROUND THE MEDITERRANEAN COULD READ.
LUKE AND I EXPANDED ON MARK'S STORY. I WROTE MY STORY OF JESUS'S LIFE ABOUT 15 YEARS LATER.
I MIGHT HAVE WRITTEN IN **HEBREW**, IN JESUS'S LANGUAGE OF **ARAMAIC**, OR IN **GREEK**.
IT'S A BIT OF A MYSTERY AND I'M NOT TELLING!
AND I WROTE MINE A FEW YEARS AFTER MATTHEW. I **DEFINITELY** WROTE IN GREEK.
ABOUT 15 YEARS AFTER LUKE, I WROTE MY GOSPEL.
I THOUGHT THE OTHERS HAD DONE A GOOD JOB WITH THE EVENTS OF HIS LIFE.
BUT THERE WAS A LOT MORE TO SAY ABOUT WHAT JESUS SAID AND TAUGHT.
SO MY GOSPEL FOCUSES MUCH MORE ON THE **SPIRITUAL** SIDE OF THINGS.

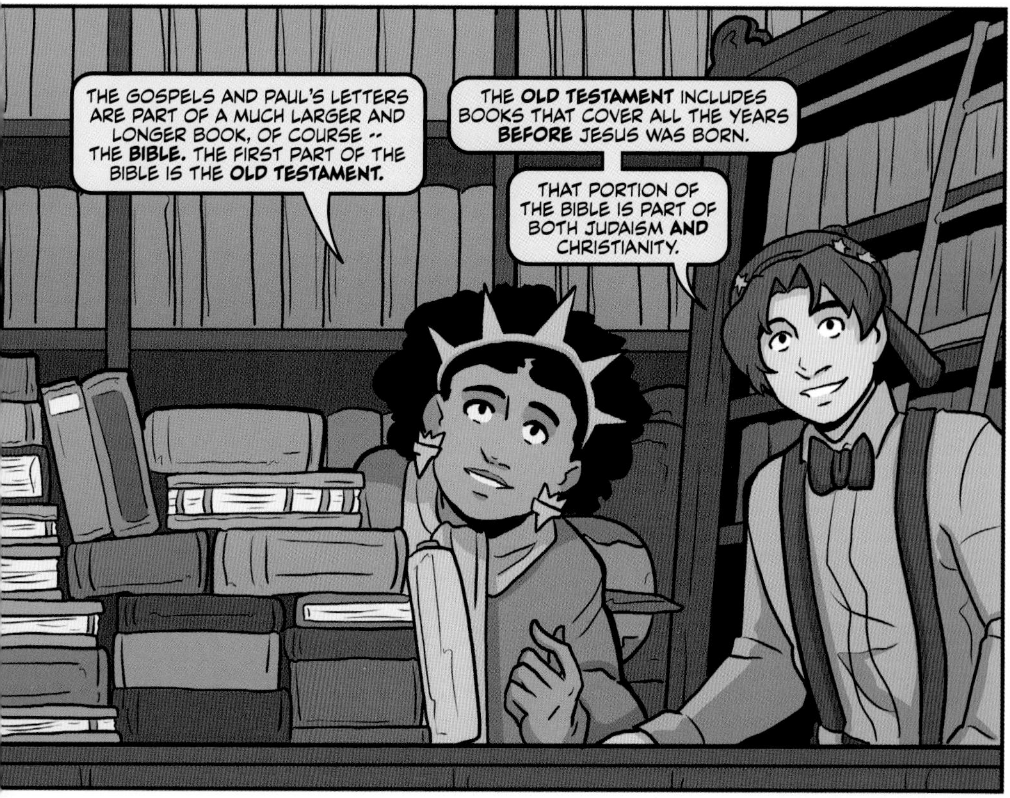
THE GOSPELS AND PAUL'S LETTERS ARE PART OF A MUCH LARGER AND LONGER BOOK, OF COURSE -- THE **BIBLE.** THE FIRST PART OF THE BIBLE IS THE **OLD TESTAMENT.**
THE **OLD TESTAMENT** INCLUDES BOOKS THAT COVER ALL THE YEARS **BEFORE** JESUS WAS BORN.
THAT PORTION OF THE BIBLE IS PART OF BOTH JUDAISM **AND** CHRISTIANITY.

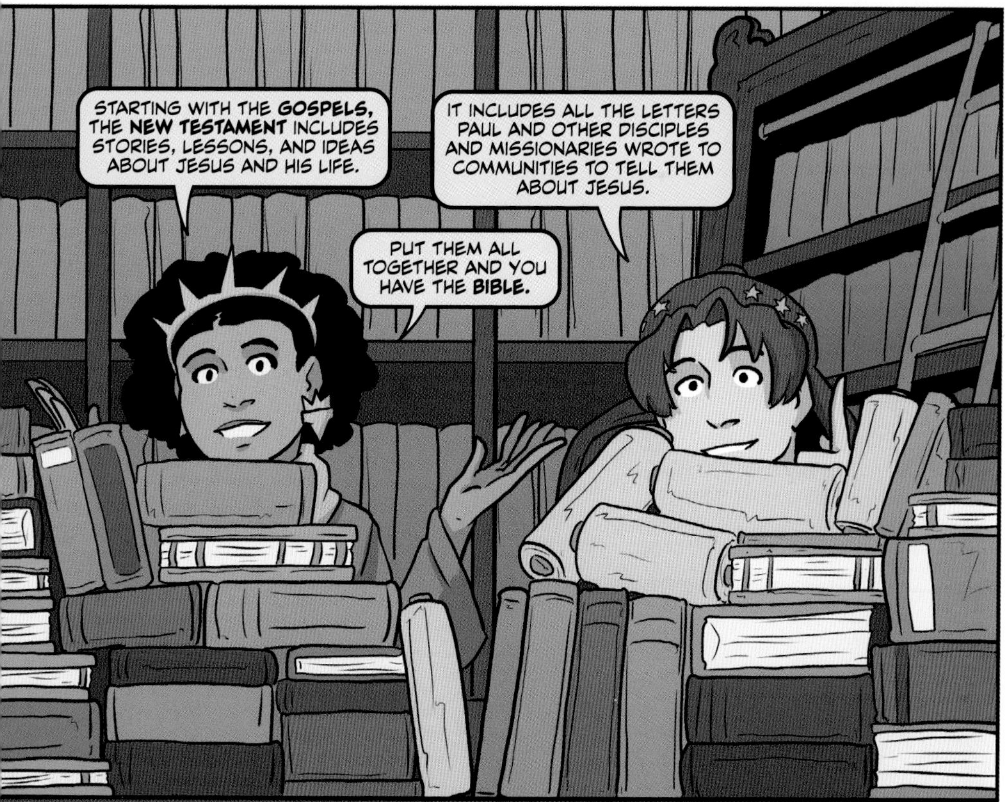
STARTING WITH THE **GOSPELS,** THE **NEW TESTAMENT** INCLUDES STORIES, LESSONS, AND IDEAS ABOUT JESUS AND HIS LIFE.
IT INCLUDES ALL THE LETTERS PAUL AND OTHER DISCIPLES AND MISSIONARIES WROTE TO COMMUNITIES TO TELL THEM ABOUT JESUS.
PUT THEM ALL TOGETHER AND YOU HAVE THE **BIBLE.**

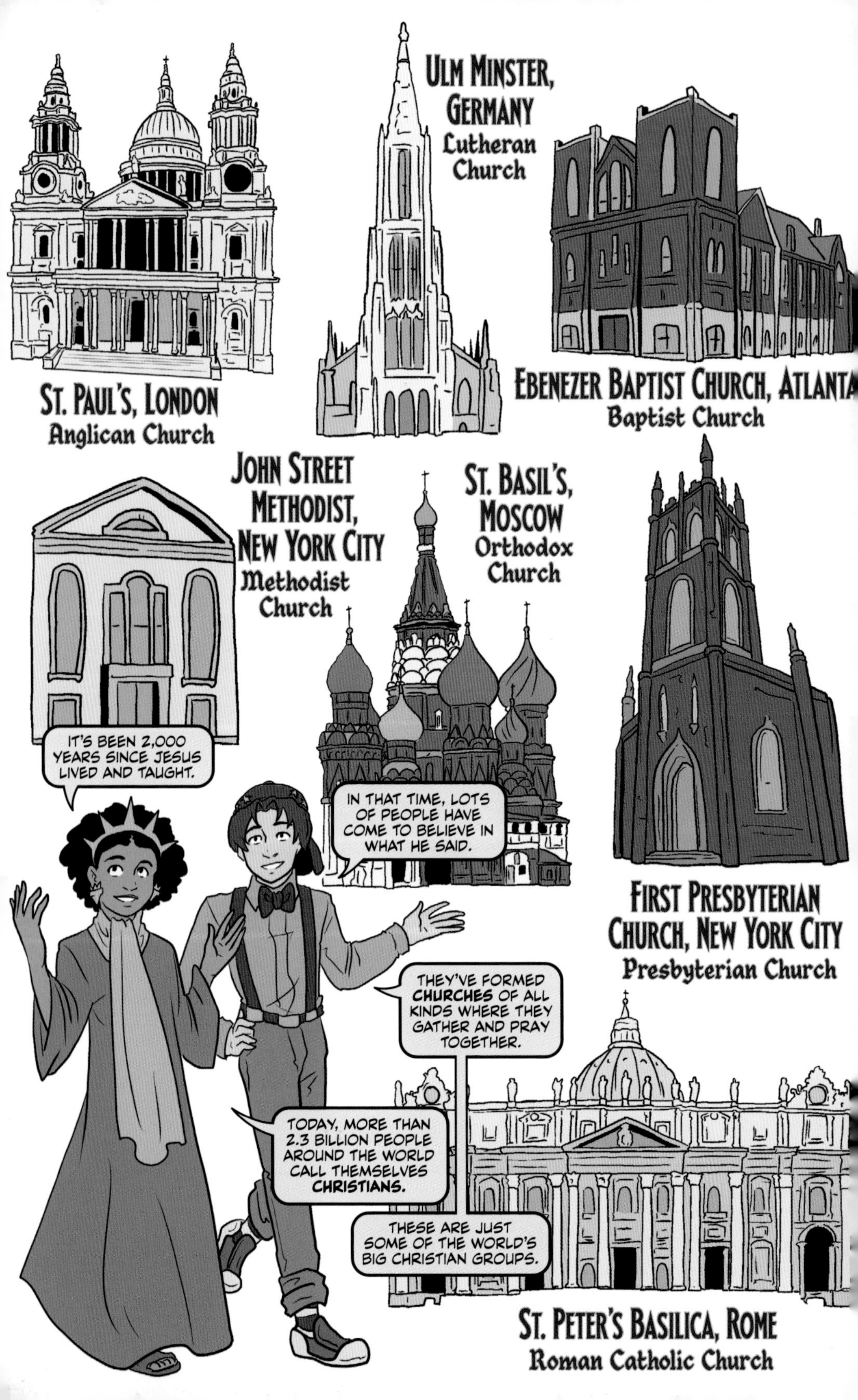

ST. PAUL'S, LONDON
Anglican Church
ULM MINSTER, GERMANY
Lutheran Church
EBENEZER BAPTIST CHURCH, ATLANTA
Baptist Church
JOHN STREET METHODIST, NEW YORK CITY
Methodist Church
ST. BASIL'S, MOSCOW
Orthodox Church
FIRST PRESBYTERIAN CHURCH, NEW YORK CITY
Presbyterian Church
IT'S BEEN 2,000 YEARS SINCE JESUS LIVED AND TAUGHT.
IN THAT TIME, LOTS OF PEOPLE HAVE COME TO BELIEVE IN WHAT HE SAID.
THEY'VE FORMED **CHURCHES** OF ALL KINDS WHERE THEY GATHER AND PRAY TOGETHER.
TODAY, MORE THAN 2.3 BILLION PEOPLE AROUND THE WORLD CALL THEMSELVES **CHRISTIANS.**
THESE ARE JUST SOME OF THE WORLD'S BIG CHRISTIAN GROUPS.
ST. PETER'S BASILICA, ROME
Roman Catholic Church

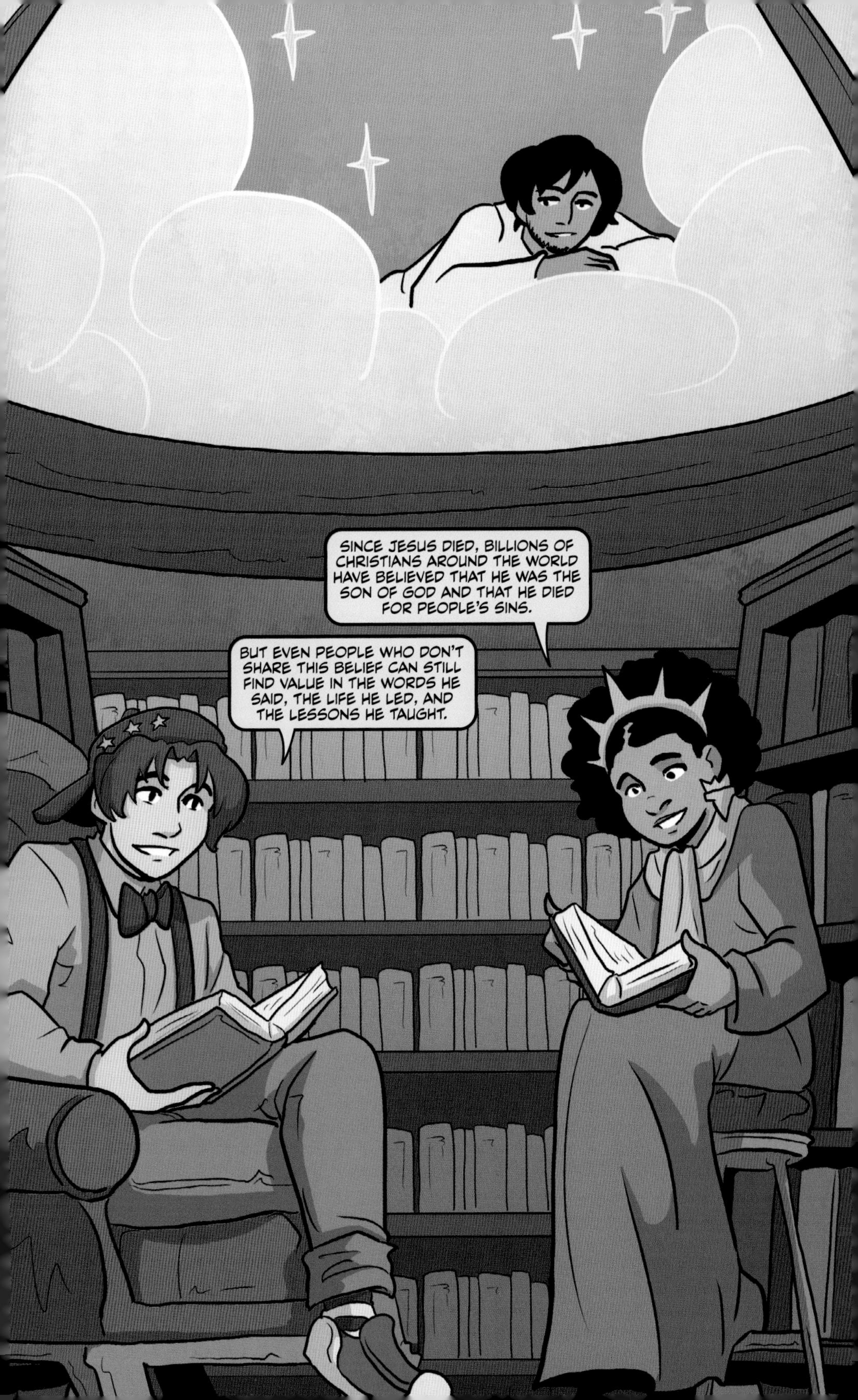
SINCE JESUS DIED, BILLIONS OF CHRISTIANS AROUND THE WORLD HAVE BELIEVED THAT HE WAS THE SON OF GOD AND THAT HE DIED FOR PEOPLE'S SINS.
BUT EVEN PEOPLE WHO DON'T SHARE THIS BELIEF CAN STILL FIND VALUE IN THE WORDS HE SAID, THE LIFE HE LED, AND THE LESSONS HE TAUGHT.

DID YOU KNOW?

THE EVENTS OF THE LIFE OF JESUS HAVE BECOME PART OF MOST ANNUAL CHRISTIAN CALENDARS. PEOPLE AROUND THE WORLD CELEBRATE THESE HOLIDAYS TOGETHER.

Christian Celebrations

CHRISTMAS: This is the birth of Jesus, celebrated on December 25.

LENT: This 40-day period of prayer and reflection comes before Easter.

ASH WEDNESDAY: This is the first day of Lent.

GOOD FRIDAY: Two days before Easter, Christians gather to remember the day Jesus died on the cross.

EASTER SUNDAY: This event focuses on Jesus's return from the dead. It is held on different Sundays in the spring.

PENTECOST: This event didn't make it into our book, but Jesus returned one more time to give his disciples the Holy Spirit, a power that helped connect people to God. Pentecost celebrates that event.

JESUS TIMELINE

1   Jesus is born in Bethlehem, the son of Joseph and his wife Mary.

12   Jesus teaches in the temple in Jerusalem.

30   Jesus is baptized by John the Baptist and begins preaching in Galilee.

        At a wedding in Cana, he performs his first miracle: changing water to wine.

30-33 Over these years, Jesus travels throughout what is now Israel and Palestine, where he teaches people, performs miracles, and heals the sick.

33   In the third year of the time of his teaching, Jesus goes to Jerusalem for Passover.

        As punishment for what the authorities see as dangerous and disruptive behavior, he is sentenced to death.

        Jesus is executed by being nailed to a cross.

        According to the Gospels, after three days in a tomb Jesus comes back from the dead for 40 days, visiting with his disciples and others before returning to heaven.

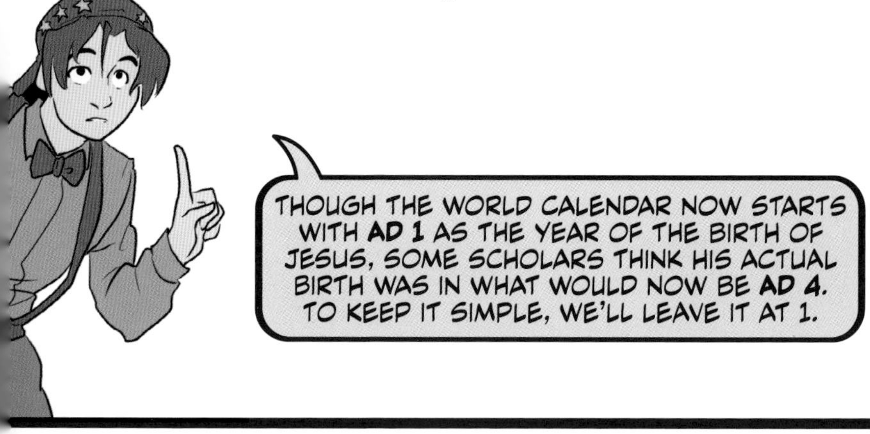

THOUGH THE WORLD CALENDAR NOW STARTS WITH **AD 1** AS THE YEAR OF THE BIRTH OF JESUS, SOME SCHOLARS THINK HIS ACTUAL BIRTH WAS IN WHAT WOULD NOW BE **AD 4.** TO KEEP IT SIMPLE, WE'LL LEAVE IT AT 1.

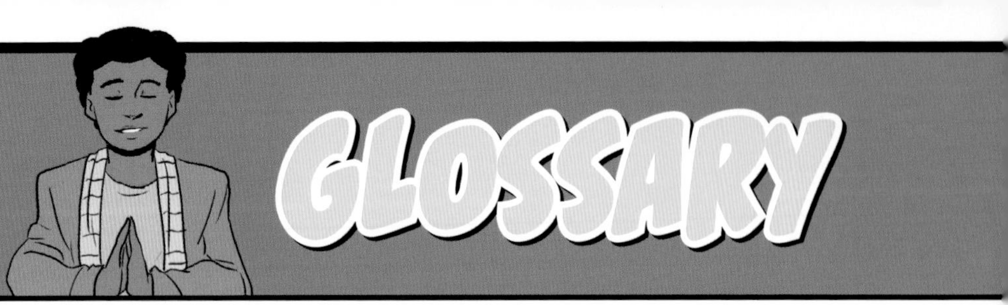

GLOSSARY

BAPTISM: A ceremony involving water in which a person joins the Christian church and affirms their faith.

CRUCIFY: To kill by nailing to a wooden cross.

DISCIPLE: A person who closely follows and often helps a religious leader.

FAITH: Believing in something without physical proof.

GOSPEL: With a capital G, the story of the life of Jesus as told in the Bible.

PARABLE: A story told to share a lesson or moral.

PASSOVER: An important annual celebration for the Jewish people, remembering a time that God saved them from danger.

PRODIGAL: Wasteful, spendthrift.

SILK ROAD: An ancient overland route from the Middle East toward China and Asia.

SOWER: A person who plants seeds.

TEMPT: Try to get a person to do something they don't want to do or shouldn't do.

VACANCY: Emptiness, availability.

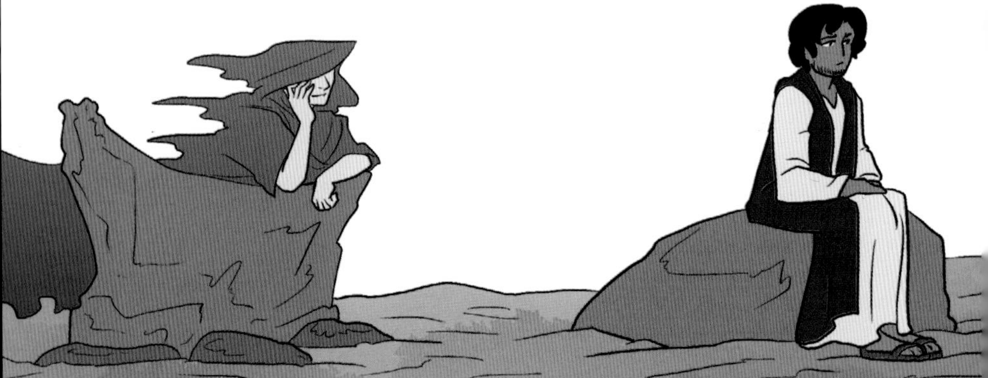

FIND OUT MORE

BOOKS

Isbouts, Jean-Pierre. *Jesus: An Illustrated Life.* Washington, D.C.: National Geographic, 2015.

Morgan, Ellen. *Who Was Jesus?* New York: Penguin Workshop, 2013.

Olson, Marc. *The World Jesus Knew: A Curious Kid's Guide.* Minneapolis, MN: Sparkhouse Family, 2017.

Sanders, Nancy I. *Jesus.* New York: Zonderkidz, 2014.

Tertrais, Gaelle. *Who Is Jesus? His Life, His Land, His Time.* San Francisco: Ignatian Press, 2018.

VIDEOS

Jesus: His Life. Biography. Santa Monica, CA: Lionsgate, 2005.

WE USED THE KING JAMES VERSION OF THE BIBLE FOR THE QUOTES IN THIS BOOK, THOUGH WE MODERNIZED SOME OF THE LANGUAGE FOR BETTER UNDERSTANDING.

OTHER POPULAR TRANSLATIONS OF THE BIBLE INCLUDE THE CONTEMPORARY ENGLISH VERSION, NEW INTERNATIONAL VERSION, AND THE NEW AMERICAN STANDARD BIBLE.

SHOW ME HISTORY!

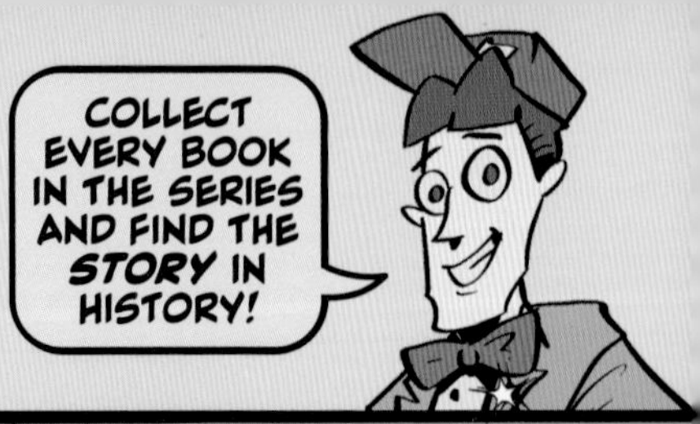

COLLECT EVERY BOOK IN THE SERIES AND FIND THE *STORY* IN HISTORY!

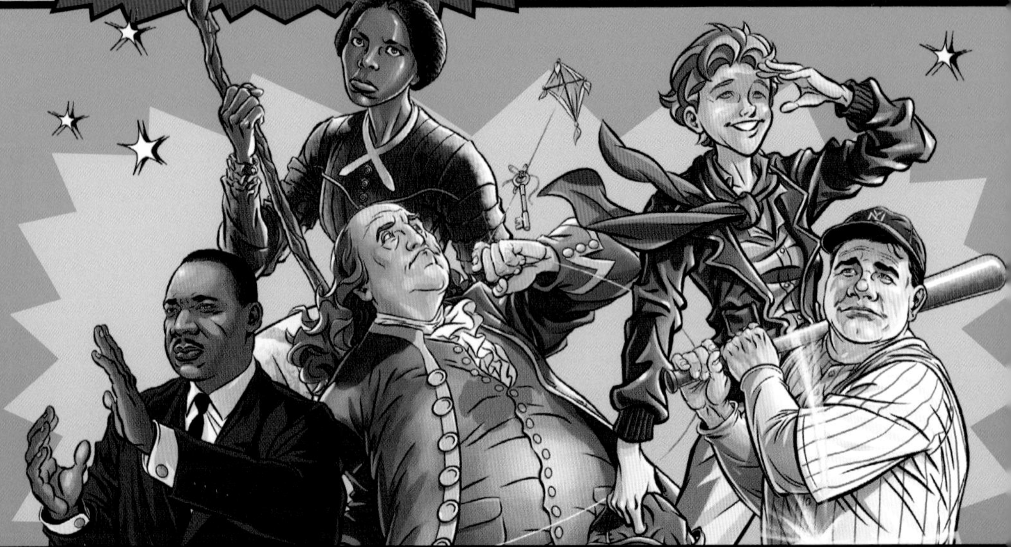

ABRAHAM LINCOLN
DEFENDER OF THE UNION!

ALEXANDER HAMILTON
THE FIGHTING FOUNDING FATHER!

AMELIA EARHART
PIONEER OF THE SKY!

BABE RUTH
BASEBALL'S ALL-TIME BEST

BENJAMIN FRANKLIN
INVENTOR OF THE NATION!

HARRIET TUBMAN
FIGHTER FOR FREEDOM!

JESUS
MESSENGER OF PEACE!

MARTIN LUTHER KING JR.
VOICE FOR EQUALITY!

MUHAMMAD ALI
THE GREATEST OF ALL TIME!

SUSAN B. ANTHONY
CHAMPION FOR VOTING RIGHTS!

WALT DISNEY
THE MAGICAL INNOVATOR!

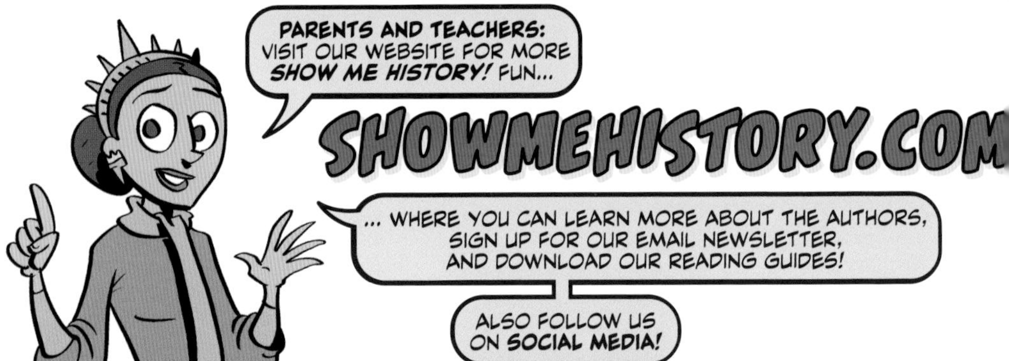

PARENTS AND TEACHERS: VISIT OUR WEBSITE FOR MORE *SHOW ME HISTORY!* FUN...
SHOWMEHISTORY.COM
... WHERE YOU CAN LEARN MORE ABOUT THE AUTHORS, SIGN UP FOR OUR EMAIL NEWSLETTER, AND DOWNLOAD OUR READING GUIDES!
ALSO FOLLOW US ON **SOCIAL MEDIA!**

@showmehistorybooks | www.facebook.com/portablepress | www.pinterest.com/portablepress | @portablepres

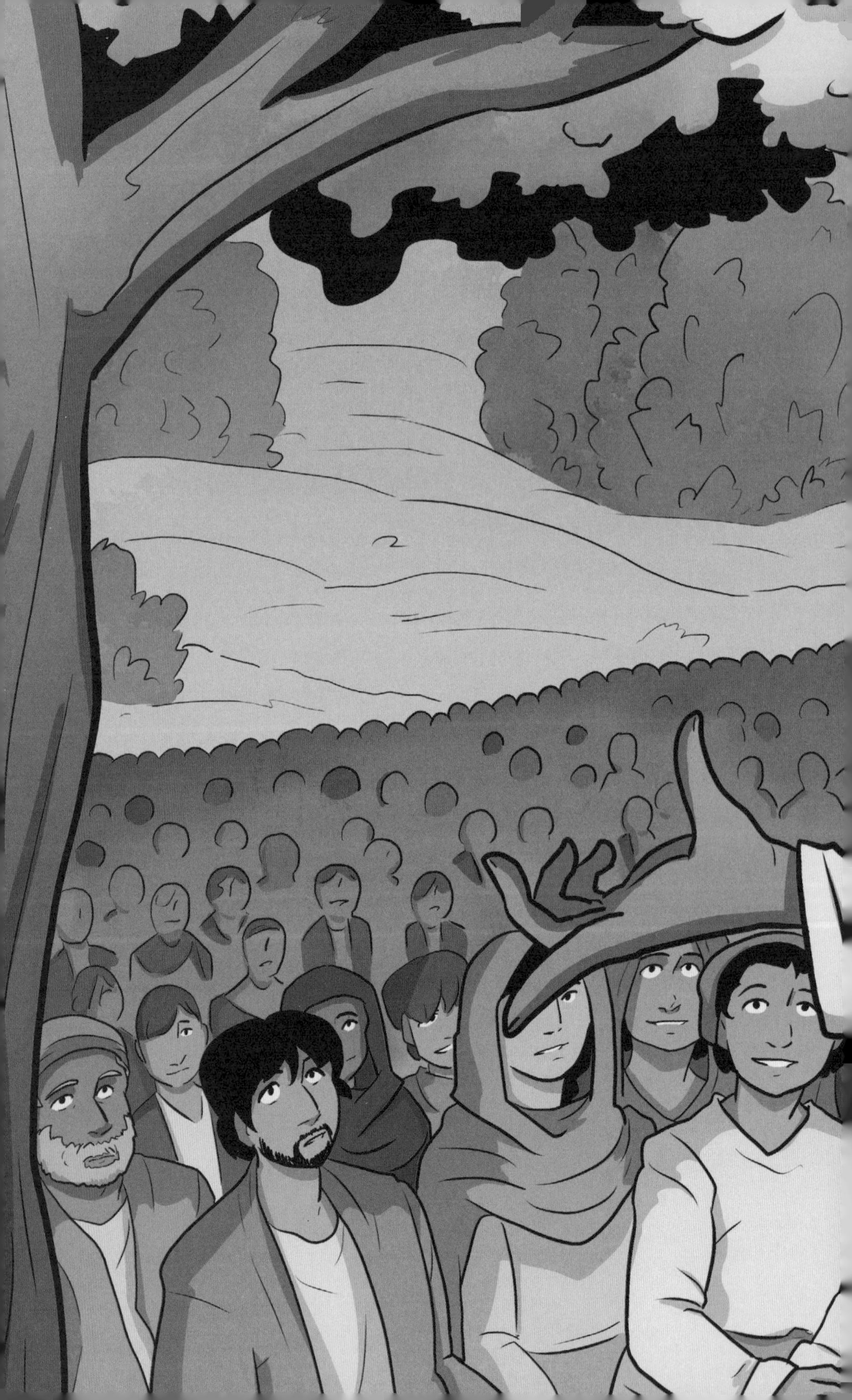